STUDIES IN CHILDREN'S LITERATURE, 1500–2000

Studies in Children's Literature,
1500–2000

Celia Keenan & Mary Shine Thompson

EDITORS

FOUR COURTS PRESS

Published by
FOUR COURTS PRESS LTD
7 Malpas Street, Dublin 8, Ireland
email: info@four-courts-press.ie
http://www.four-courts-press.ie
and in North America by
FOUR COURTS PRESS
c/o ISBS, 920 N.E. 58th Avenue, Suite 300, Portland, OR 97213.

ISBN 1–85182–853–2 hbk

A catalogue record for this title
is available from the British Library.

Printed in Great Britain
by MPG Books, Bodmin, Cornwall.

Contents

Preface

This book, consisting as it does of selected papers from the inaugural conference of the Irish Society for the Study of Children's Literature (ISSCL), is the result of the collaboration of very many people who should be thanked here. The book could not have come into being without the help of all those involved in organising the inaugural conference of ISSCL, the members of ISSCL, those who submitted papers, the selection committee that selected the papers, and all those who attended the conference and contributed to the development of these studies by their valuable and constructive comments. ISSCL executive committee members, Valerie Coghlan, Carole Dunbar, P.J. Mathews, Mary Shine Thompson and Pádraic Whyte gave enthusiastically of their time and expertise.

Members of the committee of the International Research Society for Children's Literature (IRSCL) lent real support and weight to the enterprise, both by their valued attendance at the conference and their contribution of papers. Special thanks are owed to Executive Committee member Valerie Coghlan who, in her role as secretary of IRSCL, liased between both organisations.

A number of people at St Patrick's College, Drumcondra, Dublin helped to make this all possible. They include the President of St Patrick's College, Dr Pauric Travers, who gave unstinting support to this project; the Secretary Bursar, Martin Ward; the members of the college research committee along with director of research Mary Shine Thompson; and the chairperson of the taught MA programme board, Tom Halpin. The head of the English department, Brenna Clarke, and all the members of the English Department contributed in a great variety of ways. The editors also acknowledge the financial contribution of St Patrick's College MA programme board and the College Research Committee towards this publication.

Poetry Ireland gave most needed support through the efforts of its education officer Jane O'Hanlon, as did the editorial staff at Four Courts Press.

The book is a new and exciting departure in the Irish context, opening up an interesting dialogue between Irish and international studies in children's literature, exploring the boundaries of what may be considered children's literature and promising fruitful development in the future.

Celia Keenan

Introduction

MARY SHINE THOMPSON

Scanning the bibliographies, an outsider might be forgiven for conclud-
ing that the Irish literary pantheon was populated more or less exclusively by Yeats, Synge, Joyce, Beckett, Flann O'Brien and Northern Irish
poetry.[1]

'Fred's studies are not very deep', said Rosamond, rising with her
mamma, 'he is only reading a novel'.[2]

This collection of essays, about half of which address Irish subject matter, and half
matters relevant but not specific to the Irish context, challenges presumptions that
children's literature and Irish studies are fixed, self-contained discourses. The dialogue that the collection creates confirms that the fields are both contested and
interrelated. As the omission of the work of Eilís Dillon from the *Field Day anthology of Irish writing*'s fourth and fifth volumes[3] suggests, rigorous study of children's
books is a discipline lately arrived in the academy. Mary Warnock's comment on
seeing an undergraduate read Frances Hodgson Burnett's *The secret garden* confirms that the prejudice is not confined to Ireland: '[o]ne feels inclined to ask how
they can be so intelligent if they are so ready to switch their minds off when they
are not actually working'.[4] Indeed, it might be said that children's literature enjoys
the doubtful status of the novel in the late nineteenth century: many consider it,
like Fred's studies in *Middlemarch*, 'not very deep'. Whether or not an exploration
of children's literature can make a signal contribution to literary and Irish studies
has yet to be firmly established, because it has yet to be fully integrated into the
work of the academy. However, at the most fundamental level this collection takes
Irish literature beyond the canonic pantheon, and onto roads and flight-paths less
travelled. Equally, it underlines how the trajectories of these routes parallel and
intersect each other in numerous ways.

   A number of factors have interacted to create a receptive critical environment
for children's literary studies, both globally and within the Irish context. As western democracies move towards rights-based societies, international bodies such as

1 Terry Eagleton, *Crazy John and the bishop* (Cork: Cork UP 1998), p. ix.   2 George Eliot,
Middlemarch, ed. W.J. Harvey (London: Penguin 1972), p. 129.   3 Angela Bourke et al. (eds),
The Field Day anthology of Irish writing, vols 4 and 5 (Cork: Cork UP, 2002).   4 Quoted in
Peter Hollindale, *Signs of childness* (Stroud: Thimble Press 1997).

the United Nations and the European Union have consolidated minority and marginal groups' (including children's) rights to representation in civic arenas. This
challenge to traditional patriarchal perspectives in turn has prepared the ground
for and been impelled by the inclusion of civil and political discourses, of which
the study of children's literature is one. Not that such disquisitions are uniformly
optimistic: as we shall see, some critics are profoundly despondent about even the
possibility of children's literature. However, it may be argued that the current
awareness of children's right to equal humanity has informed and extended such
debate.

Although the issue of identity has to some degree receded from the current theoretical agenda, multiple constructions of childhood continue to vie for attention
and are uniquely explicated in texts intended for children. Children's literature
critics and publishers construct children variously as readers, consumers, producers of meaning, as gendered and class-inflected, as politicized or as its opposites,
erased, unspoken or passive. Books also play a significant role in the acculturation
of children, and they draw upon residual concepts of otherness and difference that
are the staples of post-colonial theories, in order to offer insight into their real and
ideal existences. Perhaps worthy of particular mention in the context of identities
is the ebbing tide of classic Piagetian and Eriksonian psychology that provided the
dominant lens through which childhood was perceived, particularly in Ireland in
the last forty years (this school of psychology comes under the scrutiny of
Kimberley Reynolds in this book), and the more puritan, traditional model which
it struggled to replace (vividly presented in Mary Flynn's article on the religious
publications of the Talbot Press). The current emphasis on constructivist principles within education has removed from childhood the taint of developmental and
moral inadequacy, since it affirms children's ability to construct knowledge. It may
be useful to perceive children's multiple and conflicting identities as 'embracing
metonymies — names of attributes of one's identity that do not require a stable
metaphoric whole to define themselves'.[5] The essays here implicitly and explicitly
explore these myriad, imbricating cultural, individual and communitarian
metonymies.

Among them is that of the much-maligned golliwog, long an image of political
incorrectness and prejudice, whose identity, on further investigation by David
Rudd, turns out to be much more complex. Rudd differentiates between the golliwog and another black character, Sambo, and he observes that the former is mischievous, likeable, and connotes the subversion of constraining norms: in short, the
golliwog has been an example of Bakhtinian carnivalesque, in some respects comparable to Hoffman's *Struwwelpeter* (variously translated as 'slovenly' or 'shock-
headed' Peter). Anne Alston's essay suggests that fat is not just a feminist issue, but
in children's books can be a measure of abnormality and sexualization. By contrast,

5 Virginia Kuhn, 'Postmodern space and reception readers', http://www.uwm.edu/
~vkuhn/maspace.html. Accessed 18 September 2003.

A.J. Piesse's review of English Renaissance texts indicates the role of books in acculturating children, and by implication, in demarcating class boundaries.

A central motif repeated in this book is that of gender, more often than not perceived as a cultural and social construct that is in complex interplay with class and nationality, and, to a lesser extent, with race.[6] Jane O'Hanlon explores how the traditionally patriarchal genre of the fantasy novel has evolved in the hands of Tolkien, Ursula Le Guin and Philip Pullman. Within their work, the stereotypes that associate male heroes with victory and activity, and females with defeat and passivity, give way to a heroism that eschews binarism in favour of interdependence, ageing and ordinariness. Áine Nic Gabhann notes the somewhat sinister overtones of adult female sexuality in the children's writings of Frances Hodgson Burnett. Carole Dunbar and Pádraic Whyte politicize gender, showing how sexual and national identities conjugate: Dunbar relates female education to the feminisation of the nation, a topic which has attracted considerable attention in Irish literary discourse, and Whyte distinguishes between female and official histories of nation-shaping events. In addition to contributing to the established debates in Irish studies, these essays also offer multiple perspectives on how childhood is gendered.

A factor that has raised awareness of children's literature has been the continuing dismantling of the oppositions between high and popular culture, and with it recognition of the semantic possibilities of non-canonic texts. The work of Frederic Jameson and Janice Radway[7] among others has cleared the way for children's literature to be studied as a form of popular literature that explores issues of hegemony and subalternity, and the work of John Fiske has indicated the emancipatory possibilities,[8] albeit at the micropolitical level, of the oppositional meanings that can be generated in popular texts. The writings of Eilís Dillon and Patricia Lynch, for example, may be placed in this category: they have enjoyed considerable popularity among Irish children in the mid-century, and it may be argued that they offered children an opportunity to negotiate conflictual meanings. While these novels have attracted some critical accolades, their value as cultural capital outside that limited field of children's literature remains under-recognized. Declan Kiberd's exploration of Grey Friars and the Remove reveals some semantic possibilities latent in the humble school story: his analysis attends, for example, to the linguistic games that form the plots of many of the stories, which in turn

6 Anne McClintock, *Imperial leather* (London: Routledge, 1994): 'race, gender and class are not distinct realms of experience, existing in splendid isolation from each other; nor can they be simply yoked together retrospectively like armatures of Lego. Rather, they come into existence in and through relation to each other – if in contradictory and conflictual ways.' http://www.postcolonialweb.org/poldiscourse/am1.html. Accessed 18 September 2003. 7 See for example, Frederic Jameson, *The political unconscious: narrative as a socially symbolic act* (London: Methuen, 1981); and Janice A. Radway, *Reading the romance: women, patriarchy, and popular literature* (Chapel Hill: U. North Carolina Press, 1991). 8 'A text is the site of struggles for meaning that reproduce the conflicts of interest between the producers and consumers of the cultural commodity. A program is produced by the industry, a text by its readers.' John Fiske, *Television culture* (London: Methuen, 1987), p. 14.

disclose the central roles of adult language codes. Children's texts, it seems, can perform semantic functions more often associated with 'high' culture.

Crossover texts, that is, books read by both adults and children, are not a recent phenomenon. In fact, they have always been with us: note that the Renaissance children's reading texts cited in A.J. Piesse's essay were all conceived as adult reading matter; *vide* also Jonathan Swift's *Gulliver's travels*, J.D. Salinger's *The catcher in the rye* or Jostein Gaarder's *Sophie's world*. They are examples of texts that blur the boundaries not only between adult and child, but also between high and popular culture: within the academy they may be viewed as canonic, while versions produced for children of their nature are populist. Crossover books have in recent times created their own cluster of critical concerns. The popularity and the commercial success of such texts as Philip Pullman's *His dark materials* and J.K. Rowling's Harry Potter series have, on the one hand, added to the gravitas of children's books: if adults as well as children find them worthwhile, the logic goes, then they merit some critical attention. And because of its considerable global commercial impact, the phenomenon has also been deemed worthy of serious analysis. Furthermore, this popularity has firmly disposed of essentialist prejudice about children's reading: it is has shown that the boundaries between adult and children's reading are blurred. However, a Rowling book, for example, has become a 'media event', and discussion has focused at least as much on the phenomenon as it has on textual evaluation or politics, much of it breathlessly uncritical in tone.[9] The 'phenomenon' may also be seen as an instance of the accelerated and systematic commercialisation of childhood, a process already established in middle-class England in the nineteenth century. This market-driven logic has led to the publications especially for older children and young adults that are, in the words of Kimberley Reynolds, 'enervating and narcissistic', and leave readers feeling atomized, self-destructive and lacking in political purpose. Her essay suggests that certain texts work to dispel energy and emotion and promote passivity in the reader. The exploitation of this market has led, she believes, to a demotivating nihilism among the young.

Conversely, the focus on children's literature as possibly a legitimate area of academic study has been facilitated by certain strands in recent historiography that have extended historians' remit to include not only the normative nationalist and revisionist narratives of state-building, the topic of most Irish history in the twentieth century, but also areas traditionally outside political history. Allied to this is a recognition that literature is still, to a considerable extent, 'consciously conceived

9 Among the numerous examples that might be cited are 'a publishing phenomenon', http://news.bbc.co.uk/1/hi/entertainment/arts/823330.stm; 'The Potter phenomenon', http://news.bbc.co.uk/1/hi/entertainment/arts/820885.stm; 'The Harry Potter Phenomenon', http://arwenbooks.com/harry_potter_phenomenon.htm; 'The Harry Potter Phenomenon ... The most anticipated media entertainment event of the summer', http://www.google.ie/search?hl=en&ie=UTF-8&oe=UTF-8&q=harry+potter+phenomenon&btnG=Google+Search&meta=. Accessed 23 September 2003.

on all sides as a crucial stake in the wider nation- and state-building projects on the island', and is used 'to assert the existence of shared identities, shared historical experiences, common values and concerns'.[10] The recognition that certain groups are invisible within the state and the simultaneous acknowledgement that they constitute a category that *should* be represented within dominant discourse is a feature of current intellectual trends such as gender studies and postcolonialism. Among the marginal topics and groups that now routinely come under scrutiny, both globally and in the specifically Irish context, are local histories, women's and gender studies, ethnicity, labour and urban history – and, in more recent times, childhood. This decentering of history has facilitated Pádraic Whyte's interrogation of the originary events of the Irish state as interpreted in the contemporary historical novels of Gerard Whelan and Siobhan Parkinson, but from the perspective of child-characters. Whyte explores how historical narratives woven around these events are variously satirized and commodified; how some legitimize violence; how public and private histories intersect; how popular history can deconstruct official narratives, and the extent to which these histories are gendered. Ciara Ní Bhroin's analysis moves the debate into the mid-twentieth century, and her focus on Eilís Dillon's fiction places this work firmly within the realm of postcolonial debate. She argues that Dillon employs the genre of the adventure tale more typically associated with British imperial adventure in order to create a distinctively Irish literature. She sees this as an example of a decolonizing writer attempting to stamp imperial forms with a native hallmark, who succeeds in recreating them as heroic tales typical of the attitudes of the Irish Literary Revival.

As children emerge as a discrete collective with a specific range of concerns, it is inevitable that their narratives and the forms of expression that enjoy currency among them should command attention. Some strands of children's literature criticism adopt a methodology similar to that of the gynocritics,[11] in that they concern themselves with, or are read by children, in the belief that this will not so much destabilize the children's literary canon (the range of canonic texts being almost too limited and meagre to warrant the title canon), as address what it might have contained. This critical strain constitutes a significant element of this book, as might be expected of a critical work that is mapping a relatively new field of study. Explored in this context are the works of Flora L. Shaw, Mrs George De Horne Vaizey, L.T. Meade, and the formal renaissance didactic texts that A.J. Piesse explores. Here too are Edward Thomas and Robert Frost, well-established poets,

10 Joe Cleary, *Literature, partition and the nation-state: culture and conflict in Ireland, Israel and Palestine* (Cambridge: CUP, 2002), pp 76, 58.   11 Gynocriticism sought to furnish empirical data on the 'history, themes, genres and structures of literature by women', and 'studies of particular writers and work'. However, insofar as it also proposed to reveal 'the psychodynamics of female creativity', it is not directly comparable to the critical project described here. Elaine Showalter, *A literature of their own* (Princeton: Princeton UP 1977), p. 25. Another example of this critical approach is Sandra Gilbert and Susan Gubar, *The madwoman in the attic* (New Haven: Yale U.P., 1979).

but whose foray into the field of children's prose stories will come as a surprise to many. The majority of these texts has escaped serious critical attention heretofore, not least within the Irish context. So too have many of the Talbot Press publications considered by Mary Flynn and the as yet uncatalogued, uncollected (and in some cases, unpublished) works of Patricia Lynch that form the basis of Margaret Burke's essay. Only glancing attention has heretofore been paid to the genre of British school stories in the Irish context,[12] for example, although arguably it constituted a significant section of the reading matter in Irish lending libraries of the mid-century. These essays therefore challenge the traditionally patriarchal literary canon by retrieving and reassessing texts imaginatively concerned with children, and in the process, trace a child tradition in literature. They emphasize the evolving child consciousness – and consciousness of children – constructed in literature and explore the ways in which writers for children have comprized and delineated a world of their own, to paraphrase Elaine Showalter.

In important respects, this collection interrogates the relationship between aspects of Irish studies and their British and global contexts. The tendency formerly to view Irish history as a discrete, bounded story, a self-contained history, has been replaced by a consciousness of the impossibility of perceiving ourselves alone. None of the nations of the British Isles can be explored as independently intelligible units of study, as is evident in the historiography of, for example, Ray Ryan, Richard Tompson, Hugh Kearney, Jeremy Black and Tom Nairn.[13] It is now manifest that the stories of the 'four nations'[14] that (it has been argued) comprize the British Isles interact in complex ways, not solely in terms of a core and periphery model, or in terms of Michael Hechter's 'Celtic fringe'[15] on an English carpet, but rather in certain key ways. Among them is the manner in which narratives interrogate England's civilizing and modernizing role. Another is in terms of the roles that have created the conditions of their 'mutual and reciprocal existences, but have also interacted so as to modify the conditions of one another's existences'.[16] Probing Ireland's past as one element in a complex polyphonic 'Britannic' narrative (in the geographical sense), to use Nairn's term, has deepened awareness of how English and Irish texts dialogue; and how the reception of certain texts questions narrow understandings of their function.

12 Michael Flanagan's "'For the triumph of the patriot arms": the Christian Brothers, *Our boys* and militant nationalism in Irish popular culture 1914–22', in Karen Vandevelde (ed.), *New voices in Irish criticism 3* (Dublin: Four Courts Press, 2002), pp 44–5, covers aspects of related Irish boys' school stories.   13 Jeremy Black, *A history of the British Isles* (Basingstoke: Macmillan, 1996); Hugh Kearney, *The British Isles: a history of four nations* (Cambridge: CUP, 1989); Tom Nairn, *The break-up of Britain: crisis and neo-nationalism* (London: Verso, 1981); Ray Ryan, *Ireland and Scotland: literature and culture, state and nation, 1966–2000* (Oxford: O.U.P., 2002); Richard Thompson, *The Atlantic archipelago: a political history of the British Isles* (Lewiston: Mellen, 1986).   14 Northern Ireland, of course, constitutes a fifth political entity.   15 Michael Hechter, *Internal colonialism: the Celtic fringe in British national development, 1536–1966* (London: Routledge, 1998).   16 Krishan Kumar, *The making of English national identity* (Cambridge: CUP, 2003). http://assets.cambridge.org/0521771889

As Robert Dunbar points out, Shaw's *Castle Blair* is concerned with the contentious issues of civic strife in the post-Famine period; in that respect the novel does not shy away from political, apparently 'adult' subject matter. Its main protagonist is impetuous, rebellious and romantic, in contrast with his French antagonist, whose code of behaviour is ideally imperial. The plot's subtext, concerned with *civilité*, confirms the book's Arnoldian ideology: the Irish may be eloquent, but as the protagonist's untrustworthy judgement underlines, they are incapable of self-determination; English civility is threatened by the 'barbarian' outsider. The book was well received: it ran to some seventeen editions in Britain, America and France. It represented abroad, but did not address, the 'dirty, ragged and apparently degraded'[17] Irish. It is arguable that this novel intervenes as a latecomer in many of the literary and philosophical debates of the late eighteenth and early nineteenth century, in order to forge a connection between the eighteenth-century discourse of sentiment and emergent nineteenth-century concept of British imperial, civic nationalism.

Carole Dunbar's review of the phenomenon of the wild Irish girl is a further example of a nineteenth-century novel concerned with social instability, in this case overlain with gender issues. Its intertextual reference to Sydney Owenson's *Wild Irish girl* inserts the novel into an already existing context, but in counter-satirical mode; its intention is to limit the damage of Owenson's better-known work. If the original draws on Irish iconography of the woman as Ireland, so too does its successor, but in order to deprecate the deprecating Irish. However, Carole Dunbar complicates the crude oppositions between refined English and barbaric Irish that her chosen authors would wish to promote when she points to the common currency of the simian imagery in the descriptions both of the wild Irish girls and poverty-stricken, working-class English children. Yet Declan Kiberd's alert reflection on British school stories, which draws on his own childhood reading, contains little hint of the colonial alienation that was a feature of, for example, Frank O'Connor's childhood reading of comics. Perhaps class is one defining arbiter of acceptability, and the difficulty of assigning class to the Irish is central to the nineteenth-century imperial perception of their 'otherness'.

The civic, historiographic and social conditions outlined earlier in this essay have created the agenda for discussion. However, one issue crucial and unique to children's literature is the fundamental question of whether such a discourse as children's literature is possible at all. While the issue inimitably and exclusively belongs to the realm of children's literature, in terms of category it might be classified with the feminist disquisitions of the 1970s[18] which perceived women to be repressed and excluded from western philosophic discourse, or the postcolonial scholarship that links language, discourse, representation and the institutions of power, and that has informed much recent Irish historiography. It has been well

/sample/0521771889WS.pdf. Accessed 15 September 2003.   **17** Bell, *Shaw*, p. 171.   **18** For example, the work of Luce Irigaray and Helene Cixous.

established in the Irish context and elsewhere that conceptualizations of otherness are not automatically transferable from one specific context to another. Transience and change are integral features of childhood, while membership of certain subaltern groups is predicated upon certain givens, such as gender or race, for example, which are relatively fixed. Childhood is a state that accounts for perhaps only one quarter or less of the average person's lifespan; furthermore it is universal – everyone, whether empowered or oppressed, has been once a child. So while it may be asserted that ideological constructions of childhood have kept children subordinate, the specifics of children's subalternity[19] are unique and create unique dynamics.

This issue, as it relates to children's books, has been well rehearsed by Jacqueline Rose, Peter Hunt, Roderick McGillis[20] and others, and topics under discussion in several of the essays in this book reflect their concerns. That the tradition of 'childness' in literature might be shared between adults and children is a fraught proposition. Responses range from Rose's radical rejection of the possibility because, as she puts it, it 'hangs on … the impossible relation between adult and child' to therapeutic 'solutions' to the problem, to Peter Hollindale's more serenely optimistic theory. For him, childness 'is shared ground, though differently experienced and understood, between the child and adult'.[21]

Sebastien Chapleau's essay confronts this hydra, but several other contributors also acknowledge its existence. Chapleau proposes at least one possible ground for the resolution of the difficulty, and some optimism about the issue may be found in others' writings also. Sandra Beckett reviews of the work of Warja Lavater, Katsumi Komagata and Bruno Munari, originally creators of adult art books who strayed into the world of children's books, and who have been surprised at children's ludic readiness to go with the flow of their visual narrative experimentation. Howard Hollands and Victoria de Rijke point to the nakedness, blanks and absences that are a feature of the picture books of Dutch artist Max Velthuijs. By alerting the reader to the parallels between them and both the silent musical compositions of John Cage and the white paintings of Rauschenberg, the overloaded meanings of these texts become apparent. The radical narrativizing of Lavater, Komagata, Munari and Velthuijs tacitly acknowledges the difficulty of telling the tale that is at the heart of modernism, and the fun in how they respond to the

---

19 This writer has explored childhood subalternity in 'Give tongue its freedom: children as citizens of Irish civic society', ed. Marian Lyons and Fionnuala Waldron [untitled] the second series of Seamus Heaney lectures, forthcoming.   20 See for example Peter Hunt, *Criticism, theory, and children's literature* (Oxford: Blackwell, 1991); Karín Lesnik-Oberstein, *Children's literature: criticism and the fictional child* (Oxford: Clarendon Press, 1994); Roderick McGillis, 'Self, other, and the other self: recognizing the other in children's literature', *The Lion and the Unicorn*, vol. 21 (1997), pp 215–29; Jacqueline Rose, *The case of Peter Pan or the impossibility of children's fiction* (London: Macmillan, 1984).   21 Rose, *Peter Pan*, p. 1; Peter Hollindale, in *The Cambridge guide to children's books in English*, ed. Victor Watson (Cambridge: CUP, 2001), p. 145.

problem bespeaks a postmodernist playfulness. Their very puckishness testifies to possible future modes of telling tales. So too do the works of Robert Frost and Edward Thomas: Deborah Thacker suggests that the little-known children's tales of these respected poets' stories are characterized by elements inimitable to modernism. It seems that some of the experimental techniques of contemporary and high art are not necessarily resistant to a child audience.

Other critics are less buoyant. Áine Nic Gabhann, for example, persuasively accumulates evidence to suggest that Burnett's preoccupation with childhood had some sinister overtones. Implicit in her analysis is the unavoidable possibility that a dialogue among equals, adult writer and young reader, is improbable for many reasons: because of the writer's objectification of children; because of the manner in which she constructs the child in the image of her own erotic desire; and because of the reversal of roles that sees the adult dependent on the child. Kimberley Reynolds attends to the manner in which books can be instruments of coercive acculturation, and her reflection implicitly raises the question as to whether young adult literature should be restricted or censored. Can it be that there are subject matters or modes or genres (or, more likely, combinations of these) that are, of their nature, off limits to childhood? A bleak, nihilistic writer such as J.M. Coetzee is the recipient of literary accolades when he writes for adults, yet we recoil from presenting his kinds of subject matter to children. The achievement of Nabokov's *Lolita* is widely acclaimed, but few are likely to tender it as a text for children. Is the challenge, as some of Reynolds' examples propose, to find forms amenable to difficult subject matter?

The pessimistic *frisson* discernible in this essay is not exclusive to Reynolds's post-millennial consciousness. There is also more than a hint elsewhere that some respected writers themselves suspect that writing for children is an emblem of inferiority, that it draws a veil over reality to protect their vulnerable readers. That may be so in the case of Patricia Lynch, one of the most famous and respected writers for children at the mid-century. Margaret Burke points out that Lynch believed that the most important element of her work was not her singular, if flawed, contribution to the narrow and impoverished ground of children's literature in the early decades of the independent Irish state, but her writing for adults. Imbued with the prejudice of her times, she failed to value her own writing.

Notwithstanding these reservations, there is ample evidence to suggest that the young's capacity for understanding the world ought not be underestimated. As Yevtushenko noted, they 'know what you mean',[22] and the proof is in the existing body of children's books, because '[t]he history of children's literature is written, for the better or for the worse, about books which children actually read'.[23]

22 Yevgeny Yevtushenko, 'Lies', *Selected poems*, Trans. and introduced by Robin Milner-Gulland and Peter Levy (London: Penguin, 1962).   23 Maria Nikolajeva, 'How to create a success: the Harry Potter phenomenon', *Opsis Kalopsis* No. 1 (2000). http://www-rohan.sdsu.edu/dept/english/childlit/showcase/harry_potter.html. Accessed 17 September 2003.

Whatever the complex motivations of adult writers, publishers, educators and parents, for children reading is an opening to the flux and consciousness of history; for them books remain possible emancipatory spaces.[24]

---

24 I am grateful to Celia Keenan for constructive comments on and contributions to this introduction.

Reading English renaissance children and the early modern stage

A.J. PIESSE

Knowing what renaissance children read, what they were obliged to read at school, what their guardians were encouraged to encourage them to read, what they chose to read themselves, and what they remembered from among what they had read, is an invaluable tool in the investigation of renaissance constructions of childhood in the drama. This essay is a preliminary investigation of the first three items in the list, and focuses, in the main, for its source on one particular text, William Kempe's *The education of children in learning* (1588). There is no shortage of printed advice for the education of young people in the renaissance, and similarly, no shortage of lists of suggested reading, or indeed, of the order the books should be read in and why these books appear on the lists they do. Recently a considerable amount of work has been done on recovering this information;[1] as yet, however, less has been done on how that knowledge might be applied to an understanding of the social realities of childhood in the period, or to the relationship between those realities and the kind of fictional or representational child constructed for the renaissance stage. An examination of the available information, however, and the advice that surrounds it, reveals a quite particular notion of the envisaged end product. What kind of a child did books build in the renaissance? And how might that knowledge inform our readings of the construction of child characters for the renaissance stage?

II

On 1 September 1528, Cardinal Wolsey caused to be written a curriculum for the grammar school he intended to found at Ipswich. The school was intended to function as a foundation for students who would then proceed to his newly found-

---

1 See, for example, Rebecca W. Bushnell, *A culture of teaching: early modern humanism in theory and practice* (Ithaca and London: Cornell UP, 1996); David Cressy, *Literacy and the social order: reading and writing in Tudor and Stuart England* (Cambridge: CUP, 1980); Anthony Grafton and Lisa Jardine, *From humanism to the humanities: education and the liberal arts in fifteenth and sixteenth-century Europe* (Cambridge: CUP, 1986). No such study could be undertaken without reference to T.W. Baldwin, *William Shakespere's small Latine and lesse Greeke,* 2 vols (Urbana: U. Illinois P., 1944).

ed Cardinal's College, the building of which had begun following the clearance
from the site of St Frideswide's Abbey in 1525, later to become Henry VIII's
College, and, ultimately, Christ Church, Oxford. Wolsey's curriculum for Ipswich
advocates the learning of good pronunciation in first form (boys would probably
enter at around seven years of age) with good Latin speaking learnt from Lily and
Cato in the second form. Aesop, for humour, and Terence are recommended for
third form, while Virgil, both for its fine verse and its practical 'instruction in soldiership' is especially apt for the fourth. The fifth class will learn epistolary style
from Cicero, the sixth, history from Julius Caesar and Sallust, while the greater
challenge of Horace's *Epistles* awaits the seventh form, who will also ponder
notions of identity and change through the medium of Ovid's *Metamorphoses*. For
the eighth class, the grammars of Donatus and Valla are recommended.[2]

Wolsey had previously been president of Magdalen, an Oxford college with a
choristers' school whose founder, William of Wayneflete, had been a former
provost of Eton. It is a later president of the same college, Laurence Humphrey
(1561–89) who, on Watson's report, 'made a determined protest against the reading of Ovid and other authors "in whom [scholars] study strange tongues to the
decay of godliness" '.[3] Humphrey's preferred course included rather Cicero's
Epistles and the more recent, indeed current, colloquies of Erasmus and Castillion.
The latter's chief advantage was that he turned scripture stories into Latin dialogues for the purpose of learning Latin grammar – the telling detail being that
Castillion was a French-speaking Genevan who wrote these works 'in the time of
Calvin', works designed specifically 'timely to sow the seeds of godliness and virtue
in their tender hearts'. Humphrey also took exception to other items traditionally
on the curriculum at college: Terence was to be studied

> but [meaning 'only'] with riper years and judgement. If any filth be inter-
> meddled let the teacher use sounder authors as treacle to expel it. Nor
> would I yield Terence this room but for I saw Cicero so much esteem him,
> who took not the least part of eloquence of him, as Chrysostom of
> Aristophanes the eloquence of the Attic tongue, a poet nevertheless both
> nipping in taunts and wanton in tales … Not little helpeth it, even at first,
> to learn them Greek and Hebrew, preposterously do all universities, schools
> and teachers that contrary it. For about the bush run they to arts, who
> understand not the original tongues.[4]

2 See Foster Watson, *The old grammar schools* (London: Cass, 1968), p. 16. He represents
Wolsey's curriculum in the following way, but, frustratingly, with no clear indication of the
source for the quotations within it: 'Class i: Good pronunciation. Class ii: Latin speaking from
Lily's *Carmen monitorum* and Cato's *Precepts*. Class iii: 'Who more humorous than Aesop? Who
more useful than Terence?' Class iv: Virgil, for instruction in soldiership and the majesty of its
verse. Class v: The epistles of Cicero. Class vi: History: Julius Caesar and Sallust. Class vii:
Horace's *Epistles* and Ovid's *Metamorphoses*. Class viii: Donatus, and Valla (grammars).   3
Watson, p. 93.   4 Laurence Humphrey, *The nobles or of nobilitye: The original nature, dutyes,*

The preoccupation with the instigation of a proper morality, and the ability to read texts in the original languages, thereby avoiding dependence on the translation and interpretation of others,[5] is not only apparent in terms of reading choices being made, but in the choice of teacher too. Some thirty years later, in 1592, the statutes of Giggleswick school in Yorkshire declare the following:

> 1. FYRSTE The scholemaister to be chozen from tyme to tyme shalbe a man fearinge God, of a trewe Religion and Godly conversacion, not geven to dycinge, cardinge or other unlawfull games but beinge admitted to the chardge of the sayd schoole shall faythfullye followe the same. 2. SECOND-LY he shall instructe his Schollers in godly aucthors for Christian religion, and other meete and honest aucthors for more knowledge in the liberal sciences, and also shall once everye weke catachise [sic] his sayd scholers in the knowledge of Christian religion and other godlye duetyes to thende there obedience in lyfe may answere to there proceedings in godly literature. 3. THIRDLY he shall not teach his schollers any unsavorye and popishe aucthors which may eyther infecte the younge wittes of his shollers [sic] with heresyes or corrupte thewre lyfes with unclennes. 4. FOURTHLY he shall not use in schoole any language to his schollers which be of ryper yeares and procedinges but onelye the lattyn, greeke or hebrewe, nor shall willingly permitte the use of the Englishe tongue in the schoole to them which are or shalbe able to speake latyne. 5. FYFTLYE he shall indifferently in schoole endevour himselfe to teache the poore aswell as the riche and the parishioner aswell as the stranger, and as his sayd schollers shall profitt in learnynge, so he shall preferre.[6]

right, and Christian institucion thereof three bookes. Fyrste eloquentlye writte[n] in Latine by Lawrence Humfrey D. of Diuinity, and presidente of Magdaleine Colledge in Oxforde, late englished. Whereto for the readers commoditye [sic], and matters affinitye, is coupled the small treatyse of Philo a Iewe. By the same author out of the Greeke Latined, nowe also Englished (London: In Fletestrete nere to S. Dunstons church by Thomas Marshel [1563]); pub. Basle 1560 in Latin as Optimates. Humphrey, cit. Watson, cit. Watson, p. 94. Humphrey is commenting on the late sixteenth-century undergraduate curriculum at Magdalen College Oxford here, but the comments are still apposite to children, since during the sixteenth century there was considerable overlap between the ages of grammar school boys and university undergraduates, it being not uncommon for undergraduates to enter university at the age of twelve or thirteen. 5 This observation is in keeping with the reformation drive towards individual ability in translation and interpretation. Compare, for example, William Tyndale, in his address 'To the reader' at the beginning of *The obedience of a Christen man* (1528) where he lays out the arguments why scripture should be available in the mother tongue. For an accessible, modern-spelling edition, see William Tyndale, *The obedience of a Christian man*, ed. David Daniell (London: Penguin, 2000). For the earlier Lollard drive towards the greater use of the vernacular, see 'The notion of vernacular theory' by Ruth Evans, Andrew Taylor, Nicholas Watson and Jocelyn Wogan-Browne in Jocelyn Wogan-Browne, Nicholas Watson, Andrew Taylor and Ruth Evans, *The idea of the vernacular* (Exeter: University of Exeter Press, 1999), pp 314–30. 6 Canon J.S. Purvis, *Educational records* (York: St Antony's Press, 1959), p. 17.

A number of things about the way in which the reading of renaissance children is being directed become apparent even from these preliminary observations. Firstly, style is almost as important as substance, and conduct books for children from the beginning of the sixteenth century are quite insistent that children from the earliest age be taught to speak properly, both in terms of accent and proper grammatical construction, even before they begin to read (from the moment a child begins to lisp its first words, says William Kempe, 1588, debar all 'barbarous nursses [sic], clownish playing mates, and all rusticall persons').[7] This strong connection between speaking and reading has philosophical, social and pedagogical import. 'Language most shows a man', says Ben Jonson, in *Discoveries*, 'Speak that I may see thee', an apothegm almost as common as the Delphic oracular *nosce teipsum*, know thyself, in high Renaissance English writing. Socially, as the following brief examination of book lists will show, rhetoric and oratory, or the arts of proper speaking, are central to the curriculum, and clearly important to social advancement. In terms of learning to read, though, proper pronunciation, and a subsequent recognition of the way in which a word is constructed of its constituent parts, has a special import, as recorded in both Francis Clement's *The petie schole with an English orthographie* (1578) and Kempe's *The education of children in learning* (1588).[8] Both demonstrate how proper pronunciation leads to the proper acquisition of reading by building words:

> Beware he missound not these vowels after *cl*, or *gl*, for commonly they pronounce amisse *cla, cle, cli, clo, clu* as if it were *tla, tle, tly, tlo, tlu*, where *cl*. should sound as *kl* ... for *ing*, ending a word, let him not pronounce in, leauing out the g, as: *speakin*, for *speaking*.[9]

Both Kempe and Clement are in agreement about the necessity of breaking words into appropriate syllabic groupings in order to spell them properly. Says Kempe,

> Wherein let him not learne by rote, spelling one sillable of a worde, and shuffling up the rest without distinct spelling. As if he had to learne this worde *mercifulnes*, suffer him not, as some would, to go on thus: *m-e-r, mer,*

---

7 William Kempe, *The education of children in learning: declared by the dignitie, vtilitie, and method thereof. Meete to be knowne, and practised aswell of parents as schoolmaisters* (London: Thomas Orwin, for Iohn Porter and Thomas Gubbin, 1588). Facsimile reproduction in Robert Pepper, *Four Tudor books on education* (Gainsville: Florida: Scholars' Facsimiles and Reprints, 1966), p. 218. Likewise Thomas Elyot, in *The education or bringinge vp of children, translated oute of Plutarche by syr Thomas Eliot knyght* (London: Thomas Berthelet, 1533), advises gentlemen to surround their children with people who 'can perfectly and truly speke and pronounce your country language' (Facsimile, in Pepper, p. 13).   8 Facsimile reproductions of both texts can be found in Pepper, 1966.   9 Clement, in Pepper, p. 61. Interestingly, in terms of Tudor phonetics, he continues 'Loke also that he pronounce the *w*, before *r*, as: *wrath, wringeth*, the *wrangler*, and not *rath, ringeth*, the *rangler'*.

c-i-f-u-l-n-e-s, *mercifulnes*. But according to the letters and syllables, whiche are as precepts in this behalfe, let him learne it by reason thus: *m-e-r, mer: c-i, ci: f-u-l, merciful: n-e-s: mercifulnes*. For if he repeate the former sylla-bles with every other added unto them, he shall have all in perfect memorie when he commeth to the ende: whereas otherwise he may erre or forget.[10]

These exhortations to be able and exact in English speaking are particularly inter-esting, because from the lists of authors suggested, it is plain that in the main what is being read is being read in Latin, in Latin translation from the Greek, and some-times in Greek too, to the extent that one contemporary observer, Palsgrave, lamented that while there was no shortage of masters able in the Latin tongue, many petty school teachers were in fact not particularly able in an elevated English tongue:

> since they have not had occasion to be conversant in such places of your realm where the purest English is spoken, they be not able to express their conceit in their vulgar tongue, nor be sufficient perfectly to open the diver-sities of phrases between our tongue and the Latin …[11]

This would seem to be borne out by the exhortation at the end of the Giggleswick statute ('he shall not use in schoole any language to his schollers which be of ryper yeares and procedinges but onelye the lattyn, greeke or hebrewe, nor shall willingly permitte the use of the Englishe tongue in the schoole to them which are or shalbe able to speake latyne') and to raise a series of questions about the connection of scholarly reading to everyday language usage. What exactly is this anxiety about the use of the vernacular? Is it a moral anxiety – the idea that while a pedagogue has little control over a student's contact with vernacular lan-guage on a daily basis (*pace* the warnings of Elyot and Kempe regarding the com-pany that young people keep, as cited above), control over classical reading and therefore the acquisition of a classical vocabulary is absolute, rendering it impossi-ble for the young protégés to use an improper vocabulary? Is it a mark of class anx-iety – that rendering a student uneloquent in the vernacular through lack of custom in effect renders him more likely to converse only with those able to com-municate in the same classical language? Or is it rather to do with an absolute sep-aration between the natural self and the tutored self, the idea that there is one argot for private exchange and another for public, teaching by extrapolation that each individual is in effect the sum of two selves so utterly different that two sets of lan-guage are necessary? As John Gleason argues in his biographical study of John Colet, founder of St Paul's School at the beginning of the sixteenth century, it may be that the emergence of an early modern notion of individuality is to some extent

10 Kempe, in Pepper, p. 224.   11 Watson, pp 10–11. Palsgrave had compiled a French gram-mar, *Lesclarcissement de la langue francoyse* (London: Iohan Haukyns, 1530).

dependent on such a separation of selves: 'The modern sense of the word [individual] implies such dividedness as may be necessary for self-realisation'.[12] If any or all of these questions have any significance, how does that significance change when the social class of the students in question is taken into consideration?

III

There is a substantial number of texts concerning the rearing of children throughout the sixteenth century, the most famous of them probably being Ascham's *The scholemaster* (printed 1570; Ascham died in 1568) and Thomas Elyot's *The book named the governor* (1531). Elyot is also responsible for *The education or bringing up of children* (1533); also in existence are Colet's *Aeditio* (printed 1527; Colet died in 1519, and this text, with revisions by Erasmus, became the *Eton Latin grammar*, printed in 1549); Francis Clement's *The petie schole with an English orthographie* (1578); Dudley Fenner's *The artes of logicke and rethorike* (1584); and Kempe's treatise *The education of children in learning* (1588). Where Ascham and Elyot are preoccupied with the education of the governing classes, Clement and Kempe in particular concern themselves quite explicitly with the merchant classes. Alongside these deliberately constructed advice manuals, there exists a surprising degree of specific information about desirable grammar school and university curriculum reading, thanks mostly to documents such as the accounting records for 1570–7 kept by John Whitgift, Master of Trinity College Cambridge 1567–77, for the 'at least 46 junior members in his care'[13] – among them the young Francis Bacon and his brother Antony.[14] This is a list of books purchased by Whitgift, and so is by no

12 John B. Gleason, *John Colet* (Berkeley: U. California Press, 1989), p. 210.   13 See Philip Gaskell, 'Books bought by Whitgift's pupils in the 1570s', *Transactions, Cambridge Bibliographical Society*, no. 7 (1970–80), 1981, pp 284–93. The social make-up of the students mentioned is interesting: '8 Fellow-Commoners … 17 pensioners … 12 sizars … and 9 men of unknown status'.   14 The following list is extrapolated from Gaskell's article, which lists the books in alphabetical order by author, giving details of the students for whom each book was bought and the sum that was paid in each case. Sometimes the price of the same title differs, suggesting perhaps secondhand copies. Aristotle: Works, Ethica, Organon, Physica; the Bible (Latin), Psalms, New Testament (Greek); Caesar, Gaius Julius, Commentarii; Caesarius, Johannes Consentinus, Dialectica; Castellion, Sebastian, Dialogi; Cicero ('Tully') Works, Orations, Rhetorica, De Officiis, *Tusculanae quaestiones*, Letters; Clenardus, Nicolaus, Institutiones in linguam Graecam; Cooper, Thomas, *Thesaurus linguae romanae et britannicae*; Demosthenes, Orations; *Dialogues on the Eucharist*; Donatus, Bernardinus; Erasmus, *Apothegmata, Colloquia*; Hermogenes, *Ars Rhetorica*; Homer, *Iliad, Odyssey*; Isocrates, *Orations*; Justinius, *Ex troio Pompeio historia*; Livius, Titus, *Works*; Lucian of Samosata, *Dialogues*; Plato, Works, *Leges*; Ramus, Petrus, *Praelectiones in Ciceronis orations*; Sallustus Crispus Gaius, *Works*; Seton, John, *Dialectica*; Sophocles, *Works*; Sturm, Johann *De universa ratione elocutionis rhetoricae*; Valerius, Maximus, *Works*; Velcurio, Johannes, *Commentarii in universam physicam Aristotelis libri quatuor*; Wolffhart Conrad Lycosthenes, *Apophthegmatum loci communes*; Xenephon, *Works*.

means an exhaustive account of what was set to be read. As Gaskell points out, 'the list of books is most unlikely to include all of the titles owned or even bought by these pupils ... books were certainly passed from student to student'.[15] A much more copious list of recommended reading is available from Kempe's 1588 text, *The education of children in learning*. Kempe's exhaustive list of recommended authors is scattered about his carefully constructed treatise, but a count through the text yields up some forty-two 'ancient teachers' (that is, classical writers)[16], eleven or so of the 'Christian school'[17] and another seven or so of the 'Old English school'.[18]

Among the ancients, he singles out a few for special praise, separate from their place in the list:

> But of all other, for varietie in learning, and paynfulnesse to set it foorth in writing, Marcus Cicero a worthie Prince also hath deserved much prayse. Whose bookes, as also the histories of Iulius Caesar, Terences Comedies, together with the bookes of the three Poets Virgil, Ouid and Horace, and also of Quintilian the Rhetorician, are the only Latin Schoolemaisters to all good students even at this day.[19]

Kempe tells how Virgil had the people do reverence to him, how Virgil and Horace were 'the only darlings to Augustus the Emperor', and how 'Ouid's learning, like Orpheus' musicke' brings savage tribes 'to use a great humanitie towards him'. (206)

Kempe's text works on a tripartite basis, as in common in the sixteenth century. The sections of the book are 'Of the dignity of schooling', 'Of the utilitie of schooling' and 'Of the method of schooling'. He divides the reading he suggests into 'The schoole of the hebrewes' (Old Testament examples of scholarly activity), 'the school of the gentiles' or 'the schoole of humanitie'(classics) and 'the school of christianitie' which takes in the church fathers and the Old English tradition, as we have just seen. The functions of each, and the necessity of learning at least a little from each, are clearly defined;

15 Gaskell, p. 285.   16 An extrapolated list of 'ancient teachers' looks like this; the quotations in brackets are passing comments made by Kempe. He mentions Hellanicus, Democritus, Anaxagoras, Aristagoras, Pindarus, Esthylus, Sophocles, Euripides, Socrates ('the ornament of schooling'), Plutarch, Plato, Aristotle, Xenocrates, Xenophon, Eudoxus, Euclid, Socrates, Demosthenes, Menander, Ptolemy, Philadelphus, Livius Andronicus, Linnius, Plautus (who 'wrote his eloquent comedies by night'), Nenius, Statius, Pacuuis, Accius, Terence ('by whose comedies the learned men then and our schooles now have great helpe for puritie and eloquence of the Latine tongue'), Julius Caesar (who 'with a most pure style set foorth the histories of his times, and certeyn bookes of Grammar'), Virgil, Horace, Quintilian, Ovid, Callidus, Callius, Corniscius, Sallust, Seneca, Livius, Persius, Lucan.   17 Pantenius, Clemens, Origen, Cyprian, Athanasius, Gregory, Chrysostom, Basil, Hierome, Ambrose, Austin.   18 Gildas, Joseph of Arimathea, Sigebert of East Anglia (who 'set up schooles in the Greke and Latin tong'), Egbert of Kent, Ethelstan, Alfred (who ' did shut up the dore of climing to any dignitie in the Court against such as wanted the furniture of learning'), John Scot.   19 Kempe, in Pepper, pp 205–6. All other quotations in this section are from Kempe, pp 206–37.

> The Schoole of the Hebrewes hath the chiefe praise of most auncient and
> true godliness: the Schoole of the Gentiles, of framing an artificiall way and
> method to attaine learning by: the School of the Christians, of manifesting
> the true practise [sic] of all learning, referring it to the right end. (210)

He argues that all social classes should be educated; that a good material life is
the product of, and also ameliorated by, being learned, and that it is more important to educate children than to leave them wealth.

> Let thy children be nourtured up in all good knowledge, accordinge to their
> capacitie. Thou seest that the Schoole doores are open, teachers giue atten-
> dance, that there want no bookes, nor any other commoditie necessarie to
> make a good scholler, neither canst thou leave thy children any possession
> or patrimonie, either for value, or for certeyntie, comparable unto learning.
> (214)

But, he warns, not every child from every class can be expected to be fit for this:
our 'understanding in our Childhood' is 'verie slender and feeble', so we need the
'breefest and easiest way to be used in this discipline' and the schoolmaster must
first 'consider what children are fit for the same'; (217) we need a 'Scholler both
apt and willing to receive the seede of this good doctrine', and just as Xenophon
and Socrates suggest, scholars should be 'quick of understanding, sure of memorie, and desirous of good learning', and there is no point in a master trying to get
good results out of 'a dulhead, nor of a foole, nor yet of an unwilling mind'. (218)
The 'first degree of teaching' is *prosodia*, or 'pronouncing of letters', then syllables,
then words, 'with the mouth': and *orthographia*, 'writing of them with the hand'.
(223) Reading and writing by this method is all a child should be taught until the
age of seven, but a child should write only for three hours a day, and the rest of the
time be taken up with reading. (226)
　　Then comes Kempe's formal curriculum, and it is interesting to align it with
Wolsey's in terms of both distribution and content, and with Whitgift's accounts
list in terms of content. The first form, says Kempe, 'shall begin to learne the
Grammar in the Latin toong ... learne by hart the parts of speach with their properties ... and being about eight yeeres old, let him moue foorth into the second
fourme ...' (226–7) Once in the second form, the scholar's chief business is 'to
practise the precepts of Grammar in expounding and unfolding the works of Latin
Authors ... because Children learne first to talke familiarly with their fellowes or
others, Dialogs are most easy for their capacitie, as are the Dialogs of *Corderius* and
Castalion [sic]' The student is to learn 'number and persons' with an exemplary
sentence ('a good father loves an honest son', 'good fathers love honest sons'.)
Kempe goes on, 'This kind of exercise will both leade him to understande the con-
gruitie and syntaxes of speach, and also make him expert in forming of Nouns and

Verbes. And so hauing ended his yeare, let him march forward into the third four-me.' (227–9)

In the third form, 'which besides the harder Dialogs, shall reade also *Tullyes* Epistles collected by *Sturmius*', the student 'shall begin to practise without an example of imitation ... heed being taken that he be reformed when he useth bar-barous words'. (229–30) The fourth form requires further study of these more advanced authors, with, perhaps, an eye to an economical retention of students by using the same books again: 'Yea, the same bookes of Dialogs and Epistles may serve for the fourth fourme also, so that the hardest of both sorts be chosen' (230), and 'Then to the fifth fourme shall be read *Terences* Comedies, Tullyes treatises of friendship and of old age, which are a more artificiall and harder kind of Dialogs, whereunto, let *Ouid de Tristibus* ... be added for Poetrie... If the scholler shall be a *Graecian*, let him learne the Greeke grammar while he is yet in this fourme... and likewise... in the Hebrewe, if he will be an *Hebrician*. And so I conclude the sec-ond degree of schooling with the ende both of this fifth fourme, and the twelfth yeere of the schollers age.' (231–2)

The third degree of schooling begins in sixth form. 'Then shall follow the third degree for Logike and Rhetorike ... wherein he shall employ the sixth part of his studie, and all the rest in learning and handling good authors: as are *Tullies Offices*, his *Orations, Caesars Commentaries, Virgils Aneis, Ouids Metamorphosis, and Horace* ... he must observe in authors all the use of the Artes ... the method of the whole treatise, and the passages, whereby the parts are ioyned together ... the Rhetoricall pronounciation [sic] and gesture fit for euery word, sentence, and affection'. (232–3) This all being mastered, 'After a three yeeres exercise in this degree of studie, he may ascend to the fourth degree, of Arithmetike and Geometrie. And according to the same manner, easely passe through these Artes in halfe a yeere, and so before the full age of sixteene yeeres be made fit to wade without a schoole-maister, through deeper mysteries of learning, to set forth the glorie of God, and to benefite his Countrie.' (237)

In summary then, it would seem that the following observations can be made: fact is clearly more abundant than fiction, and concentration on form valorized over content. There is a preoccupation with propriety of expression, with knowl-edge of history, with exemplar, with the giving and receiving of advice, and with the transitional nature of life.

IV

The question of what Renaissance children were led to read, how and in what order they read what they read, and the kind of self that is expressed as an appar-ent result of this formative experience might lead to a reassessment of how the twenty-first century views sixteenth-century accounts of childhood or individual representations of children. Initially, five texts in particular, the Marian moral interlude *Jake Jugeler* (attributed to Nicholas Udall), Shakespeare's *King John* and his *Titus Andronicus*, Phyllis Rackin's *Stages of history* and Merry Wiesner-Hanks' *Gender and history*, prompted questions about the nature of the formation and expression of identity in children, and their relationship in society to each other and to adults. Both Rackin and Wiesner-Hanks[20] investigate the relationships of gender, history, status and power to each other. The work that Rackin has done on alternative readings of Shakespeare's histories, and that Wiesner-Hanks has done on the gender/generation axis of power can be usefully adapted to inform the way in which one might read the creative characterisation of children in the sixteenth and early seventeenth centuries. But, given the masses of information available, and the welter of methodologies by which this information might be read, what is the relationship between the child that books build[21] (to borrow a phrase from Francis Spufford) and the child that dramatic works of the period create and present to our view?

V

Shakespeare rarely uses his child actors to represent children. There are of course exceptions that prove the rule: the crowd of punitive children who, dressed as supernatural little beings, pinch and pummel Falstaff at the end of *The merry wives of Windsor*; the more obvious individuals, the little Macduffs in *Macbeth*, Mamilius in *The winter's tale*, the young princes in *Richard III*, Arthur in *King John*, young Lucius in *Titus Andronicus*, Coriolanus' son; there is also a group of young people, somewhere between childhood and adulthood, who are made to feel their status in relation to their parents very strongly, and all of whom invoke a story of their childhood to defend themselves: Helena (*A midsummer night's dream*), Marina (*Pericles*), Miranda (*The tempest*). There are other plays of the period that need investigation too, most obviously Beaumont's *The knight of the burning pestle*, which plays with the idea of generic knowledge of dramatic and literary forms among the apprentice cohort in early seventeenth-century London, and has its apprentice players able to quote extempore (if inaccurately) from both *The faerie queene* and *Henry V*.

When Shakespeare does use children as important characters, though, he always relates them to either a literary text, to the question of historiography, or to the question of knowing self by being told stories. His children are always precocious, they always know or want to know just a little more than is good for them, and the knowledge puts them in a position where they have to act with a maturi-

---

20 Phyllis Rackin, *Stages of history* (London: Routledge, 1991); Merry Wiesner-Hanks, *Gender in history* (Oxford: Blackwell, 2001).   **21** Francis Spufford, *The child that books built* (London: Faber, 2002).

ty, and with a knowingness, beyond their years. His representation of young children seems to me to be inextricably bound up with the idea of gaining knowledge through narrative, or with self-redemption through the art of good speaking, not just in terms of good rhetoric but in understanding the innate structures of communication.

In *King John*, for example, there is a moment when the young Arthur – whom Shakespeare turns into a much younger character than was historically true[22] – saves his eyesight – and probably his life – by reciting the personal history of the relationship between himself and the man-servant who has been detailed to blind him.

> Have you the heart? When your head did but ache,
> I knot my handkercher about your brows
> (The best I had, a princess wrought it me)
> And I did never ask it you again:
> And with my hand at midnight held your head;
> And like the watchful minutes to the hour,
> Still and anon cheered up the heavy time,
> Saying, 'What lack you?' and 'Where lies your grief?'   4.1.41–8

At this moment, both Rackin's and Weisner-Hanks' positions can be seen to be borne out. Arthur understands that the balance between the sympathy he can invoke as a dependent child is in crucial balance with his higher social status; he also understands that speaking will delay the moment of action (usually, though not always a feminine ploy in Shakespeare); and he also seems to realize that the invocation of an individual history, an intimate private history between himself and Hubert, might, at the right rhetorical pitch, overrule the generic historical perception of him within the current power structure as threat to the throne. The tensions of authority between age and status are also clearly seen, and it might be argued that there is a gender issue here too, in the not unusual concept that a young boy is more likely to be thought of as feminine than masculine. But it is an understanding of the relationship between state history and the representation of the individual, and the noble power to speak well and to invoke lineage and status almost coincidentally, subtly, that saves him at this instant.

In *Titus Andronicus*, young Lucius is seen to solve the mystery of the rape and terrible mutilation of his aunt Lavinia because of the knowledge she shared with him by reading to him as a young boy. Lavinia is violated as an act of revenge, and because her hands have been cut off and her tongue severed, she can neither name her violators nor describe what has happened to her. There is a whole scene at the beginning of Act IV where Lucius is urged not to be afraid of his grotesquely dis-

---

22 'Arthur, a young warrior in Holinshed, becomes a helpless child in the play.' E.A.J. Honigmann, *King John*, The Arden Shakespeare (London: Methuen, 1986), p. lxiv.

figured aunt and is reminded how often she used to read to him when he was very small. He is urged to perform the same labour of love for her to assuage her suffering. In this scene, which is dreadfully macabre and horribly comical, Lavinia pursues Lucius with a copy of Ovid's *Metamorphoses* clasped between her bleeding stumps, entreating him to recognize, though their shared knowledge of the Procne and Philomel myth, the nature of what has happened to her. Lucius is caught in the moment between childhood story-telling and adult recognition of responsibility as he unravels the mystery by dint of his knowledge of the *Metamorphoses*. Moments later, Titus has his knowledge of the rapists' guilt revealed to them by having the same young Lucius deliver a scroll to them containing a quotation from Horace which they recognize: 'O, 'tis a verse in Horace, I know it well; I read it in the grammar long ago', says Chiron.

VI

These moments in *Titus Andronicus* raise a series of questions about the status of the *Metamorphoses*, about the nature of apophthegmatic knowledge learnt in school, and about the clear relationship between the child, the knowledge of literature and the knowledge not only of history but also of historiography, the forms in which history can be received, in Shakespeare. What is Shakespeare's idea of the relationship between the child and the book? Why does Shakespeare posit so clearly the usefulness of both knowing, and knowing the value of, certain texts, the mechanism of the telling of stories, the importance of histories and historiographies, the recall of what his characters learnt unthinkingly from books as children? Is this how nascent renaissance men and women come to know themselves, or to recall an earlier, more innocent version of themselves? Why is it that these elements of self-knowledge are lent such importance, rather than reliance on received informal information from the parent-figures in these plays?

    An examination of such records as exist of grammar school and university curricula show that there is a clear preoccupation, in the early modern project of education, with four areas of a child's/young person's education: rhetoric, history, proper social conduct and processes of change. It is clear that the import of that knowledge is held to be important not only in terms of academic knowledge, but in terms of recalling the self to understanding. How do these elements inform the notion of the child as presented through the drama? What is here is only a beginning, but I think the questions formulated might turn out to be of huge importance.

Rebuilding *Castle Blair*:
a reading of Flora Shaw's 1878 children's novel

ROBERT DUNBAR

In nineteenth-century Dublin families comprising mother, father and fourteen children were not all that unusual: rather less common, though, would have been one where the fourteen children included six daughters named Alice, Flora, Lulu, Marie, Mimi and Thomasina. But such was the Shaw family, living in some style in a beautiful home on sixty-nine acres of land, a residence originally known as Kimmage House, subsequently to become more widely known as Kimmage Manor. It had been bought in 1829 by one Sir Frederick Shaw, a prominent figure in Irish political life, who for a period had been a Member of Parliament at Westminster before becoming Recorder of Dublin. In a short space of time, according to Patrick Ryan in his history of Kimmage Manor, Shaw had remodelled the property and extended the grounds, creating a building in the Tudor style, complete with 'triangular gables, spiral turrets and tall chimneys'.[1] His second son, George, was an army general who, while serving in Mauritius in 1848, had met and married Marie de Fontaine, daughter of the island's governor. Theirs were the fourteen children, the third of whom was Flora, more exactly Flora Louise, born in December 1852. Although stationed for part of the time in Woolwich barracks in England, the Shaws and their children generally moved to Kimmage in May of each year, remaining there until October. Flora's only biographer to date, E. Moberly Bell, writes in 1947 of the children: 'They spent long happy days out-of-doors, wading up the little stream that ran near the garden, exploring all the wonders of the garden and the countryside.'[2] Clearly, these were idyllic times and Flora's memories of them were to serve as background for many details of the natural world in the setting of *Castle Blair*,[3] her first children's book, to be published in 1878 when she was twenty-six. Some years previously, while at Woolwich, she had met, and become good friends with, John Ruskin, to whom she would later send an outline of this first novel. 'I am delighted with the idea of your tale,' he responded, 'and do not doubt your power of making it entertaining to children.'[4]

Ruskin's optimism was justified, to the extent that when *Castle Blair* eventually appeared it enjoyed wide success and between 1878 and 1907 ran to some eight

1 Patrick Ryan, 'The missionary college – Kimmage', *Go teach all nations*, ed. Enda Watters (Dublin: Paraclete, 2000), pp 405–45, p. 410.   2 E. Moberly Bell, *Flora Shaw* (London: Constable, 1947), p. 15.   3 Flora L. Shaw, *Castle Blair* (London: Hart-Davies, 1966). All references to the text in this article are to this edition.   4 Bell, *Shaw*, p. 30.

editions in Britain; there were also five American editions and three from France between 1889 and 1894. The financial rewards were small but the book brought invitations to contribute to the then significant and influential *Aunt Judy's magazine*, edited by Margaret Gatty, in which many Victorian children's authors had their work first published. It was here that Flora's second novel, *Hector*, first appeared, in 1881, in serialized form: this was set in France and based on holidays spent there with her French cousins. These, together with a third novel, *A sea change*,[5] first published in 1885, were her only writings of any importance for children, for her subsequent distinction was in journalism, a career which saw her appointment, while still a young woman, as the first woman special correspondent of the *Times* and which took her, as her specialized interest and expertise in colonial politics developed, to virtually every corner of the then British Empire: Gibraltar, Egypt, South Africa, Australia, Canada.

In 1902, at the age of fifty, she married the colonial administrator Sir Frederick, later Lord, Lugard, in whose company her travels, to places such as Nigeria and Hong Kong, continued. Such were the prevailing conventions of the time that, as her biographer succinctly expresses it, 'When she ceased to be Flora Shaw she also ceased to be a woman with a career'.[6] In the entry on Shaw in *Women in world history: a biographical encyclopaedia* (2002), Kenneth J. Orosz concludes: 'Despite many unusual accomplishments Flora Shaw proved unable to escape from typical Victorian notions that women and their contributions were less important than men. Convinced that her own life was unworthy of being recorded she spent her final days working on a biography of her husband, leaving it to future chroniclers to piece together the enormity of her own impact on British public opinion and imperial affairs'.[7] Part of this 'enormity of impact' arose out of her continuing interest and involvement in contemporary Irish matters, particularly the ongoing controversy about Home Rule, and her emergence as a strong and public spokesperson for the cause of those Ulster (and indeed) Irish Protestants opposed to it. She died in 1929 at the age of seventy-seven, by which time Kimmage Manor had become a novitiate and scholasticate for the Irish province of the Congregation of the Holy Spirit. 'The story of Kimmage,' Ryan concludes his history, 'is a story of change'.[8] In an account of the only return visit that I have been able to confirm that Flora made to Kimmage – this was in 1895, some twenty years after she had left for England – she records how she found the place 'changed in detail, unchanged in the abiding lines of hill and stream; the principal trees standing still, the low wall under the chestnut gone, but the tree itself still there ... one wonders

5 Mrs A. [Margaret] Gatty (ed. 1866–73), *Aunt Judy's Magazine*, eds H.K.F. Gatty and J.H. Ewing 1874–6; H.K.F. Gatty 1877–85; Flora L. Shaw, *Castle Blair: a story of youthful days* (London, 1878); Flora L. Shaw, *Hector: a story for young people* (London: Bell, 1883); Flora L. Shaw, *A sea change* (London: Routledge, 1885).   6 Bell, *Shaw*, p. 250.   7 Kenneth J. Orosz, 'Flora L. Shaw', in *Women in world history: a biographical encyclopaedia*, 15 vols, ed. Anne Commire (Waterforth, CT: Yorkin, 2002), vol. 14, pp 213–20.   8 Ryan, 'Kimmage', p. 445.

which changes most, oneself or the old surroundings.' One does, indeed. Of the 1895 Dublin of which Kimmage was part she writes: 'I cannot remember to have seen in any country in the world a people so dirty, ragged and apparently degraded.'[9]

Shaw's children's novel *Castle Blair* initially enjoyed, as has been commented, much popularity. Subsequently, however, it almost totally vanished from public awareness and apart from a 1929 edition from Oxford University Press, for many years was out of print. Until 1966 in fact, when the British publisher Hart-Davis reissued it as part of a series called 'The Keepsake Library'.[10] The book's first return to public notice may be traced to a couple of paragraphs by Anne Thaxter Eaton in *A critical history of children's literature*, an American reference book dating from 1953, where it is described as a 'spirited account of a houseful of children living very much according to their own sweet will in their uncle's home in Ireland while their parents are in India'.[11] While some later 'overview' surveys of children's literature include some brief reference to Shaw's book, the majority, especially the more recent ones, do not: it does not, for example, figure in Townsend's *Written for children*, in any of the various Peter Hunt histories or anthologies, or in Victor Watson's *Cambridge history of children's books in English*.[12] The only critical commentary of any length remains Gillian Avery's, in her 1965 study, *Nineteenth century children*. Avery is primarily interested in the way in which Shaw's portrait of her child characters sets the book apart from other children's literature of the period: given some other children's literature of the period, this is not a particularly contentious notion to propose. 'It uncovers,' she writes, 'the savageness in children, their capacity for a terrifying degree of hatred, in a way no other author has cared to do.'[13] But neither the Irish nor the political dimension to the story is given any particular emphasis by Avery; the reasons for the children's 'savageness' or their 'terrifying degree of hatred' are not discussed.

The only Irish reference which I have seen to Flora Shaw as a children's author is a one-line mention in Janette Condon's essay 'Children's books in nineteenth-century Ireland' in *The big guide 2: Irish children's books* published in 2000. Condon includes her as one of four late nineteenth century Anglo-Irish writers who 'adopted the socially acceptable feminine role of educator ... and wrote "Edgeworthian"

9 Bell, *Shaw*, p. 171.   10 This edition is now also out of print, though it is reasonably easily available in second-hand condition: at the moment these words are being drafted there are twelve copies available on the abebooks.com site on the internet.   11 Anne Thaxter Eaton, 'A broader field', in *A critical history of children's literature*, ed. Cornelia Meigs (New York: Macmillan, 1969, rev. ed.), p. 175.   12 Peter Hunt, *An introduction to children's literature* (Oxford: OUP, 1994); Peter Hunt (ed.), *Children's literature: an anthology, 1801–1902* (Oxford: Blackwell, 2001); Peter Hunt (ed.) *Children's literature: an illustrated history* (Oxford: OUP, 1995); Hunt (ed.) *International companion encyclopaedia of children's literature* (London: Routledge, 1996); John Rowe Townsend, *Written for children* (London: Kestrel, 1983 second rev. ed.); Victor Watson, *The Cambridge guide to children's books in English* (Cambridge: Cambridge UP, 2001).   13 Avery, *Children*, p. 180.

tales of the civilizing influence of English culture and education in Ireland'[14] – a remark which, whatever its relevance to the other writers named by Condon, has little to do with the essential spirit of Castle Blair, in which the 'civilizing influence' is shown to be resisted with such vigour. Interestingly though, in a further essay, ' "A quaking sod": Ireland, empire and children's literary culture', also published in 2000, Condon writes in general terms: 'The Ireland of children's literary culture in the nineteenth and early twentieth century is ... dependent upon and conditioned by the presence of empire, whether Ireland is seen as part of it or struggling to escape from it',[15] a remark which is extremely pertinent to Shaw's novel. Indeed, it is precisely what the book is about and, given the later political sympathies of its author, it assumes a particularly distinctive role in the novel.

For *Castle Blair* is, in fact, the nearest we have in children's literature to the 'big house' novel of much Irish literature and, like its adult counterparts, is largely concerned with juxtaposing English and Irish perspectives, seen here, however, through children's eyes. The principal children are the five lively young Blairs, staying with their uncle at his slightly decaying pile in County Tipperary. He is not, technically, an absentee landlord but, because of his absorption in his bookish interests, he entrusts the day-to-day running of his house and young charges to his housekeeper-with-a-heart-of-gold, Mrs Bridget Donegan, and of his estate to the much firmer Mr Plunkett. 'He's so wrapped up in books, and stones and pictures, he puts all his duties on one side,' (152) says hoity-toity Cousin Jane at one point, not completely without justification. The story, set in a time more or less contemporary with its date of publication (1878), has as backdrop those contemporary events which make this post-famine period of land wars, financial crises and civil dissension, in the words of the historian Gearóid Ó Tuathaigh, 'one of the most eventful and tragic epochs in Irish history', a time when, to quote Ó Tuathaigh again, 'violence was never far from the surface of everyday life in rural Ireland', and not least in County Tipperary, which was particularly notorious for agrarian unrest.[16] Little wonder that soon after her arrival the Blairs' French cousin, Adrienne, is 'beginning to think that Ireland was an unsafe place to live in'.[17] Shaw, then, very courageously for a children's novel of her time, takes on strictly contemporary political events – she is not writing historical fiction – and, incidentally, deals with a period which has remained virtually untouched since then in any children's literature emanating from, or dealing with, Ireland: strange, given the influence of so many events of these decades in determining the course of future Irish history. Perhaps the twenty or so children's novels we now have about the famine have sapped our creative energies.

14 Janette Condon, 'Children's books in nineteenth-century Ireland', *The big guide 2: Irish children's books*, eds Valerie Coghlan and Celia Keenan (Dublin: CBI, 2000), pp 53–9, p. 57.   15 Janette Condon, '"A quaking sod": Ireland, empire and children's literary culture', *New voices in Irish criticism*, ed. P.J. Mathews (Dublin: Four Courts, 2000), 189–96, p. 197.   16 Gearóid Ó Tuathaigh, 'The struggle for emancipation and independence, 1809–1918', *The Irish world*, ed. Brian de Breffny (London: Thames and Hudson, 2000), pp 171–98, pp 172, 185.   17 Shaw, *Castle*, pp 152.

Castle Blair derives much of its power from the fact that events soon develop into what is essentially a highly concentrated battle of wills between two intractable forces, Mr Plunkett and eleven-year-old Murtagh Blair, who must have a serious claim to be one of the most arresting creations in any children's fiction set in Ireland. By nature impetuous, rebellious and romantic, Murtagh early makes it clear to everyone – including the very puzzled visiting French cousin – that in any sort of dispute about Irish and English matters his sympathies will be very much with the native Irish and that his most energetic contempt will be reserved for the 'agents' – Plunkett being one such – whom he, endorsing the viewpoint of the 'native Irish', identifies as being the chief cause of the people's hardship. ' "I say, Murtagh," says his brother Bobbo early on, "we must do something to that old Plunkett. He is getting worse and worse." "I think I'll kill him some day!" burst out Murtagh.' (29) By the time events have played themselves out Murtagh has come close to being involved in doing just that, principally through his growing attachment to the cause of some of the local families, the Dalys and the O'Tooles particularly. He shows at all times an understanding of the larger Irish world of which his own hostilities are a part: his symbolic role as the colonized engaged in battle with the colonizer comes to the forefront as the novel's essential motif. Plunkett has, in Mrs O'Toole's formulation, been 'a blight an' a curse upon the country since the day he first set foot in it'. (176)

Murtagh's anger with Plunkett is rooted in controversies about ownership: the tropes between which the narrative moves relate to appropriation and dispossession, to subjection and freedom, to tameness and to wildness. Even the children's 'secret place', their hut on an island, becomes, in one of the novel's most convincing combinations of the literal and the figurative, a significant metonymic focus of dispute when Plunkett demands its destruction. Similarly, the 'old tower' where Adrienne is to be initiated as a member of the children's 'tribe' serves as backcloth for one of their most uninhibited expressions of political intent. 'Oh, wouldn't it be glorious,' says Winnie, 'if we could live up here really with our tribe ... To be perfectly free ... and one day when we get older we would rise and set Ireland free. Oh, I would like to be queen of a tribe and I'd lead them into battle and shout "For Ireland and Liberty!" ' (140) The effervescence of the moment reaches its climax when all present burst into song: 'We'll pluck the laurel tree,/ And we'll call it Liberty, /For our country shall be free ...' (150) At such moments of intensity as these, Avery's comment that 'On the whole [Shaw's] sympathies are with the children, who certainly gain the moral victory at the end of the book ...'[18] seems perfectly valid as a summary. The perspective of the 'downtrodden Irish' has a very good run – perhaps a better one than the author may have intended: there is something in the sheer enthusiasm of the young voices, and especially in Murtagh's cool arrogance in his verbal confrontations with Plunkett, that is very engaging and

18 Gillian Avery, *Nineteenth-century children* (London: Hodder and Stoughton, 1965), p. 180.

infectious, even if they contribute to what Shaw herself was to call the 'rather fancy politics' of the novel.[19] At the very least there is an ambivalence which, as often in discussions of Irish 'freedom', centres on the legitimacy, or otherwise, of the steps it may be necessary to take before it is to be attained.

When, early in the story, Murtagh needs to leave a note secretly in the Daly household, he recommends to his sister Winnie that they might 'poke it under the cottage door the way the Fenians do their warnings about shooting people'; (56) later, when the same sister asks, following an attempt on Plunkett's life, 'why they always shoot people,' Murtagh's immediate response is: 'Because they're agents ... and I don't really know what agents are, but it's something very bad. They're tyrants, and they oppress everybody. That man that was fishing with me and Pat O'Toole said Ireland would never be free till all the agents were killed.' (66)

That sentence of Murtagh's – 'I don't really know what agents are' – becomes the crux of the whole business, as Shaw slowly directs her story towards educating him concerning the authorial perception of what, at least, Plunkett 'really' is – though with what degree of conviction remains problematic. The principal medium through whom more 'gentlemanly' notions are gradually instilled in Murtagh is the visiting French cousin, whose initial bewilderment and detachment eventually give way to candid criticism of what she sees as Murtagh's limitation: his capacity to hate and to rage as violently as he does. (It should be said, in passing, that notions of what constitute 'gentlemanly' attitudes provide an intriguing subtext to the novel: the word becomes a key element in the ongoing dialectic which also involves scrutiny of such words as 'savage' and 'civilized'.)

Adrienne at first tentatively recommends to Murtagh a response of 'peace on earth, good will to men', while simultaneously growing to appreciate the new situation – 'the wildness, the enthusiasm, the restless, passionate courage' (149) – in which she finds herself, and sees parallels between it and Sicily's history in throwing off French domination. But by the time she hears that, as part of Murtagh's intended revenge on Plunkett, killing will be involved – and, moreover killing of what Murtagh already feels may be a treacherous, as distinct from an open, kind – she is insisting, in Plunkett's defence, that 'he is not robbing them ... and even if he were it's too dreadful hating like that and watching to kill people. I'd rather be oppressed all my life than be guilty of a cowardly murder'. (209) And as for the Sicilians, 'They fought a brave hand-to-hand struggle: they did not secretly murder a man who was going fearlessly about amongst them; and what they did they did only after having tried every other means in their power.' (241) A few pages earlier, the authorial voice has intervened, as young Pat O'Toole spills out his sense of grievance to Murtagh, to tell us, explicitly, that 'Neither of the boys really knew anything of what he was talking about. They only heard that people had to pay more than they had ever paid for their homes, and that in some cases they were turned out of them altogether. They did not hear that where rents had been raised

19 Bell, *Shaw*, p. 31.

it was in consequence of expensive and necessary improvements; where tenants had been turned out it was always for a solid reason. Rigorous justice had been dealt to all.' (241) By the time Murtagh and Plunkett are, as the book closes, shaking hands and talking about there being, perhaps, 'faults on both sides', (237) Murtagh concludes: 'I didn't know how wicked it was. I thought it would be a great thing to do, because I thought ... you were oppressing the people and I would set them free'. (254–5) The now magnanimous Plunkett, who 'knew himself to be one of the best agents in Ireland', responds: 'I have made mistakes with you; but we must start afresh, and perhaps we shall get on better now.' (255)

It is an attempt at the kind of balanced conclusion which, in 1878, might well have seemed honourable and justified; 125 years on, with the benefit of hindsight, we may feel that its optimism seems misguided. *Castle Blair* is not a literary masterpiece: its weaknesses – its awkward moments of piety, its occasionally unwise (and often entertaining, even if unintentionally so) attempts to reproduce Tipperary speech patterns – are largely the weaknesses of its time. But it has the supreme merit of tackling political complexities in a way that respects differing viewpoints and, as I have suggested, in a way which, accidentally or deliberately, gives the children, if not quite the last word, then the word that is most generous.

The wild Irish girls of L.T. Meade and
Mrs George De Horne Vaizey

CAROLE DUNBAR

This essay is concerned not with the earlier, and perhaps more famous, 'wild Irish girl' novel written by Sydney Owenson, Lady Morgan, but with a selection of novels written in the genre by two later authors, L.T. Meade and Mrs George De Horne Vaizey, who wrote mainly for a female adolescent readership. Meade, who was born in Co. Cork in 1844 and moved to England in adulthood, was a prolific and hugely popular writer of stories for girls. Vaizey was born in Liverpool in 1856 and wrote books and magazine stories for a similar audience to that of Meade. They, together with several other authors of the late Victorian period, helped popularise the genre of the 'wild Irish girl'.

While sharing a literary designation, the novels of Meade and Vaizey differed radically from Owenson's novel, *The wild Irish girl*, which was published in 1806, in the same decade as the Act of Union, a piece of legislation which formalized Ireland's status as an English colony came into force. As Kirkpatrick observes, Owenson's work 'seeks to provide a genealogy for a separate identity at a historical moment when that identity seemed lost'.[1] This is a book, therefore, which smacks of defiance, insisting, as it does, on defining Irish identity through reference to a Gaelic past and a Gaelic culture. Such a definition automatically excludes the Anglo-Irish Protestant ascendancy, imposed by England, in whom was invested much of the country's power and the ownership of most of its assets.

The novel's protagonist, Glorvina, an Irish princess, is portrayed as learned and cultured, her qualities being depicted as 'both natural and national'.[2] Alongside these rare and laudable traits there exist characteristics more stereotypically associated in the public mind with her race and her gender, 'natural impatience and volatility', and an unpredictability, a 'union of intelligence and simplicity, infinite playfulness and profound reflection'.[3] Glorvina acts as tutor to the English visitor, Horatio, the allegorical relationship suggesting the superiority of the native Irish and the prejudice and ignorance of Ireland's colonial oppressor.

Such radicalism from both a nationalist and gender perspective was not universally welcomed. Phillips, Owenson's publisher, describes the sentiments that

---

1 Kathryn Kirkpatrick, 'Introduction', Sydney Owenson, Lady Morgan, *The wild Irish girl* (Oxford: OUP, 1999), p. 7.   2 Owenson, *The wild Irish girl* (Oxford: OUP, 1999), p. 120.   3 Ibid. p. 92.

underpin *The wild Irish girl* as 'too strongly opposed to the English interest in Ireland'.[4] Whelan reminds us that objections were not merely confined to political issues: 'Croker admonished her to find a book on domestic economy [...] "she might then hope to prove, not indeed a good writer of novels, but a useful friend, a faithful wife, a tender mother, and a respectable and happy mistress of a family"'.[5]

In a real sense it is the instilling of the qualities that Croker catalogues, along with a conviction of the superiority of the English nation, that is at the centre of Meade and Vaizey's 'wild Irish girl' novels. As the generic title the wild Irish girl suggests, the perspective from which the books were written is, despite Meade's nationality, not an Irish one. Indeed, the very *raison d'être* of the novels is to extol English civilization, contrasting it with what is viewed as Celtic barbarism. This is done by attempting to transform exuberant, demonstrative, garrulous and spontaneous Irish teenage girls from middle-class or landowning families into English ladies. The contrast between the supposed cultured and genteel English colonial power and the primitive nature of the colonized Irish is at one with a preoccupation of the turn of the century period in which the books were written. The age was, as Ledger and Luckhurst assert, obsessed by 'fantasies of decay and degeneration'.[6] One thinks of Bram Stoker's *Dracula* and Oscar Wilde's *The picture of Dorian Grey*, both, of course, Irish novels. In the stories of Vaizey and Meade written for the young, Irish decadence, although suggested, is muted. What is implied however is that only the most flimsy layer of civilization hides the primeval in the Irish.

Throughout the nineteenth century the scientific establishment interested itself in theories surrounding the origins and development of mankind, Darwinism being the most celebrated. Both Meade and Vaizey repeatedly use the word 'savage' to describe their Irish protagonists. It was a term also commonly applied to the English working classes, especially to its younger members. Hodgson Burnett uses it of Ann, the street child, in *A little princess* (1905), for instance. Interestingly, in the light of suggestions of the moral degeneracy of both the English working classes and of the Irish inherent in the application of the term savage, Darwin in *The descent of man* claims that there is 'a vast distance' in morality 'between the highest man of the highest race and the lowest savage'.[7]

The word 'lowest', used in the sense of one having an affinity with the soil, has strong echoes in the portrayal of the Irish protagonist in Vaizey's novel *Pixie O'Shaughnessy*.[8] The author tells us that Pixie 'is a botanist in a small way, could discourse like any farmer on crops and tillage, was most sporting in her descriptions of shooting and hunting, and had an exhaustive understanding of, and sym-

4 Kirkpatrick, 'Introduction', p. xvi.   5 Kevin Whelan, 'Writing Ireland reading England', in Owenson, Sydney, Lady Morgan, *The wild Irish girl* (London: Pickering and Chatto, 2000), p. xxiv.   6 Sally Ledger and Roger Luckhurst, *The fin de siècle: a reader in cultural history, 1880–1900* (Oxford, OUP, 2000), p. xiii.   7 Hugh Cunningham, *The children of the poor: representations of childhood since the seventeenth century* (Oxford: Blackwell, 1991), p. 125.

pathy with, the animal world'. While this is ostensibly a celebration of Pixie's achievements, the author uses it as a contrast to English values, 'civilized' values, what Vaizey calls 'the hundred and one restrictions and obligations of society'. Without these, Pixie is 'no more than a South Sea Islander dancing gaily upon the sands, and stringing beads in her dusky locks'.[9] The association of the Irish with the earth and nature is used as an indication of the nation's backwardness and the rudimentary and lascivious nature of its people.

Meade, in her novel *A wild Irish girl*, suggests a similar primitivism by employing images of water. Despite being described as 'a wild creature from the woods',[10] Patricia, the wild Irish girl of the title, is associated with the sea and recounts with relish on several occasions her love of swimming, diving, fishing and sailing in what she describes as the 'darling Atlantic'. (129) Ireland is described by one character as 'all bog' (179) with the inherent notion of the primeval swamp. Patricia's lack of sophistication, by implication, is accounted for by her recent emergence from that primeval swamp. This idea is illustrated by the author's use of the image of the sea anemone, a rudimentary form of animal life, so primitive that it still carries characteristics of a plant, and, as its name suggests, has not evolved enough to reside on land.[11] The dead sea anemones found in an aquarium that has been allowed to run dry are used as a metaphor for Patricia and her physical deterioration as a result of her being removed from Ireland, the bog, the environment which gave her life and sustains her.

From Meade's evocation of the primeval Irish swamp, we move to her use of images arising from the Darwinian assertion that apes and man have a common ancestor. In the novel under discussion Patricia is taken to London Zoo the day after her arrival in England. She escapes from her two English peers and their governess and is later found in the monkey house – 'the first nice place I've been in since I left Carrigraun'[12] – in which, significantly, Patricia says with affection, that one of the apes looks like her beloved grandfather, a comparison which vividly recalls popular cartoon images of simian Irish[13]. The governess discovers her charge with a monkey perched on her shoulder. The intimacy of the two is suggested in the image of Patricia's hair entwined around the ape's fingers.

Vaizey, in a bizarre scene in *Pixie O'Shaughnessy*, which seemingly has little relation to the rest of the novel, takes up a similar theme. Pixie assembles her friends in one of the schoolrooms and announces she is going to make a circuit of the room without touching the ground. It is, we are told, a mode of travel in which her whole family is proficient.

8 Mrs George De Horne Vaizey, *Pixie O'Shaughnessy* (London: The Religious Tract Society, 1920).   9 Ibid., p. 51.   10 L.T. Meade *A wild Irish girl* (London: Chambers, n.d., *c*.1910), p. 21. 11 Ibid., pp 225–6.   12 Ibid., p. 95   13 L.P. Curtis, *Apes and angels: the Irishman in Victorian caricature* (Washington: Smithsonian Press, 1971), provides extensive evidence of this phenomenon.

> From one chair to another, from chair number two to the shelf of the old
> bookcase which filled the middle space of the wall, from the bookcase with
> a leap and a bound on to the oak chest, from chest [...] to another chair and
> thence with a whoop and wildly waving hands to the end of an ordinary
> wooden form [...] It was easy enough to run along the blackboard, but what
> about the space between it and the shelves on the other side of the fire-
> place... What if there was no article of furniture within reach, there was a
> shelf overhead to which one could cling and work slowly along hand over
> hand until the coal-box offered a friendly footing.[14]

The ape-like athleticism of Pixie's escapade is underlined by the author's explanation, which again alludes to the closeness of the Irish girl to her primeval ancestors: 'When one had been accustomed to climb trees all one's life, what could be
easier?'[15] The reader is reminded of Swift's description of the Yahoos, themselves
a debased form of humanity, in *Gulliver's Travels*, in which he says 'they climbed
high Trees, as nimbly as a squirrel [...] They would often spring, and bound, and
leap with prodigious Agility.'[16]

Meade and Vaizey were not of course the first writers of fiction for children to
associate the Irish with apes. Several decades earlier, on the fourth of July, 1860, nine
months after Charles Darwin sent him a copy of *On the origin of species by means of
natural selection*, Charles Kingsley, while on a visit to Ireland, in a very short diary
entry, describes the Irish poor as 'human chimpanzees' and 'white chimpanzees'.[17]
It is an image that reappears in his description of the young English chimney sweep,
Tom, in his children's novel, *The water babies*, first published in 1863, the year in
which Kingsley describes himself as 'a convert to Darwin's views'.[18] Descending the
wrong chimney, Tom finds himself in the virginal surroundings of the 'sweet young
lady's room'. Catching his reflection in a mirror, he sees not a boy covered in soot,
but 'a black ape'.[19] Kingsley is deliberately ascribing to the working-class child, as
he did to the Irish, a degraded and primitive form of humanity.

Kingsley's linking of the Irish with the English working classes finds echoes in
Meade's work. In *A wild Irish girl*, the newly-arrived Patricia is unable to relate to
the governess, whom she tells: 'You'd be a very nice woman if you were wild and
ragged, and had big holes in your stockings and great brogues for shoes.' Musing
over the approaching meeting with the person who was to prove her salvation,
Patricia 'had a wild desire deep in her heart that Hope de Lacey might prove to be
a poor girl. If so – if so – life might be tolerable.' The only real poor person Patricia
actually meets is Sparkling Tim, whom, alluding to her feelings of kinship, she
describes as her 'brother'.[20]

---

14 Vaizey, *Pixie*, pp 290-1.   15 Ibid., p. 91.   16 Jonathan Swift, *Selected prose works*, ed. John
Hayward (London: Cresset Press, 1944), p. 315.   17 Fanny Kingsley (ed.), *Charles Kingsley:
his letters and memories of his life* (London: Kegan Paul, Trench, 1885), p. 326.   18 Ibid., p. 253.
19 Charles Kingsley, *The water babies* (London: Puffin 1984), p. 28.   20 Meade, *Wild Irish*, pp
49, 104, 339.

In the portrayal of women in nineteenth-/early twentieth-century novels immorality is often signified by vulgarity of dress. The critic Harriet Guest argues that prostitutes were characteristically represented in gaudy clothes.[21] It is a convention for which Mrs Sherwood provides a source. Her novel, *The history of Susan Grey*, provides its readers with a biblical reference, which exhorts women to 'adorn themselves in modest apparel'.[22] Given the authority behind the directive, it would have been construed as sinful not to comply.

While the wardrobes of all the Irish protagonists in the Meade and Vaizey novels are criticized for their alleged incongruity in an English setting, it is Meade's wild Kitty who is forbidden by her English guardian to go out in public in her 'spangles, and jewels, and beads, and all the other fal-lals'.[23] Meade's depiction of Kitty's sartorial vulgarity implies the girl's, and by extension her nation's, lascivious inclinations. For in a real sense, of course, the wild Irish girls are symbols of their country. The title of the last chapter of *Wild Kitty*, entitled 'Kitty "Go-Bragh" ', is a confirmation of this.

The identification of Ireland and the Irish with sexual licence finds an echo in Irish writing for adults. Kitty sports the red hair commonly associated with her race. In Swift's *Gulliver's travels* a sub-group of the Yahoos, debased humans, are described thus: 'the red-haired of both sexes are more libidinous and mischievous than the rest'.[24] Contemporaneous with the novels of Meade and Vaizey is Yeats's play of 1902, *Cathleen ni Houlihan*, in which the eponymous protagonist's sexual advances are linked to her marked loquacity. Cathleen ni Houlihan, the personification of Ireland, is seen to go from house to house seducing young men by her talk. 'Bewitched' is what Yeats's character Michael, is, listening to Cathleen ni Houlihan speaking. His mother describes him as having 'the look of a man that has got the touch'.[25] A similar fluency is emphasized in the depiction of the Irish characters in both Meade's and Vaizey's novels. In *Wild Kitty* Meade entitles one chapter 'The Blarney Stone'. The protagonist maintains that to have kissed the stone makes one irresistible. 'There's not a man, a woman, nor a child, no, nor a beastie either, that can resist you. You bewitch 'em.'[26]

The critic Seamus Deane points out that the attribution of stereotypical oral fluency is not without its dangers. 'A reputation for linguistic extravagance is dangerous, especially when given to a small nation by a bigger one which dominates them. By means of it Celts can stay quaint and stay put.'[27] Deane is right. What the 'wild Irish girl' novels do is to reduce their Irish characters' complexity, and therefore their humanity, and render them in many ways caricatures, at their worst, stage 'Oirish'.

21 Harriet Guest, 'The deep romance of Manchester: Gaskell's Mary Barton', in D.K.M. Snell (ed.), *The regional novel in Britain and Ireland, 1800–1900* (Cambridge: C.U.P., 1998), p. 91. 22 Mary Martha Sherwood, *The history of Susan Gray* (London: Houlston, 1838), p. 7.   23 L.T. Meade, *Wild Kitty* (London: Chambers, 1897), p. 26.   24 Hayward, *Swift*, p. 356.   25 Richard Allen Cave (ed.), *W.B. Yeats: selected plays* (London: Penguin, 1997), p. 27.   26 Meade, *Kitty*, p. 21.   27 Blake Morison *Seamus Heaney* (London: Methuen, 1982), p. 36.

In addition to caricature in relation to species, gender and language there is the fact that the protagonists of these novels, the symbols of Ireland, are portrayed as children. Contemporaneously with their publication, Benjamin Kidd, referring to colonized peoples, asserted that Britain was dealing with people who represent in the history of the development of the race what the child does in the history of the development of the individual.[28]

The Irish, then, could be dismissed as debased, immoral and children, obviating the need to take them seriously. At the heart of these novels is the conviction that Ireland is barbarous, and that to be civilized is to be English, of the right class. Both Vaizey and Meade in their respective novels depict an English man of the right class buying an ancestral estate whose previous Irish owners had found themselves incapable of maintaining. In the fashion of the best colonial powers, the new owners avow that they have procured the country's assets for the sake of the natives who are not advanced enough to manage their own affairs.

Interestingly, in the case of Meade's *Wild Kitty*, the earliest of the books under discussion, the novel ends, not with the promised assimilation of the reformed Irish girl into English society as do the later stories, but with Kitty along with her companion, the disgraced and impoverished English girl who emanates from the 'narrow-minded, the vulgar and the low',[29] being expelled from school, and, symbolically, from English society. The representatives of the two elements of the United Kingdom which in the nineteenth century threatened revolt, the English working-classes and the Irish, are, like Oscar Wilde, that wild Irishman, forced into exile, because they are all, in Meade's words, 'too wild for England'.[30]

The wild Irish girl with her exuberance, forcefulness, independence and originality embodies the qualities of the New Woman, beginning to appear in the adult fiction of the period. But as Kimberley Reynolds points out, what was innovative and daring in the portrayal of the contemporary female could be subverted to become conservative.[31] Both Meade's and Vaizey's novels seek to quash notions of the New Woman and extol the model of a more constrained female. In the early 1800s a sizeable English adult readership guaranteed the success of Owenson's largely anti-English, anti-colonial novel, which linked Irish culture to that of the ancient Greeks.[32] *The wild Irish girl* ran to nine editions in the first two years of publication in England. Yet a century later English teenage girls who made up the readership of Meade and Vaizey were still encouraged to view their Irish counterparts – and the indigenous working classes – as essentially primitive, immoral, vulgar and inferior. The only salvation envisaged for these recalcitrant Irish young women, as for their country, was in their submission to English rule.

28 Cunningham, *Representations*, p. 90.   29 Meade, *Kitty*, p. 329.   30 Ibid., p. 364.   31 Kimberley Reynolds, *Children's literature in the 1890s and the 1990s* (Plymouth: Northcote House, 1994), pp 32–3.   32 Whelan, 'Writing Ireland', p. xx.

The voyeur

ÁINE NIC GABHANN

'What do we know of that which lies in the minds of children? We know only what we put there.'[1]

Living in a rapidly changing world in which many of the former certainties had been eroded, Victorians increasingly looked to the child both as a source of comfort and as a symbol of security. Linda Pollock attributes their interest to society's insecurity predicated upon a world that was changing too quickly:

> Perhaps the wish to retain childhood was linked to the wish to revert back to a predominantly rural society rather than live in an urban technological one? It is possible too that the upheaval caused by the Industrial Revolution, the French Revolution and (for Britain) the wars with France – all of which deeply affected society – influenced attitudes to children.[2]

Although there is abundant documented evidence of the victimisation of working-class children in the Victorian age,[3] the middle classes in particular appropriated and sentimentalized romantic constructs of childhood. The 1842 Children's Employment Commission published details of the horrors to which children were exposed as they worked in the mines, and this 'newly publicized image of the victimized, exploited child of early Victorian England did not sit comfortably with the romantic inheritance of innocence and frailty.'[4] As evidence of this, Michael Benton refers to the popularity in the Victorian era of Gainsborough's pictures of the 'deserving' poor,[5] which presented idealized versions of the lives of the impoverished.

Delighting in sentimentality, many Victorians embraced a romanticized construct of childhood. The popularity of John Millais' paintings of children is testament to this. In 'Bubbles' (1886) the solitary, beautiful child is locked forever in

---

1 Valerie Sanders, *The private lives of Victorian women* (London: Harvester Wheatsheaf, 1989), p. 50.   2 Linda Pollock, *Forgotten children: parent-child relations from 1500 to 1900* (New York: O.U.P., 1983), p. 110.   3 James R. Kincaid, *Child-loving: the erotic child in Victorian culture* (New York: O.U.P., 1983); Linda Pollock, *Forgotten children*; and Ronald Pearsall, *The worm in the bud: the world of Victorian sexuality* (London: Penguin, 1972), provide insights into this subject.   4 Benton, Michael, 'The image of childhood; representations of the child in painting and literature, 1700–1900', in *Children's Literature in Education*, vol. 27, no. 1 (1996) pp 35–60, pp 51–2.

a moment of wonder as he gazes at the suspended bubble. This portrait, an adult construction of the perfect child, offers a poignant symbol of the fragility of innocence. The ethereal nature of the bubble becomes symptomatic of childhood itself and perhaps suggests something of the Victorians' relentless quest to capture the elusive state of innocence. Kate Greenaway's paintings are also typical of the Victorian predilection for nostalgic, sentimental portraits of the child. A sense of regression, of returning to a past age, untrammelled with worries or anxiety, is a defining feature of Greenaway's work. Her portrayal of the child as somehow quaint is facilitated by the archaic, rustic style of dress that Greenaway favoured in her paintings. This served to lock the child into a particular image designed to satisfy adult obsession with innocence.

Often beneath the veneer of an interest in childhood purity were darker obsessions. This was an age that promoted a repressive, ultimately unhealthy attitude towards sexuality in the official culture, resulting in the suppression of many normative expressions of adult sexuality. However the proliferation of pornography and prostitution reveals the unofficial, hidden side of Victorian sexuality. This is substantiated by the increasing revelations of child prostitution and the homosexual scandals of the 1880s. The official reaction to such scandals was to repress sexuality by mounting fierce 'social purity campaigns', culminating in the adoption of 'restrictive legislation and censorship'.[6] Perhaps the channelling of adult desire towards the child was inevitable in an age that, Benton notes, regarded 'explicit sexual imagery as unacceptable'. Benton informs us that 'the art market became increasingly aware of the saleability of the imagery of childhood, both for its sentimental appeal and, in Victorian times, as a covert expression of sexuality'.[7] Images of scantily clad, cherubic children, which were cherished by a society bent on capturing the essence of innocence, paradoxically provided a rich and acceptable source of erotic stimulation for the repressed adult. As Jackie Wullschlager observes, 'in a society which refused to accept mature sexuality ... the pre-sexual child became an obvious ideal'.[8]

Such ambivalence is the keynote of the attitude of Charles Dodgson, *aka* Lewis Carroll, towards the child. Carroll's preface to *Alice's adventures underground* depicts a worthy adult reverence for the sanctity of childhood innocence: 'Any one that has ever loved one true child will have known the awe that falls on one in the presence of a spirit fresh from God's hands, on whom no shadow of sin ... has yet fallen.' Yet even a cursory reading of Charles Dodgson's diaries reveals a very different side to the author and establishes that he was inexorably drawn to children. A reference to seeing 'nice-looking children' followed by 'I am suddenly growing rich in child-friends here', reveals a man who sought out the company of children.

5 Ibid., p. 53.   6 Elaine Showalter, *Sexual anarchy: gender and culture at the fin de siècle* (London: Virago, 1992), p. 3. One consequence of this repression was the infamous trial of Oscar Wilde in 1895.   7 Benton, 'Image', p. 37   8 Jackie Wullschlager, *Inventing wonderland* (London: Methuen, 1995), p. 23.

This is substantiated by accounts in his notebooks of children he met. Dodgson desired to link himself as closely as possible to the purity that childhood seemed to offer. Such a connection allowed him to immerse himself in a world less complex than that of adults. Dodgson confirms this in a letter dated November 1886: 'The friendship of children has always been a great element in my enjoyment of life, and is very *restful* as a contrast to the society of books, or of men.' His biographer, Cohen writes that Dodgson 'clung to the simple affections of childhood, refusing to trade them in for the duplicities of Victorian adulthood'.[9] Yet Dodgson's penchant for sketching and photographing nude children reveals the erotic attraction they held for him.

The relationship between John Ruskin, art critic and Kate Greenaway, aspiring artist, also highlights the prevalent duality in attitudes towards children. Ruskin's relationship with Greenaway was initially conducted in correspondences between them, with the former acting as adviser, often offering his protégée advice on the use of line or colour. However, Ruskin's emerging interest in Greenaway's depictions of young girls, or 'girlies', as he called them, is clear.[10] A letter of 1884 reveals this:

> Of course the Queen of them all is the little one in front – but she's just a month or six weeks too young for me. Then there's the staff bearer on the right turning round!!!! But she's just three days and a minute or two too old for me. Then there's the divine one with the dark hair, and the beatific one with the brown – but I think *they've* both got lovers already.[11]

Ruskin was smitten by Greenaway's 'Child–Utopia'. In a letter dated July 5 1880 he wrote the following about 'one of those three sylphs': 'Will you – (it's all for your own good!) make her stand up, and then draw her for me without her hat – and, without her shoes … and without her mittens, and without her – frock and its frill? And let me see exactly how tall she is – and how – round.'[12]

A voyeurism emerges in a study of many of these seemingly respectable Victorians. This is particularly the case when the child begins to fill some craving in the adult. In many novels of the period the idealized relationship is that between adult and child. A sense of the world-weary adult being revitalized by the child is a central motif in Victorian fiction, with *Silas Marner* being a prime example of the genre. Noteworthy also in the literature of the time is a tendency to reject adult sexuality and its ensuing responsibilities. This is evident in the work of James Barrie and Kenneth Grahame, both of whom attempt to create a world that is devoid of sexual pressures. It is indeed arguable whether either succeeds.

Frances Hodgson Burnett (1849–1924), a prolific author of fiction for both adults and children, is primarily remembered today for her romantic portrayal of

9 Morton N. Cohen, *Lewis Carroll: a biography* (London: Papermac, 1996), pp 85, 174, 117. 10 Ruth Hill Viguers (ed.), *The Kate Greenaway treasury* (London: Collins, 1968), p. 78. 11 Pearsall, *Worm*, p. 440. 12 Viguers, *Greenaway*, pp 47, 73.

childhood innocence. Yet a closer study of this author's work reveals that it reflects the prevailing ambiguity surrounding the channelling of sexual energies towards children. It is the purpose of this paper to examine the darker side of the adult-child dynamic both in Hodgson Burnett's autobiographical writing and in her fiction for children. By focusing so exclusively in her work on the celebration of a particular concept of childhood beauty, Hodgson Burnett creates a dangerous and unsettling force field in which the adult is often cast into the role of voyeur, with the child as the object of the sexual gaze. A 'voyeur' may be defined as a person who gains sexual gratification or satisfaction from watching the sexual acts or nakedness of another. Various strains of deviant sexuality may be found in Hodgson Burnett's work, notably in the objectification and eroticization of childhood. Unequivocally the adult gaze is drawn towards the child. Conforming to the Victorian predilection for sentimental portraits of childhood beauty already noted, Hodgson Burnett persistently fixed the child in a particular pose, the object of an adoring adult's gaze. While each image in itself may appear innocent, it is the cumulative effect of the repetition of similar images that makes Hodgson Burnett's attraction to childhood beauty so problematic. There is a palpable sense of the author lingering over certain child poses that is reminiscent of the voyeuristic cameraman adjusting his lens.

That Hodgson Burnett was drawn to a romantic idyll of childhood is clear. Her obsession with boyhood beauty is repeatedly portrayed in her fiction. Her ideal boy-child invariably possesses 'a tumbling mass of long curls';[13] his legs must be plump and his eyes dark. Cedric Errol, the child protagonist of *Little Lord Fauntleroy*, conforms to this template. She describes him in sensual terms, as having 'soft, fine, gold-coloured hair, which curled up at the ends'[14] and he of course possesses the requisite dark eyes and long eyelashes. In the story 'Eight little princes', Eitel, her favourite, possesses similar physical attributes. The author's attraction to this child is evident: 'I cannot tell you how pretty Eitel's bare legs in his short socks look drawn together in that grand military way.'[15]

Hodgson Burnett's attraction to a five-year old Roman beggar in her largely autobiographical *Children I have known* illustrates the degree of her fascination with childhood beauty. She consistently refers to the boy using the possessive adjective 'my', which both displays affection and hints at a wish to appropriate him as her own: 'My little Roman, so far as beauty goes, is one of the most perfect small pictures I remember.' (37) This boy also possesses many of the physical features that Hodgson Burnett favoured, including 'full, silky, curling hair' and is described by her as her 'favourite'. (40) One might imagine this to be the mere indulgence of a lonely mother, as at the time the author was on an Italian tour with a female friend and was thus separated from her two sons. Yet the language used by the

13 Hodgson Burnett, *Children I have known and Giovanni and the other* (London: Osgood, McIlvaine, 1892), p. 3.   14 Frances Hodgson Burnett, *Little Lord Fauntleroy* (London and New York: Penguin, 1994), p. 5.   15 Frances Hodgson Burnett, *Children*, pp 53–4.

author has certain erotic connotations: 'He had such soft, round cheeks, the colour of a very ripe peach – an Indian peach perhaps, with the red showing through the downy brown'. (40) This image is reminiscent of the peach that is a symbol of eroticism in Marvell's 'The Garden'. That it is Indian is highly suggestive of the charmed, sensual world of the Orient that Edward Said described as 'a place where one could look for sexual experience unobtainable in Europe'.[16] It is the choice of the word 'downy', however, which endows the image with ambivalence, with its dual connotation of innocence and dawning sexuality.

In the story, Hodgson Burnett shies away from any overt display of sexuality and chooses a safe, maternal image which both cloaks the sexual or erotic and invests her with ultimate power: 'He looked soft and warm all over, as if he would feel like a rabbit, or a squirrel if one took him in one's arms'. (44) The natural impulse of a rabbit or squirrel is to escape. So the narrator's desire to caress the child is merged with a need to tame him, in effect to exert control. Hodgson Burnett proceeds further, indulging herself in a fantasy in which she would 'coax the leading gentleman' into her carriage and take him on her knee 'for a drive'. (45) Having just given the child some money, the narrator concludes this particular encounter with a most revealing comment: 'What an astonishing thing it would have seemed to the passers-by to have seen a Signora Inglese take a little Roman beggar suddenly in her arms, hold him on her knee and kiss his velvet cheeks – but to me that would have seemed the most natural thing in the world to do'. (44) This fantasy, in its sensuality, merges the images of the son and lover and encapsulates a recurring veiled desire of the author's.

The payment of children, a motif in both the above story and in 'Giovanni and the other', is unsettling. The latter concerns 'a handsome Italian boy about fourteen years old', (147) who sings to two American ladies (namely the author and her friend), in return for payment. The ladies in this story refer possessively to Giovanni as 'our boy' (155) and Hodgson Burnett focuses yet again on capturing the essence of the boy's attractiveness. The language chosen to describe Giovanni's body is imbued with sexual overtones: 'His brown eyes had the golden clearness one sees in the eyes of some fine young animal, he had a glowing olive skin and a body that was full of grace and strength.' (213) The story was written in the year after the death of her consumptive son Lionel, and is thus charged with the emotional intensity of the grieving mother. Nonetheless a clear attraction to the young, virile boy is undeniable and the fact that the admiring women pay him money creates a link between the young boy and a gigolo. The climactic moment of thundering applause in response to Giovanni's singing, when the house is 'throbbing with delight', (214) has unmistakable sexual connotations, and the notion of subsequent emotional release is confirmed by the reaction of the 'lady in black' whose 'eyes were wet ... but ... filled with a shining smile which was strangely happy'. (214) This ecstatic moment could be seen as a further variation on the motif of the

16 Showalter, *Sexual anarchy*, p. 81.

adult as voyeur, since the gratification gained is dependent to a large extent on the author's attraction to the young boy's physical attractiveness. Yet the contrast between the healthy Italian boy, who was 'strong and plump and well built' (147) and the narrator's tubercular son, referred to in the story as Leo, whose 'brown eyes closed so softly', creates both tension and poignancy in this story. (162)

Adult titillation is also evident in another story from *Children I have known*, 'The little fawn', which employs the fawn as a metaphor for a young, dancing boy whom the narrator likes to observe. Particular importance is attached to her first glimpse of the child: 'At that moment I only saw the most beautiful, unwashed, half-clothed little creature one could imagine.' (93) The adult's keen interest in the child is manifested by her persistent observation of the boy from her window. She explains that she became 'accustomed to watching him' (94) and descriptions follow of her delight in this activity. While the dancing boy conjures a romantic motif of liberated childhood, an unwholesome interest in the child's near nakedness is also apparent: 'He had on nothing but a fluttering little calico slip ... As he danced his dingy calico slip fluttered about, and I could see his round bare limbs on which he wore nothing at all.' (93) This particular description highlights the gratification gained from watching another and such vicariousness is the essence of voyeurism.

James Kincaid suggests that voyeurism 'concentrates not only on the position of seeing, but on avoiding the opposite position'.[17] A description of raindrops falling on the young boy's curls is sexualized as the author imagines that 'each drop on his cheeks or his curls seemed like a little kiss'. This is a projection of the narrator's desire, confirming the eroticism in the act of watching this child. One sentence toward the end of the story betrays a distinctive dynamic between them: 'My own [children] were used to be held and petted ... but holding this one was like holding a rabbit.'[18] This episode offers an interesting variation on the pet motif, identifying it as an image of control: this child squirmed and resisted the narrator's petting and restraining gestures. The maternal impulse to hold the child, coupled with the sexual undertones in the descriptions of the boy's body, point to a complex, cloaked eroticism in which the concept of desire is linked to a need to dominate the boy by reducing him to the status of a petted animal. Ultimately, adult desire suffocates the child, or object of desire.

A similarly erotic indulgence in boyhood beauty is found in *Little Lord Fauntleroy*. Mr Havisham, the 'ceremonious rigid old lawyer' is clearly affected by Cedric Errol's beauty.[19] Apparently Cedric awakens desires and impulses within him which had long lain dormant or which had been repressed. On first seeing the young boy 'curious sensations' passed through Mr Havisham and we are told that 'he experienced a revulsion of feeling which was quite exciting.' (29) The word 'revulsion' points to a hidden impulse that proves to be simultaneously exciting and abhorrent to Mr Havisham. His response to observing Cedric and his friends com-

17 Kincaid, *Child-loving*, p. 304. 18 Hodgson Burnett, *Children*, pp 94, 101. 19 Frances Hodgson Burnett, *Little Lord Fauntleroy* (London: Penguin, 1994), p. 25.

peting in a race suggests that he is drawn to particular images of Cedric that have erotic overtones: 'He never really remembered having seen anything quite like the way in which his lordship's lordly little legs flew up behind his knickerbockers.' (31) Tropes of the boys' 'red legs' and 'brown legs', we are told, 'made him feel some excitement'. (31) Clearly, such youthful virility has stirred Mr Havisham. This is confirmed when a more overt erotic attraction to the boy is articulated: 'There rose up before his mind's eye the picture he had left at Court Lodge – the beautiful, graceful child's body lying upon the tiger-skin in careless comfort – the bright tumbled hair spread on the rug – the bright, rosy boy's face!' (68) That Mr Havisham stores this particular image in his mind in order to return to it is significant. The sheer abandonment of the child's pose underlines the boy's unawareness of his being observed by the older man. The adult, thus placed in a position of power, is the archetypal voyeur. The tiger skin takes on a particular significance with its dual association with eroticism and hunting or possession. In Hodgson Burnett's expression of sexuality, the erotic is inextricably bound up with the establishment of relationships of control. The hunting metaphor, therefore, is particularly appropriate and redolent.

The dangers of intense and exclusive adult–child relationships are clearly portrayed in *A little princess*. This full-length novel offers an exploration of the father-daughter theme as its central relationship. Initially Sara Crewe is wholly dependent on her 'young, handsome, rich, petting father', who we are told, seemed to be the only relation she had in the world. Sara, however, is cast in the role of companion rather than daughter: 'She had liked to think of that. To keep the house for her father; to ride with him and sit at the head of his table when he had dinner parties; to talk to him and read his books.'[20] The lavish clothing that Captain Crewe buys for Sara mirrors his excessive love for her. We are told that she possessed 'a wardrobe much too grand for a girl of seven'. Sumptuous descriptions follow of velvet dresses 'trimmed with costly furs, lace dresses and embroidered ones and lots with great ostrich feathers and ermine coats and muffs and boxes of tiny gloves and handkerchiefs and silk stockings in such abundant supplies that the polite young women behind the counters whispered'.[21] Such items of clothing are hardly suited to a seven-year-old and would be more appropriate for a society lady embarking on a romantic adventure. The references to feathers, fur, lace and silk are imbued with sensuality, as one can readily imagine such delicate textures caressing the skin. Yet the garish quality of some of the items of clothing – the costly furs and the great ostrich feathers, for example – draws attention to the young girl's appearance in a manner that deliberately sexualizes her.

20 Frances Hodgson Burnett, *A little princess* (London and New York: Penguin, 1994), pp 2, 4.   21 The whispering women characters speculate as to whether Sara is a foreign princess or the daughter of an Indian rajah. One cannot therefore assume that they suspected an improper relationship between Captain Crewe and his daughter, although clearly they were conscious of the inappropriateness of the shopping.

Once Sara's father has been dispensed with, Hodgson Burnett is free to explore the surrogate father/seducer in the persona of Mr Carrisford, 'the Indian gentleman'. Carrisford, we are informed, harboured 'a very tender place in his heart for all children, and particularly for little girls'. (172) This gentleman allows the author to fully exploit the traditional role of the female as nurturer as he awakens such qualities in the ever-benevolent Sara. 'I wish you had a "Little Missus" who could pet you as I used to pet papa when he had a headache. I should like to be your "Little Missus" myself, poor dear!' (172)

A study of *Sara Crewe*,[22] Hodgson Burnett's earlier version of *A little princess*, reveals that the author deliberately altered the relationship between Sara and Carrisford, resulting in a more unsettling dynamic being written into the later text. In *A little princess* we observe her being looked after by the maternal Mrs Carmichael prior to going to live with Mr Carrisford. In a touching scene we witness Mrs Carmichael tucking Sara up in bed. Details are not included about the length of time Sara spent with the Carmichael family: it is merely stated that 'Mr Carrisford did not die, but recovered, and Sara went to live with him'. (274) One can deduce that at least a short amount of time elapsed, thus allowing for the natural development of their relationship. However, in *A little princess* the adult–child relationship is charged with a greater intensity. The first encounter between Sara and Mr Carrisford is extremely emotional. The language used is extraordinarily needy and suggests a much more intimate relationship than that intimated in the earlier version: 'He looked at her with the look she remembered in her father's eyes – that look of loving her and wanting to take her in his arms'. (272) This look has the effect of making Sara 'kneel down by him, just as she used to kneel down by her father when they were the dearest friends and lovers in the world'. (272) The language is charged with sexual connotations of submission. Furthermore Mr Carrisford's actions smack of the possessive. On his first encounter with Sara he draws her to his side and patting her hand, peremptorily remarks that she is not going home as her home for the future will be with him. The subsequent actions of Carrisford confirm our suspicions, as they are more appropriate to a lover than a father; yet it seems that Hodgson Burnett has difficulty in distinguishing between the two roles.

In *Sara Crewe*, Carrisford sometimes placed 'a new book on her pillow'. (75) This type of fond parental gesture has been altered in the subsequent book so that the 'whimsical little gifts' are 'tucked under pillows' in *A little princess*. (290) The change in emphasis is more suggestive of the exchange of gifts between lovers. The adjective 'whimsical' has that light-hearted quality associated with romantic love in the early stages. It is equally clear that Sara's role is not that of a surrogate daughter. We are told that Carrisford 'had never had a companion he liked quite as much'. (289) Indeed Hodgson Burnett provides us with a scene of amity between them, more redolent of that between a mature married couple: 'But the hours

22 Frances Hodgson Burnett, *Sara Crewe, little Saint Elizabeth and other stories* (New York: Screibner, 1925).

when Sara and the Indian gentleman sat alone and read or talked had a special charm of their own'. (290) This child, whom Carrisford renamed 'Missee Sahib' is essentially denied her selfhood and absorbed into an exclusive relationship with this older man. Indeed, it can be argued that Sara is more constrained in her new situation than she was in the attic room, where she discovered within herself a wonderful ability to transform the world through the magic of story. In the all-female environment of the attic Sara was empowered: in being saved by Carrisford she is ultimately imprisoned.

Hodgson Burnett persistently refers to Carrisford as 'the Indian gentleman' when his identity is known and it is clear that he is not an Indian gentleman at all. The effect of this is to accentuate the exotic attraction and potential danger that he may hold for the young girl. One of the final images we are left with is of Carrisford requesting his princess, Sara, to sit on a footstool. He then 'drew her small dark head upon his knee and stroked her hair'. (292) This image conjures two disparate ideas. The veiled sexual reference in the drawing of the child's head upon the man's knee is fused with an image of an obedient dog being petted. Both images underline the child's submissive role and highlight the adult's exercise of power.

The role of Ram Dass in *A little princess* is ostensibly that of the benign helper of the fairy tale genre; however his actions have a covert, surreptitious quality and encapsulate the motif of the adult as voyeur. He is described as slipping 'across the slates' to 'look at her [Sara] many nights to see that she is safe'. (199) A particularly telling remark is the following admission: 'I can move as if my feet were of velvet … And children sleep soundly – even the unhappy ones.' (202) It is the use of the plural, children, that is most worrying. It seems that this activity is not confined only to his nocturnal visits to Sara's bedroom. More than any other character in Hodgson Burnett's writings, Ram Dass conforms unequivocally to the role of voyeur. His utterance that 'we are both lonely', (201) is highly significant, as it intimates that it is his lonely state which draws him to Sara. This loneliness is accentuated by his cultural difference, which places him more firmly in the role of an outsider or loner. Ram Dass's obsession with Sara goes beyond the bounds of duty: 'I watch her from my window when she does not know I am near … All her life each day I know … Her going out I know, and her coming in.' (199)

The dangers of an adult-child dynamic, in which the adult gaze is focused exclusively on the child, are abundantly clear.[23] It is noteworthy that the solitary child of Romantic poetry is a recurring motif in the work of Hodgson Burnett. Not one of her child-protagonists has siblings and the Victorian motif of the orphan child is fully exploited in order to focus on the exclusivity of the adult–child relationship.[24] The orphan child, when separated by necessity from

23 The short story, 'Little Saint Elizabeth', and the novel, *The lost prince*, offer fascinating insights into this subject. It can also be argued that it is the relative freedom from adult interference in *The secret garden* that allows the children to discover their own creative potential.
24 See Judith Plotz, *Romanticism and the vocation of childhood* (New York: Palgrave, 2001), on the negative implications of the romanticization of childhood.

parents and siblings, creates an unsettling dynamic in terms of power, particular-ly for the adult who is often drawn to the child because of a particular lack in him-self. Indeed it is arguable that the author's negative view of marriage as 'a hideously grotesque position'[25] is mirrored by the absence of satisfying relationships between adults in her work. Instead, both emotional and erotic gratification is derived from the adult-child relationship. While the concept of liberation underpinned the Romantic construct of childhood, Hodgson Burnett's depiction of the adult-child dynamic reveals that the child, rather than being liberated by the adult, is drawn into the dark world of adult desire which is ultimately imprisoning. The insistent and regressive motif of the adult's life revolving around the pivot of the child expresses the sinister and more obsessive side of Romanticism. The dilemma therefore in Hodgson Burnett's portrayal of adult-child relationships, is that it is perhaps inevitable that issues of control, desire and need become the defining fea-tures of a relationship that has its basis in inequality.

25 Ann Thwaite, *Waiting for the party: the life of Frances Hodgson Burnett* (London: Secker & Warburg, 1974), p. 192. Burnett's marriages to Swan Burnett and Stephen Townsend ended acrimoniously.

School stories

DECLAN KIBERD

Childhood has always been a zone of moral ambiguity and, as such, irresistible to a certain kind of writer. Our feelings in western culture about all this lie buried very deep and they help to explain our social and philosophical conflicts. The notion that humankind is innately weak and evil is epitomized by the Christian theory of original sin, which necessitates an act of ritual purging, even of a newborn baby, in the sacrament of baptism. Against all that, however, may be set the more modern, secular, and optimistic theories of Rousseau and the Enlightenment – that the child is born sinless and spotless, in a state of unselfconscious grace, until the fallen social world coarsens and darkens its personality.

The feelings of ambivalence even enact themselves *within* each of these traditions. In Christian practice, the child is presumed to be near enough to godliness to be still innately holy – as Wordsworth would say, it comes trailing clouds of glory from God who is our home – but also with a sufficient propensity for evil that it must be whipped off to the nearest baptismal font for shriving. The same ambiguity haunts the debate surrounding first holy communion, as to the age at which it is best administered: on the one hand, the child should still be essentially pure, unsullied by worldliness, and thus very young, but on the other it should have a sufficiently developed analytic and imaginative power as to be able to understand the complex enough meanings of the Eucharist.[1] Hence the longstanding division between Roman Catholic and Protestant opinion as to the preferable age. Equally, however, within the humanist tradition, the theory of original goodness and innocence has come up for critique as a sentimental secularization of the Christian doctrine of holy childhood – and a new kind of knowingness has supervened. The century that began with William Blake's idea of the child as a spotless lamb, free as the wind, ended with Sigmund Freud's analysis of infantile sexuality,[2] and, in between, ran the gamut of modern emotions about childhood, from the death of Little Nell (which Oscar Wilde said he could never read without bursting into laughter) to the murder of siblings by Old Father Time in Thomas Hardy's *Jude the obscure*, a horrible but all too apt prophesy of the child murderers of Jamie Bulger.

Of all the nineteenth-century writers who addressed the theme, Wordsworth seems one of the most balanced. His child trails clouds of glory at once Christian

1 Philippe Aries, *Centuries of childhood* (London: Penguin, 1973), chapter 1 and passim.   2 Peter Coveney, *The image of childhood* (London: Penguin, 1967), passim.

and Renaissance, but then shades of the prison-house of a fallen world and fallen modern language surround the growing boy. That prison-house is, of course, school itself, which initiates the child in the language of the father, and which, by calibrating progress from year to year, measures the degree of socialization, before marking the moment of final access to adult codes. Throughout the nineteenth century, because of the progress in science and knowledge, these experiences changed greatly. As fewer and fewer children died in early life, parents, spurred on by romantic cults of feeling, became even more intense and melodramatic in their relations with their offspring. Under the influence of Rousseau's ideas on the noble savage, educators and parents tried increasingly to imagine and address the inner world of the child, and not just the adult that he or she might one day become. This, it was often pointed out, was a move by no means inimical to Christian values, which had long told adults that unless they become as little children, they would not enter the kingdom of Heaven. Once this statement was taken with full seriousness, it was inevitable that a forty-year old adult like Picasso would try to paint like a child – and in this moment, a key form of modernism was born.

But the vastly increased amounts of knowledge to be mastered at school also had the effect of extending the years of childhood beyond primary level and well into the teens, so that by the end of the nineteenth century it was lasting up until the age of seventeen or eighteen, when formal schooling came to an end. This extension had the inevitable effect of adding to the original feelings of ambivalence – for now, whatever about infantile sexuality, rather well-developed adolescents with the voices and bodies of adults must nonetheless submit to being treated as children.

All of these forces may be held to lie behind the emergence of the school story in the Victorian period. They also explain the radical uncertainty of tone with which these stories addressed such issues as bullying, fagging, sexuality and even honour. The post-romantic focus on the child as not only a subject but also a reader certainly sounded the death knell for the more naive sort of Sunday School literature that had gone before. Mark Twain's books helped, more perhaps than any others, to explode that old worldview. If *Huckleberry Finn* was an attack on the evil of slave-holding in the American South-West, then *Tom Sawyer* was an assault on the stunted religion of the same region. Its raucously satiric accounts of Sunday School meetings, obscene feats of bible-memorizing, or the dreary routines of the Temperance Revival, all speak of Twain's disgust with the Calvinist ethic with its black-and-white moral options. That juvenile literature, like its counterpart among non-conformists and even Anglicans back in England, had presented the youth of America with paragons of unbelievable goodness as heroes to be emulated by every Yankee boy. The Model Boy was hard-working at school, respectful of teachers and parents, and incorrigibly clean and honest – in short, super straight, utterly lacking in complexity. The bad boy, on the other hand, was known by his proclivity towards sin, debauchery and social deviance. A clear illustration of the doctrine of original sin, he went on the lam from school or played hookey from work. He was an artist in evil and committed unspeakable outrages against the community, such as swearing, stealing, whistling at girls, lying, drinking etc., and – sometimes, though this was yet the most extreme perversion known to the writers – smoking. This boy was not of the Calvinist elect; he grew up, committed a murder, and was summarily despatched to Hell.

By 1862 the public was tiring of such high-minded tosh and Henry Ward Beecher wrote in a New York review: 'the real lives of boys are yet to be written. The lives of pious and good boys, which enrich the publishing societies, resemble a real boy's life about as much as a chicken on a spit resembles a free fowl in the fields.'[3] The change in public taste was becoming clear and Twain helped to create it. By 1867 he published 'The story of the good little boy who did not prosper' and by 1870, 'The story of the bad little boy who did not come to grief'. These are obviously the sources for *Tom Sawyer*, which likewise inverts all the conventions of the puritan genre – the goody-goody kid instead of being the hero is now the villain, while Huck and Tom steal jam, lie and smoke under the stars on Jackson's Island, being rewarded with riches beyond their dreams. Twain is however, sufficiently aware of the ambiguities surrounding childhood literature to feed them at every turn. It's never clear whether Tom and Huck are boys or adolescents (Tom fancies Becky Thatcher and Huck seems to pass for fourteen or fifteen in his own book), but it is clear that Tom is not really bad, just pretending, expressing those high spirits now necessary to an attractive hero long before some young woman like Becky Thatcher tames him for bourgeois marriage. This is obvious in the message that he leaves for his aunt Polly when he escapes to a life of freedom on Jackson's Island: 'we ain't dead – just off being pirates'.[4] Aunt Polly eventually names the new stereotype herself – 'he wasn't bad, so to say, only mischeevous. Only just giddy and harum scarum.' (131) And in this definition lurked the genesis of all future American anti-heroes – of Elvis who wagged his outlawed pelvis for a year before joining the imperial army and cutting his hair; of Jack Kerouac who scored with angel-headed hipsters on a thousand highways before going back to live respectably with *his* aunt Polly and die; of James Dean, the rebel without a cause who tried for revolution and settled for Natalie Wood; and of Bob Dylan who called the armies of revolution out into the plains and then slunk off to marry a nice Methodist girl. It is nothing but the same old story of a seeming rebel who turns out to be super-straight, of the rock-star who proclaims his sympathy for the devil into camera one but takes time to file full tax statements by April the fifth. In short, the kind of healthy high-spirited boy of whom every mother dreams.[5]

For all that, what is most remarkable about Twain's classics is just how seldom they are set in classrooms. There is a funny account in *Tom Sawyer* of the removal of a teacher's wig, as well as routine mockery of Tom's wayward sense of facts: 'In

3 Walter Blair, *Mark Twain and Huck Finn* (Berkeley, U. Calif. P., 1961), p. 78.   4 Mark Twain, *Tom Sawyer* (London: World Classics, 1967), p. 131.   5 On the good-bad boy syndrome, see Leslie Fiedler, *Love and death in the American novel* (London: Cape, 1967), passim.

Geography class, Tom turned mountains into rivers and rivers into mountains, until chaos was come again',[6] and the Shakespearian echo is the knowing, patronizing wink from one adult to another, superior to the childish subject matter at hand, which of course Tom will one day triumphantly transcend and master. But generally, the stories of how young men and women in America become adults are located less often in classrooms than in the open air. They grow, as Emerson said they would, by opening a direct relation to nature, whereas in England they grow mostly indoors in schools that allow for a developing relationship with one another.

When schools feature in American texts, they tend to be day schools: but the quintessential English establishment is a boarding school that contains both a knowable community and a range of personality types. Such advantages to a writer are obvious, but they do not fully account for the central place occupied by such schools in the English fictional imagination – a place far deeper and more rooted that that occupied in the psyche of other western European peoples. It is, of course, a feat of history that a good boarding school became an essential element in the lives of families devoted to imperial and missionary work overseas – and that the so-called public schools were prestigious training grounds for many of the rulers of the empire. But this in itself would still not account for the extent to which even the stay-at-home British sometimes sent their children away, and often at remarkably early ages, to board at schools.

Doubtless, many a stern *paterfamilias* felt that it was an essential phase in the formation of a manly, self-reliant character, that his sons, even more than his daughters, should be educated in this way. A culture which taught stoicism out of Roman classics like Seneca, as well as an ideal of heroic state service out of Virgil, might feel a strong necessity to curb the emotional excesses of a parent-child relationship – and the boarding school may have represented one attempt to control a sentiment that might otherwise have caused all stiff upper lips to tremble in the aftermath of the romantics, who did so much to intensify that relationship.

Boarding schools did not just teach epics of Greece, Rome and ancient Britain: it was in its own way a version of the epic world, so familiar as to scarcely need description, but filled with strange unexplained taboos and often formulaic tests of courage and audacity. It offered, like epic, a total world in itself. This is true of English schools, as of no other schools in the world: a fact brilliantly spotted by D.W. Brogan who wrote that England was the only country in the world where being a schoolboy was an end in itself.[7] The highest ideals of traditional English culture – fair play, not peaching on a fellow, giving everyone a chance, self-discipline imposed more from within than without under a leadership too subtle to actually say what the implicit rules are – all these were epitomized by the schools, which became not just institutions for the transmission of those values, but imagined communities in which those values could be put to the test by the young.

6 Twain, *Sawyer*, p. 67.   7 Quoted by Steven Marcus, *Representations: essays on literature and society* (New York: Random House, 1975), p. 65.

Often the values did not survive such strenuous moral scrutiny, which exposed also cheating, boot-licking and wanton cruelty from authorities who never seemed to have to account for themselves – a trope which links *Tom Brown's school days* to its Irish version in Joyce's *A portrait of the artist as a young man*, when Stephen discovers that Clongowes Wood College does not really believe in its own codes and has senior masters who are quite capable of laughing behind their backs at those literal-minded boys who do believe.

This – or something like it – may be the deeper source of the attraction of school stories for British children. Compared with the adventures on the open road or open raft enjoyed by children in a Walter Macken or a Mark Twain story, the British school offered a rather circumscribed world, a lot more predictable in its routines – but no less morally strenuous in its demands. It is the fact that school stories deal with ideals which explains their perennial effect not just to the young, but also to the vast numbers of adult readers who saw in them a projection of their own ideal self-image *and of their own communities.*

So the Billy Bunter tales of Frank Richards contained all possible types – from the foolish glutton Bunter to the gimlet-eyed master Quelch, from the unassuming bravery of Harry Wharton to the solid dependability of Johnny Bull, from the American materialism of Fisher T. Fish to the polysyllabic artifice of Hurree Jamset Ram Singh. The bounder of the Remove, Vernon-Smith, was as addicted to the public house and betting shop as the most weak-minded member of the communities described by Richard Hoggart in *The uses of literacy* – it required only a little effort for readers to map the lives of the Famous Five of Greyfriars School onto their own school or their own community.[8]

Part of the appeal was of a world that never changed – the boys in Greyfriars never left the Remove and Bunter was a perfect embodiment of Aristotle's definition of comedy – a fool incapable of change or reform who delights us by repeating the same set of mistakes many times over. This same unchangeability applied even to his verbal trademark 'yarroo!', 'I say, you fellows!' and so on, just as the slang used by the Famous Five – 'frabjous' 'jape', 'my hat' also stayed forever the same. All this had a powerful attraction for children who, growing very fast, love things that remain the same (hence the conservative insistence on endless eating or re-eating the same food – crumpets, jam and so on, much favoured by Bunter). In the early years of universal education and mass literacy, the stories of Frank Richards in *The Gem* or *The Magnet* entranced a wholly new kind of audience with escapades which were sufficiently like the school life of millions to carry that appeal, yet sufficiently more affluent and more upper-class to carry the glamour of aristocracy. In an England which was both democratic and at the same time obsessed with minor and major calibrations within the class system, this was a perfect formula. For if each class likes in its dream life to live out a fantasy of an exis-

8 Jonathan Rose, *The intellectual life of the British working classes* (New Haven: Yale U.P., 2001), pp 323–35.

tence in a more cushioned section of the community, that is precisely what Greyfriars supplied, in much the same way as the weekend supplements now entertain the masses with images of cars, furniture and houses to which they can aspire but in all probability will never possess.

The spell cast was even wider, for although schoolboys are dimly aware of class from an early age, they are far more responsive to those internal youth codes which mark off one generation from another – and in magazines like *The Gem* and *The magnet*, Frank Richards created a virtual world of teenage boys which was perhaps the first manifestation of that phenomenon known later as youth culture, which would in time through magazines like *Melody Maker* and *New Musical Express* create the mods and rockers of a late era. The early antipathy among representatives of elite culture to popular magazines was based on the view that these middlebrow and lowbrow entertainments represented a dismal use of literacy, as compared with that which had been hoped for by those who taught the workers' children how to read. In his famous 1892 lecture on the necessity to de-anglicize Ireland, Douglas Hyde brought his analysis of the corrupting effects of English popular culture to a climax with an attack on penny dreadfuls and shilling shockers[9] – just the sort of magazines which thrilled the young James Joyce, if the account of the Wild West magazines read under the desk in Latin class in Belvedere College in 'An encounter' is anything to go by, 'though there was nothing wrong with the magazines and though their intent was sometimes literary, there were circulated secretly'.[10]

Hence, perhaps, the message on some of the papers published by Alfred Harmsworth in the 1890s: 'You need not be ashamed to be seen reading this.'[11] If the pietistic magazines deplored by Twain were at one end of the market, the stories of the Wild West represented the other – but Frank Richards novels filled the gap between the two, producing in time a million and a half words a year over a very long career (1 and a half million words is about twenty novels).[12]

Richards was arguably the most influential writer of his time, not only in the number of his readers but also in the traces that he left on high culture. For example, Sean O'Casey learned from Richards the technique of establishing a trademark phrase –'derogatory' for Fluther, or 'it is and it isn't' for Mrs Grogan in *The plough and the stars*, a play in which the same Mrs Grogan regards the mockery of Uncle Peter's colourful uniform in a sentence taken straight from Tom Merry and company at St Jim's: 'I have never seen anything like it before off a Christmas tree.'[13] If anyone doubts the direct lineage from Richards to O'Casey, they have only to look at posed photographs of the Irishman, in skull-cap and steel-rimmed spectacles, to know that Richards was his model in this respect too. The interac-

9 Douglas Hyde, 'The necessity for de-anglicizing Ireland', *The revival of Irish literature*, ed. C. Gavan Duffy (London: Fisher Unwin, 1894), p. 159.   10 James Joyce, *Dubliners* (London: Cape, 1967), p. 19.   11 E.S. Turner, *Boys will be boys* (London: Penguin, 1976), p. 11.   12 Ibid.,p. 221.   13 Cited ibid. p. 219.

tions between the culture of high modernism and of popular weeklies are a lot more promiscuous that we might expect, crossing lines of nation as well as social values.

At the heart of Richards' world was William George Bunter, the Fat Owl of the Remove, a truly mythical comic creation to rival those of Dickens. Some of his mannerisms were based on those of real people (often publishers' editors) known to Richards – one who was always on the lookout for a postal order which never materialized, another forever blinking over his spectacles. But to these Richards added the authentic dimensions of a modern anti-hero – fat beyond belief in an age when Wallis Simpson said you could not be too rich or too thin, Bunter was eternally strapped for cash as he rolled into a classmate's study. He had no compunction about stealing food from other boys, or claiming credit for the bravery of others – and he could, like any caricature, be kicked or thumped at will, since the wounds he felt were not real. In a sense, Bunter was the supreme caricature who, by his extremity and grossness, allowed the normal to define itself as such, but who also allowed the normal to become the heroic: he became a walking or rolling advertisement of the virtues of self-discipline, English restraint, modesty, honesty and sheer pluck. He was the anti-Englishman incarnate – and therefore of a piece with all these colourful foreigners who shared supplies with him – not least the Nabob of Bhanipur, Hurree Jamset Ram Singh, who liked to speak in Hindu abstractions (' the esteemfulness of dear Bunter's uncle is terrific') but who was also shown to be in search of an ideal England which was fast disappearing before the onslaught of youth culture: Hurree wished 'to induce my esteemed and ludi-crous chums teasefully to stop talking slangfully and to use speakfully only the powerful and honoured English language as taught by my learned and preposter-ous active tutors in Bhanipur'.[14]

George Orwell found a hint of racism in such a portrayal, suggesting that in Richards all foreigners are reduced to the ludicrous – the French, forever excitable wear beards and gesticulate, Arabs and Mediterranean types are sinister and treacherous, Nordics kind but stupid, and so on. The English have become more careful in more recent times and employ semi-foreigners like Clive James to engage in the same typology – but Richards was more refreshingly direct, responding that foreigners really were funny and lacked the English sense of humour. They were simply put by God in the world for the English to laugh at – so why complain?[15]

As a psychological creation, Billy Bunter was a little like the Christopher Robin of A.A. Milne, though of course much older. His self-indulgence was like that of an unsocialized infant who lacked a basic sense of right or wrong:

> Do you think the king knows all about me?
> Sure to dear, and it's time for tea, says Alice.[16]

---

14 Cited ibid., p. 225.   15 Ibid., p. 233.   16 A.A. Milne, *When we were very young* (London:

This is why people would forgive him – for only an arrant fool could ever be taken in by his clumsy acts of self-interest. And those acts bring out the best in those all around him – they become norms for the definition of true heroism. People felt free to chuckle over his jokes for precisely the same reason that they cooed over toddlers in prams. Those who have had to make the compromise of renouncing their own narcissism in order to live in culture will be forever haunted by those who refuse to make that desperate bargain with the gods. And the fact that Bunter always comes out ahead appeals to our sense of cosmic justice for clowns. As Mary Cadogan has so wisely said, Bunter is the schoolboy Falstaff,[17] just as the Famous Five normaltons who oppose him with their everyday sweetness may be the original boy band.

The utopia that is Greyfriars is that partly because the boys have no material needs. Many indeed seem to come from stately homes – including the Indian Nabob and Bunter – but even more attractive to readers attending grammar schools or day moderns would be the notion of a republic of youth, freed for each term from controlling or over-watching parents. In a world that since then has seen the ever-increasing monitoring of children's lives by anxious parents on the lookout for molesters and weirdos, this attraction can only have increased. The pleasures of self-creation in a world without parents are matched for the reader by a commensurate amenity in Richards' own style. He never condescends to the reader but rather to the character of Bunter, who allows every reader to feel wholly superior:

> There was no escape for Bunter. He was booked for a whole hour of English literature: a subject on which the Owl of the Remove took no interest whatever. 'Gray's Elegy' was the order of the day ... really it was an excellent poem: and there were fellows, even in the Lower Fourth, who could appreciate its beauties. But William George Bunter was not one of those fellows. Bunter would have given the Completed Poetical Works of Thomas Gray for a cake, and thrown in those of William Shakespeare as a makeweight and considered that he had got the best of the bargain.[18]

Even those lower-class readers who are living vicariously through the aristos of Greyfriars can displace onto Bunter any residual qualms about what they're doing – for it turns out that his parents have no stately home, merely a common villa – and so the Fat Owl becomes a comic-abject version of the fantasy of an upper-class life. Richards, like a true writer may be found to have anticipated all key objections to his work – and built them into the texts. After all, to those who say he scoffed at foreigners, he might rejoin that Greyfriars, with its Yanks, Hindus, inner-city Londoners and Irish, was the first multicultural school in fiction.

* * *

Methuen, 1926), p. 15.   17 Mary Cadogan, *Frank Richards: the chap behind the chums* (Claverley, Shrop.: Swallowtail Books, 2000), pp 64–90.   18 Frank Richards, 'The schoolboy forger', *Schoolboys' Own Library* no. 397 (1940), n.p.

Ludwig Wittgenstein once wrote that 'the limits of my language are the limits of my world', and so it is in the world of Anthony Buckeridge: most of his jokes and mistakes have a linguistic component:

> Keeping a diary for a whole year was not a task to be undertaken lightly. However, he had made the resolution and he was determined to carry it out. So far, it is true, the diary contained nothing of a confidential nature. The most recent entries read: 'Wednesday: Had bath. We won, two-nil. Thursday: Had second helping of prunes, clean socks and French test. Friday: Broke boot lace.'
>
> But after all, the year was young yet. Soon, no doubt, many pages would be covered with highly secret information.
>
> 'If only I could think of some way of doing it so no one else could read it', said Jennings thoughtfully.
>
> 'Why not write it upside down?' suggested Darbishire. 'That ought to fox them alright.'
>
> Jennings heaved an impatient sigh: 'Don't be so stark raving haywire! All they'd have to do would be to turn the book the other way up.'
>
> Darbishire pursed his lips and stroked an imaginary beard – a device he had worked out on holidays to help him think more deeply. Rather to his surprise, it worked: for at once an idea sprang to his mind. 'I've got it', he cried, his eyes lighting up with inspiration. 'Shorthand! Like that chap – what was his name? – that Mr Carter was telling us about last term. He kept a diary in shorthand.'
>
> 'Who – Mr Carter?'
>
> 'No, you clodpoll. Samuel Pepys – that's the chap. And after he was dead, it took some professor years to work out what it was all about.'[19]

Darbishire, described always as a boy who speaks in capital letters and begins every other sentence with 'my father says' or 'if you ask me', has to be dismissed, for Jennings, as usual, has a better idea. Every word is to be spelt backwards.

> 'Yes sir, it's ever so good. You pit your wits against it sir,' he urged Mr. Carter.
>
> Mr Carter read: 'Played football with Selbanev. Erih-sibred, Nosnikta and Co. Retsim Retrac reffed the game. 'Sounds as though you were playing against the Moscow Dynamos,' he commented.[20]
>
> 'Well: *Selbanev* is Venables the wrong way round, and *Nosnikta* is Atkinson in reverse.'
>
> 'I see,' said Mr Carter. 'And who is this mysterious *Retsim Retrac* who reffed the game?'

19 Anthony Buckeridge, *Jennings' diary* (London: Collins, 1960), pp 26–7.   **20** Ibid., p. 33.

'That's you, sir … Mister Carter, sir!'

The discussion was interrupted by the ringing of the dormitory bell. It was a pity, Jennings thought, as he trotted up the stairs, that Samuel Pepys was dead; he sounded just the sort of chap who would have been interested to hear of this modern improvement on the seventeenth-century method of keeping a diary.[21]

If access to adult codes, at least in the days of print culture, was measured by a child's increasing mastery of reading and writing, Buckeridge certainly knew how to milk the potential comedy for all it was worth. In *Take Jennings, for instance*, the ever-absent-minded Aunt Angela has failed to send the promised Christmas gift of a gleaming new two-wheeler bicycle. Initially, Jennings is stoical and far too polite to complain – until he realises that he will miss major school outings for want of a conveyance. Under such duress, he has to write a letter with coded reminders inserted among all the pleasantries

'Dear Aunt Angel', Darbishire read aloud.

'I hope you are well. I am quite well and having decent weather. On Saturday week we are all going on a picnic, but I am not as I have not got a bicycle. There is a boy named Atkinson who got a bicycle for a Christmas present, so he can go but not me, as you have to have a bicycle. It is a long time since Christmas. I hope you enjoyed the card with the robin on that I sent you. Almost everybody has a bicycle, except me, it is good exercise. You can send them by train, and the van brings them. It comes quite often. I expect they will all enjoy the picnic, except me. It would be nice to go as I am Chief Frog Spotter, but you can't go if you haven't got a bike.

With love from John.'

'Do you think she'll get it?' Jennings inquired anxiously.

'Of course she'll get it – if you put a stamp on it and post it, that it.'

'No, you clodpoll. I mean do you think she'll see the point?' Jennings persisted. 'I didn't like to make it too obvious, you see; that's why I've only dropped a veiled hint here and there among the rest of the news.'

Darbishire considered the matter. 'I should send it just as it is', he advised. 'If she reads it carefully she may see what you're driving at. Of course, it might help if you drew a picture of everybody starting off on their bikes, and you watching them with a sad look on your face. And then you could draw the railway van with a bicycle in … '

'This is supposed to be a letter, not a comic strip!' Jennings pointed out tersely. 'All I can do is to post it right away and keep my fingers crossed till she sends me an answer.'[22]

21 Ibid., p. 34. 22 Anthony Buckeridge, *Take Jennings, for instance* (London: Collins, 1959), p. 42.

Most of the troubles into which Jennings and Darbishire plunge themselves arise through an excess of ethical zeal. They like the school matron and attempt to organise a surprise present for her birthday – but find that in order to do so they must break immeasurable school and civic laws, sneaking off to Linbury when they should be at prep, using postage stamps to make up the price of a cake, and so on. A great deal of the comedy arises from the clash of discourses, between the metaphorical language of the masters and the more literal-minded understanding of young boys.

For instance, when Jennings overhears that Mr Wilkins is leaving on Friday week, he does not realise that the man is simply visiting a relative – instead he assumes he is quitting the school. Mr Williams, or 'old Wilkie', is a hot tempered barrel-chested man who seems forever at war with his young charges, eternally issuing threats to them which peter out for want of invective: 'If any of you little blighters puts another foot wrong, I'll ... I'll ... well, you'd jolly well better not!' The boys are fearful of his moods, but faintly suspect that he has a good heart and so Jennings overwhelms all the voiced reservations to take up a collection for a present for the departing teacher. He also initiates a be-kind-to-Wilkie-week which initially unnerves the teacher, then outrages him with the thought that it is all a giant parody, and ultimately reduces him to tears.

Ms Wilkins is of course 'ozard' – the opposite of 'wizard'. Though fiery, he has no imagination, unlike Mr Carter, who is shrewd, kind, forever undeceived. The comedy of two non-intersecting languages is usually enacted between the boys and Mr Williams, with Mr Carter as referee. For instance, in one disastrous history class, Jennings makes error after error (due mainly to tiredness after organizing a midnight feast), so old Wilkie tells him to go and put his head under a tap to see if that'll waken him up. He returns smiling, and Mr Wilkins walks suspiciously past his desk, before exploding: 'But I told you to put your head under the tap!' 'Oh I did, Sir.' 'But then boy, why is your hair not wet?' 'Sir, you never told me to turn the tap on.'[23]

Similarly, during a fire-escape drill, Jennings is instructed to act as if the threat were real and to show initiative and leadership. He promptly phones the Dunhambury Fire Brigade. They are caught off guard, take ages to repair their engine and reach the school, only to find old Wilkie trapped in a sling, half-way between the third floor and ground floor – and so it is lucky for him that they brought the rotating ladder specially requested by Jennings, even though there doesn't seem to be a flame in sight.[24]

This is one of Buckeridge's favourite narrative devices. By some act of silliness –usually the silliness of taking adults more literally than they deserve to be taken – the boys create a major crisis, but then go on to resolve its elements to the even greater glory of the little school. For instance, for one of his japes, Jennings is given

23 Anthony Buckeridge, *Jennings goes to school* (London: Collins, 1959), p. 182.   24 Ibid., pp 85–144.

a terrible punishment by Old Wilkie – he has to memorise two whole pages about Richard the Lion-Heart. All week he struggles, as Darbishire examines his progress, providing encouragement, criticism, mnemonic hints. On the Friday, a school inspector unexpectedly descends on the Form 3 classroom and Old Wilkie suffers the agonies of the damned, as the boys fail dismally to answer any of his questions for a full half-hour. Edging towards the door, the inspector, almost as embarrassed as Mr Wilkins, asks one last question – about Richard the Lion Heart – and Jennings is still reciting perfect Gibbonesque prose on the topic as the bell rings for break and the honour of the school is saved.

Buckeridge was himself a schoolmaster and seems to have drawn heavily on his experiences in recreating this little world – the scene where Jennings organized a poetry competition and was presented with a plagiarism of Lord Tennyson by one boy came straight from life. Jennings and Darbishire admitted that the poem had some good bits but still engaged in wholesale criticisms before coming upon the original in a second-hand bookstore.

Their world is a safe, innocent place, where the plots are slow-moving and most of the gentle fun comes from the language. The fire-drill episode takes up sixty pages of *Jennings goes to school*. When I read it to my son, he laughed a lot but complained of how slowly the plot turned and how it took us two long sessions rather than one to get through it. Yet that same son reveres each episode of *Fawlty Towers*, itself built around the same type of comedy of mistaken language – so much so that we must count Buckeridge a major influence on John Cleese – just as P.G. Wodehouse may have been a clear exemplar for Buckeridge, who seems to treat Linbury Court as a sort of mock-rehearsal by boys for life in the Drones' Club.

I read all of these books between the ages of nine and twelve and the great tragedy of my childhood was that I would never find in the city of Dublin a copy of *Our friend Jennings* to complete my set. What appealed, I suppose, was what would soon appeal to the young teenager in the writings of P.G. Wodehouse and Oscar Wilde, the idea of a world elsewhere. Oscar Wilde once joked that to an Irishman England is a fairyland – and to me the corridors of Linbury Court, the club-rooms of Woodhouse, the drawing rooms of Wilde were utopia, a world seemingly without conditions, in which all hierarchies were reversed. No sooner is Darbishire introduced in *Jennings goes to school* than his father is described as a carbon-copy replica of the son, only with thinner hair. In utopia, fathers defer to sons, teachers to pupils, and so on; outside utopia, as Wilde complained, the old-fashioned respect for the young is fast dying out. If Orwell could describe the average English public school as a fair imitation of and preparation for the concentration camp, to me Linbury Court seemed more like an anarchist commune – a land of cockayne, in which boys seized the initiative at every turn, confused the bumbling local policeman and always had the last word against Old Wilkie (who was, of course, secretly delighted by the brilliance shown in their victory).

Of course, I also read Blyton, Richmal Crompton, Frank Richards and the rest. The great charm of Blyton's stories lay in their depiction of children coping with complicated emergencies on their own initiative without the guiding hand of near-by adults – this might indeed be the reason why they have remained always in print and popular – for the motif of the unprotected child adrift in a grown-up world is very ancient, but it probably has more appeal than ever today, in a time when children are allowed fewer and fewer unmonitored activities by parents understandably fearful of molesters and abusers. But I always half-suspected that there was something ultimately unrealistic about a boarding-school like Malory Towers which allowed you to keep pets – in *Jennings*, the pets were always kept unofficially, rather like Manuel's hamster in *Fawlty towers*. However, it's worth reminding ourselves of the more radical, subversive qualities in all these stories at a moment when far too many commentators worry unduly about political correctness in Blyton (the golliwog has been removed from those Noddy stories, and the eponymous hero now puts lead-free petrol into his car), class snobbery in Richmal Crompton or racism in Frank Richards

* * *

The harshest critics of the fictional world were never from the working class, but from the ranks of those left-wingers who had been to actual public schools: and chief among those was George Orwell. In his famous essay titled 'Boys' weeklies' (1939), he admits that the stories are hugely popular, by public demand, in which they contrast with the sort of popularity *enforced* by a monopolistic film and radio industry. But he marvels at the survival of their world – in which it is always 1910 – into the late 1930s.[25] This timeline however seems to be an unwritten law of school stories, for the world of Harry Potter seems vaguely 1980 rather than 2000 – certainly there are no play-stations, computers, or other paraphernalia of the contemporary child, but rather the trappings of Rowling's own childhood years. When Harry and Hermione seek information on Nicholas Flamel, they visit the library rather than a website.

Orwell was convinced that Richards was a pseudonym for a team of writers, because no one could be so productive and the general formulae would be recyclable by other authors. (In this, also, Orwell was wrong; Richards' work was all his own). Orwell put the appeal down to mob values – those for whom a posh public school was thrilling and easily purchasable for a few shillings a year rather than thousands of pounds. Here is his caricature of what he feels is a caricature to begin with:

> The year is 1910 — or 1940, but it is all the same. You are at Greyfriars, a rosy-cheeked boy of fourteen in posh tailor-made clothes [...] The King is on his throne and the pound is worth a pound. Over in Europe the comic

25 George Orwell, 'Boys' weeklies', *Essays* (London: Everyman, 2002), pp 185–211.

foreigners are jabbering and gesticulating, but the grim grey battleships of the British Fleet are steaming up the Channel and at the outposts of Empire the monocled Englishmen are holding the niggers at bay. Lord Mauleverer has just got another fiver and we are all settling down to a tremendous tea of sausages, sardines, crumpets, potted meat, jam and doughnuts.[26]

Orwell considers this is a mark of Richard's reactionary politics, but I wonder. In my childhood during the early 1960s, the stories were all of twenty years earlier, World War Two pilots defending Britain from the Nazi scourge – just as Rowling deals with the world of 1980 (and nobody would accuse this defender of unmarried mothers and Labour Party policies of being right-wing). Where Orwell's essay scores is in showing that the petty values of the white and the blue collar world of his own time are inscribed into the Greyfriars stories – where one house in a school is considered more posh than another, just as in the rivalry between Gryffindore and Slytherin in Harry Potter – and in the ways in which upper class bounders like Arthur Augustus D'Arcy (Gussy) become the targets of class anger, much as the worried but slack-jawed Draco Malfoy plays the same role in the world of J.K. Rowling, where class warfare is more openly discussed whenever Malfoy insults the Weasley family for their want of wealth and comfort. However, the ease with which so many elements of the world according to Frank Richards can be mapped onto that of Rowling (who seems to celebrate Hogwarts as a sort of 1980s comprehensive school) suggests that the Bunter books were hardly as reactionary as Orwell claimed.

Orwell in his essay did, however, detect a second strain of boys' weeklies, in *Hotspur* and *Wizard*, and these generally eschewed the routines of school life for a more global backdrop of the Wild West tales, big-game hunts in Africa, or magical trips into a future of rockets and spaceships. The two traditions appeared to him to have the same general audience, yet to be quite disconnected. It is J.K. Rowling's great intuition and achievement to have reconnected them, so that even her most caustic critics now recognize the synthesis when they call the Harry Potter series 'Bunter on Broomsticks'. In effect, Rowling added elements of magic from the world of C.S. Lewis or J.R.R. Tolkien to the existing formula of the English school story.

The train platform 9¾ through which the children enter the magical world of Hogwarts is a little like E. Nesbit's in the *Railway children* or Lewis's wardrobe in *The lion, the witch and the wardrobe.* The wild wood to which the wardrobe gives access is reflected in the forest round the school, a zone of the Unconscious, and the battle with the universal villain Voldemort is straight out of the *Lord of the rings.* Dumbledore is a Gandalf figure, while the mirror that shows Harry his parents is like the mirror of Galadriel in Tolkien. None of this is to devalue the achievement of Rowling, for it is really in her imaginative combination of so many disparate elements of previous children's literature that the brilliance of the Harry

26 Ibid., pp 198–9.

Potter conception may be found – and in the rather contemporary wit of her much pithier prose.

Another major element added by Rowling is the developmental one – unlike Bunter, Harry develops and grows from year to year, with one book for each of his years at Hogwarts. And unlike most boarding schoolers, Harry is not just temporarily deprived of his parents, but orphaned forever. Like other female authors before her, Rowling very cannily suppressed the initial evidence of her authorship by using initials rather than her Christian name, for she was told by her agent that boys would not pick up a book if they knew the author was a woman.[27] She herself surmized that a male lead and female off-lead would work better with all children than the other way around – but she was careful to show that Hermione is far more learned and clever than Harry, despite his bravery and imaginative capacity. And just as Frank Richards fed initiatives on high culture, so Rowling has fed off high culture – the hated cat of the Hogwarts caretaker being named Mrs Norris for a horrible aunt in Jane Austen's *Mansfield Park*, a favourite novel of the author. But the basic elements of school stories are still there – the establishing phrase like Hagrid's 'Gallopin' gorgons', or the sense that Potter's name has been down for Hogwarts ever since he was born to admittedly non-orthodox flower-power wizard parents of the 1960s. The book, if you wanted to be po-faced, might indeed be said to be a parable, the survival of 1960s people in a sort of underground, for one function of the ministry of magic is 'to keep it from the Muggles that there are still witches and wizards up and down the country'- a subversive quality shared with those insurgent but clandestine Borrowers of Mary Norton who live under the floorboards as an underground movement in their own land. 'Are all your family wizards?,' Harry asks Ron Weasley on the Hogwarts train. 'Er, yes, I think so,' said Ron. 'I think Mum's got a second cousin who is an accountant, but we never talk about him.'[28]

The props are, of course, pure postmodern – the Nimbus 2000 broomstick or the merchandized magic wands seeming to come straight out of the Manchester United gift shop, and the reference to Quidditch referees having 'been known to vanish and turn up later in the Sahara desert' is the old, post-modern football joke.[29]

The regime at Hogwarts is in some ways as liberal as any modern comprehensive – Dumbledore allows everyone to sing the school song to their own favourite tune, in classic, liberal, child-centred mode, with the result that 'everyone finished the song at different times'.[30] The invisibility cloak, however, comes out of the old stories in the penny dreadfuls as surely as the chess game comes from Lewis Carroll, and the nasty teacher Snape is as old and hoary a scapegoat as you could ask for. By far the most traditional element, however, held in common with other generic school stories, is the epic treatment of the war between good and evil, and the

27 J.K. Rowling, interview with Jeremy Paxman, *Newsnight,* BBC 2, 17 June 2003.   28 J.K. Rowling, *Harry Potter and the philosopher's stone* (London: Bloomsbury, 1997), p. 75.   29 Ibid., p. 133.   30 Ibid., p. 95.

notion of a special child ear-marked or hand-picked for a peculiar but unknowable greatness.

Given the rather modern ideas of Rowling, it's probable that she would have chosen a day school as setting, but for the fact that a boarding school allows for a far more extensive range of adventures and emotions. Those rare novels of artistic power set in day schools such as *Tom Sawyer* by Twain and *Reading in the dark* by Seamus Deane often deal with schools in small, claustrophobic communities where everything is as intimate and every local character as well known to us as if in a boarding school. Both Twain's and Deane's books contain strong elements of gothic – structured loosely around a series of anecdotes about boys living on the cusp between urban and rural settings, with Derry rather like Jackson's Island, in the role of a utopian otherworld. The major difference, of course, is in the fact that *Tom Sawyer* is narrated in the third person prose of a reporting adult, while *Reading in the dark* is told through the eyes and voice of a growing child.[31] Yet this is done to strange effect, because the identity of the narrator remains in many ways as shadowy at the end as at the start, as much a mystery to himself as to the reader. This is what happens when you splice the techniques of *Tom Sawyer* with those of *A portrait of the artist as a young man*. Perhaps it is only at the end, when he finally solves the mystery of the family's past, that the narrator is freed to become and develop a distinctive self. Up until that moment, the young reader of the tale, rather like the practical critic whom the younger Deane was trained to be, must withhold himself from any act of interpretation.[32] And, of course, the authority that scarcely believes in its own codes is, on this occasion, not just the schoolmasters, but also the police force itself.

It is worth noting in passing that the school in which Deane's tale is set, St Columb's in Derry, served as both a day and boarding school. Irish writers, seeking the effects of a traditional school story, often have to settle for such half-measures. In Joyce's *Portrait* for instance, the scenes are divided between the boarding school in Clongowes Wood and the later experience as a day-boy in Belvedere College. Likewise in *The dancers dancing* by Eilís Ní Dhuibhne, the four girls whose lives are in focus are students of a day school in Dublin's southside, but they are plunged into a short, intensive version of boarding school conditions by their weeks away from home in the Gaeltacht.[33] This kind of cross between American-style summer camp and British boarding school would appear to be the Irish substitute for the rite of passage which in other countries took those very different forms. It may be significant that there is a rather funny, if brief, description of a students' encounter with Gaeltacht people near the end of Joyce's *Portrait* in the famous diary entries about Mulrennan and the red-rimmed horny-eyed peasant. Perhaps in those pages lurks the emergence of a new literary form that Ní Dhuibhne has helped to bring into focus.

31 Seamus Deane, *Reading in the dark* (London: Cape, 1996).   32 I owe this point to Dr Derek Hand.   33 Eilís Ní Dhuibhne, *The dancers dancing* (Belfast: Blackstaff, 1999).

Golliwog: genealogy of a non-PC icon

DAVID RUDD

The golliwogg was a figure created by the American artist Florence K. Upton in her 1895 publication, *The adventures of two Dutch dolls – and a 'golliwogg'*[1] (with verses by her mother, Bertha), going on to feature in twelve further volumes. It is of note that Florence records that her original doll story was going nowhere until the then anonymous doll was discovered in an attic; everything then fell into place, as she puts it. The title itself carries this history, for the front cover simply states *The adventures of two Dutch dolls*; only on the title page is the real hero mentioned, as a seeming afterthought: 'and a "golliwogg"'. However, famous though the golliwogg was to become – more so than anyone then realized – it was a transient fame, with the figure subsequently being returned to the attic, if not erased from children's literature entirely.

Thus Norma Davis, Upton's biographer, notes that Longman's 250-year anniversary publication[2] omits any reference to golliwogg, though 'Florence Upton's *Dutch doll* series' is mentioned. Likewise, as she notes, in the Opies' *Treasures of childhood*, though the dolls are present, golliwogg himself has been cropped so that only his foot is visible. Perhaps most regrettably, when Davis went to Hampstead Public Library to consult records (Upton's family home was in Hampstead, and she was buried there), she asked to see archived copies of the books, only to be told that 'they had been shredded and used for packing materials'.[3] Certainly, this notion of 'the past ... brought up to date', as Orwell puts it in *Nineteen eighty-four*[4] where no 'expression of opinion, which conflicted with the needs of the moment, [was] ever allowed to remain on record', is worrying. Indeed, in considering the history of the golliwog, such 'presentism' – as Michael Banton[5] has termed it – needs to be set aside, to avoid inappropriate, impulsive reactions.

The first thing to notice about the golliwogg is the double 'g', which was soon to be reduced, by others, to a single one, as Upton never had her creation patented. So, although '[f]or the first time in the history of children's literature, a storybook character was reproduced as a doll',[6] Upton herself received no financial return for it.

1 Florence K. Upton and Bertha Upton, *The adventures of two Dutch dolls – and a 'golliwogg'* (London: Longman Green, 1895).   2 Asa Briggs (ed.), *Essays in the history of publishing: in celebration of the 250th anniversary of the house of Longman, 1724–1974* (London: Longman, 1974).   3 Norma Davis, *A lark ascends: Florence Kate Upton, artist and illustrator* (London: Scarecrow Press, 1992), pp 105–6.   4 George Orwell, *Nineteen eighty-four* (London: Penguin, 1954), p. 35.   5 Michael Banton, 'The idiom of race: a critique of presentism', in *Research in Race and Ethnic Relations*, vol. 2 (1980), p. 21.   6 Davis, *A lark ascends*, p. 23.

This said, as the character was based on a rag doll bought at an American fair when Florence was a child, perhaps the doll was never really hers to patent anyway. (The doll itself, along with its Dutch companions, was housed for many years at Chequers, the British Prime Minister's country residence, before being moved to its current home, at the Bethnal Green Museum of Childhood.) The altered spelling was but the first of many changes in the process of emasculation of the figure. In his original form, though, golliwogg is quite powerful as a 'grotesque'; that is, as one who exhibits disharmony, displaying the 'thin dividing line' between 'mirth and revulsion', between 'the comic and the terrifying'.[7] Upton herself endorsed this ambivalence, admitting his ugliness, but arguing for his endearing personality.[8] We find a similar reaction repeated in early reviews of the golliwogg books. The first substantial thing said of the golliwog is that, 'terrible as it must be to be his foe, it must be almost as nervous a business to be his friend' (*The bookman*, 1899), but, by the following year, the character is reread as possessing a 'placid beauty'.[9] This ambivalent reaction, either of horror or deep affection, continues throughout the golliwog's history. Thus Lady Clive[10] records her brother's 'paroxysms of terror of one and Tom Sharpe, the novelist, has noted his own negative reactions; on the other hand, both Eric Bligh[11] and Kenneth Clark have championed the figure, the latter claiming, 'I identified myself with him completely'.[12]

As I shall argue, this ambivalence is precisely the basis of the golliwogg's appeal, as shown by the reaction of the other main characters towards him; here is how the two main Dutch (that is, 'Deutsch', or German) dolls initially greet him:

> E'en as she spoke,
>   Peg Deutschland broke
> Into a piercing scream.

> Then all look round, as well they may
> To see a horrid sight!
>   The blackest gnome
>   Stands there alone,
> They scatter in their fright

But then,

> Their fears allayed—each takes an arm,
> While up and down they walk;
> With sidelong glance
>   Each tries her chance
> And charms him with 'small talk'.[13]

---

7 Philip Thomson, *The grotesque* (London: Methuen, 1972), pp 17–18.   8 Hubert W. Peet, 'Birth of the Golliwogg', *John O'London's Weekly* 22 Dec. 1950, p. 11.   9 Davis, *The lark ascends*, p. 34.   10 Lady Mary Clive, *The day of reckoning* (Basingstoke: Macmillan, 1964).   11 Eric Bligh, *Tooting Corner* (London: Secker & Warberg, 1946), pp 164–74.   12 Kenneth Clark, *Another part of the wood: a self-portrait* (London: Murray, 1974), pp 6–7.   13 Upton,

Throughout this first book – not just in the title – golliwogg's name appears in scare quotes, supporting the notion that he is disruptive and defies categorization. He is certainly a hybrid figure, crossing cultural boundaries. His engorged lips suggest eroticism. His frightened, or angry eyes stare and his hair stands on end as if in fright, or to scare others. Besides this, he has a monochrome body, yet is dressed in brightly coloured clothes. He mixes human and animal characteristics in that he has paws rather than hands or feet, and a mane of hair. Lastly and most significantly, given his history, he has a 'blacked up' appearance.

Though some read this as proof that he represents a stereotypical black person, the tradition of 'blacking up' has a more catholic history, which seems particularly relevant to Upton's creation. The inverted figure, with black face, has been used in a variety of carnivalesque displays, especially subversive ones, since the Middle Ages, whether in the harlequin figure of the *commedia dell'arte*, in 'plough-witching, pace-egging, mumming, morris, and May customs',[14] or amongst more politically motivated groups such as disenfranchised peasants and machine breakers.[15] As Dale Cockrell says of this 'masking in blackface',

> [it]was making a statement more about what you were not than about race. Belsnickels, callithumpians, mummers, and morris dancers were manifestly not trying to represent persons of African heritage. To black up was a way of assuming 'the Other,' in the cant of this day, a central aspect of the inversion ritual.[16]

Interestingly, he also notes 'reverse' examples of black people engaging in 'whiteface' inversions.

It seems to me that Upton's golliwogg fits far more appositely in this wider tradition of inverted figures that are often associated with festive periods. In the opening book, this is clearly identified, it being 'a frosty Christmas Eve', with the striking of

> the midnight hour,
> When dolls and toys
> Taste human joys,
> And revel in their power.[17]

This is the time of inversion, when normal rules are set aside. And since it is Christmastime, there are certainly parallels with two other black-faced figures, the

Adventures, pp 23–4.   **14** Michael Pickering, 'White skin, black masks: "nigger" minstrelsy in Victorian England', in *Music hall: performance and style*, ed. J.S. Bratton (Milton Keynes: Open UP, 1986), p.78.   **15** Natalie Zemon Davis, 'Women on top: symbolic sexual inversion and political disorder in early modern Europe', in *The reversible world: symbolic inversion in art and society*, ed. Barbara A. Babcock (London: Cornell UP, 1978), pp 178–81.   **16** Dale Cockrell, *Demons of disorder: early blackface minstrels and their world* (Cambridge: CUP, 1997), p. 53.   **17** Upton, *Adventures*, p. 2.

German *Belsnickel* and the Dutch *Zwarte Piet* (Black Peter), each with a long ancestry (going back to the Middle Ages) and each having migrated to America. The Belsnickel was a black-faced character, often in fur coat and cap, who went round on Christmas Eve. He had a bell, a whip or a rod, and some treats for children; however, as they went to get their treats he would slash at them, making them promise to be good.[18] He is related to Saint Nicholas who, especially in his more diabolic form as Old Nick, is also an ambivalent figure. Black Peter who 'appears to have little to do with Africa or black people',[19] was also traditionally a devilish figure, becoming Saint Nicholas's helper after being captured by him. Saint Nicholas was known as 'Sinter Klaas' in Holland, becoming 'Santa Claus' in America. In a role similar to that of the *Belsnickel*, and also armed with a rod, he would deliver gifts to good children, carried down chimneys in a sack. A link between golliwogg and these festive figures seems strengthened by the fact that all the Uptons' books were brought out for the Christmas market. The action of the first one actually takes place on Christmas Eve, and a later one, *The golliwogg's Christmas*,[20] depicts Golliwogg in the role of helper to Santa Claus, tumbling down the chimney in the process.

But even if none of the above parallels is accepted, it is still a shock to read Norma Davis's claim that '*The adventures of two Dutch dolls* was the first picture book to use a Negro character as its protagonist'.[21] 'A negro character' Golliwogg most definitely is not. Even if it were acknowledged that he was a minstrel figure, as Davis suggests elsewhere, this would make him a white, blacked-up character, not an African-American. But even this claim seems disputable. Golliwogg does not conform to the traditional minstrel stereotype – unlike another character called 'Sambo' who features in the book. The latter, dressed traditionally and with burnt-cork face, plays a banjo and sings, a point Davis herself notes.[22] Golliwogg is not musical, lazy, stupid, savage or superstitious, either.[23] However, there are other black figures represented, such as a black waiter in *Golliwogg at the sea-side*,[24] who *does* use a stereotypical negro dialect. In *The golliwogg's desert island*, Golliwogg, in the role of Robinson Crusoe calls Monday[25] a 'fuzzy-wuzz'. In *The golliwogg in the African jungle*,[26] the last of the thirteen golliwogg books, cannibals feature.

This racial dimension is important to note, for it would be foolish to suggest that the books stand apart from their historical context. There was undoubtedly a particular fascination with blackness at this time. Helen Bannerman's *Little black Sambo* appeared in 1899, and the first strip cartoon with a black figure as its main character appeared in 1901, in R.F. Outcault's *Lil' Mose*, in the *New York Herald*,

18 Cockrell, *Demons*, p. 36.   19 Jan Nederveen Pieterse, *White on black: images of Africa and blacks in western popular culture* (London: Yale U.P.), 1992, p. 165.   20 Florence K. Upton, *The golliwogg's Christmas* (London: Longman, 1907).   21 Davis, *Lark ascends*, p. 106.   22 Ibid., p. 109.   23 Ibid., p. 106. Cf. James Walvin, *Black and white: the negro and English society, 1555–1945* (London: Allen Lane, 1973).   24 Florence K. Upton, *Golliwogg at the sea-side* (London: Longman, 1898).   25 Florence K. Upton, *The golliwogg's desert island* (London: Longman, 1906).

with what Pieterse describes as 'a portrayal of the black that was sympathetic for its time'.[27] Black people were also used extensively in advertising, especially for products that were stereotypically associated with them such as tobacco, coffee, chocolate and soap. Also, as Marilynn Olson notes, the primitive was becoming increasingly attractive to Western culture, culminating in the 'negrophilia' of the early twentieth century.[28] In this context, it would be surprising if the Golliwogg books did not touch on any racial issues. In fact, as Toni Morrison argues, 'a dark, abiding, signing Africanist presence'[29] has always existed in American literature. But this should not allow multi-faceted figures to be mono-railed into reductive, essentialist readings; for example, Mickey Mouse has also been shown to signify blackness, especially in his early days,[30] but this does not make him a racist icon.

It should not then be surprising that the golliwog figure was drawn into the discourse of race and racism, and that his appearance and name were inflected in this way. He had after all become a hugely popular icon, copied and reworked endlessly in dolls, games, perfume, food, and in music. He also appeared in many children's books by other writers such as Ruth Ainsworth's 'Rufty-Tufty' series, Blyton's 'Amelia Jane' and Rupert the Bear. In some of these instances the associations with black people, and with minstrelsy, are clearly more overt. For example, Debussy's *The golliwogg's cake-walk* (1908) references a dance that was itself originally a parody *by* black people of the stiff way that white people danced,[31] and some golliwogs are explicitly named 'Sambo', giving the lie to claims of a completely innocent genealogy.

The point that needs emphasizing is that meaning is both socially constructed and historically variable, with signs being differently accented at different times. They also have more particular import established in the course of particular texts. Examining the history of the term 'blackness' in ancient Egypt alone, Pieterse notes that the term moves from positive to negative connotations, then back again, and bases these changes on Egypt's relations with the Nubians.[32] But even then, there would be other connotations of blackness current. For example, in ancient Greece there began the long-influential notion of the four humours, wherein blackness was associated with bile, signifying not only melancholy, but also passion and expressivity.[33] These emotions would fit Upton's golliwogg well, as, aside from his exuberance, he also suffers bouts of despondency.

To illustrate this crucial point about the semantic latitude of terms, consider another colour concept, 'greenness', which suggests not only nature, fertility and

26 Florence K. Upton, *The golliwogg in the African jungle* (London: Longman, 1909).   27 Jan Nederveen Pieterse, *White on black: images of Africa and blacks in western popular culture* (London: Yale, 1992), p. 170.   28 Marilynn Olson, 'Turn-of-the-century grotesque: the Uptons' golliwogg and dolls in context', *Children's Literature*, vol. 28 (2000), p. 79.   29 Toni Morrison, *Playing in the dark: whiteness and the literary imagination* (New York: Vintage, 1992).   30 See Pieterse, *White on Black*, p. 141; and Susan Willis, 'I want the black one: is there a place for Afro-American culture in commodity culture?' *New Formations*, vol. 10 (1990), 95–6, for a discussion of this topic.   31 Pieterse, *White on black*, p. 137.   32 Ibid., p. 23.   33 Richard Dyer, *White* (London & New York: Routledge, 1997), p. 47.

innovation, but also putrefaction, decay and sickness. The term also has powerful political connotations among the Irish. In an Irish neighbourhood of Syracuse, New York, known as Tipperary Hill, the authorities eventually had the colours of the traffic lights reversed, with the grccn hanging above the red (a colour signify-ing the British and their empire); this was the only way to keep the lights func-tional, and stop the red one from being shot at.[34]

Unfortunately, in the case of the golliwog, a presentist construction has invari-ably resulted in the doll being metaphorically 'shot at'. A racist discourse has thus been fomented where there was none before. The word 'golliwog' is itself a good example of this, assumed to be reprehensible as the source of the insulting 'wog', when in fact, the two terms have a separate history, though they were later inter-twined. Upton said that the word simply came to her. Others, though, have tried to work out possible sources, a popular one being 'pollywog', an old word for a tad-pole. In a scene in E.M. Forster's *A room with a view* where some of the male char-acters are swimming, one declares, 'Hee – poof – I've swallowed a polly-wog'. Also, Hilaire Belloc, has the following lines in his poem, 'Frog':

> Be kind and tender to the Frog,
> And do not call him names,
> As 'Slimy skin', or 'polly-wog'

The term 'polliwog' might have been associated with 'Gullah', a name for the African Americans who inhabited the islands off South Carolina; or it could have been seen as a variant on 'dolly' – which is where James Robertson of the Paisley jam manufacturers claimed that he independently heard the term. Alternatively, it might be associated with 'scallywag', which certainly captures golliwogg 's rascal-ly character. Scallywag itself was a variant of 'scalawag', once current in America to describe a white Southerner who supported the federal government following the Civil War (*Webster's English Dictionary*).

But whatever 'golliwog's' origins, the term 'wog' no more derives from *it* than from 'pollywog.' 'Wog' has a separate ancestry. Pieterse supports the notion of its being an acronym for 'western oriental gentleman', though there are alternative suggestions, such as 'working on government service'. Davis quotes a letter to the *Times* from 1945, which claims that 'The letters W.O.G.S. were worn on the arm-bands of the native workmen in Alexandria and Port Said'. The term was then ret-rospectively tied to 'golliwog', in that, because these workers were so thin, wealth-ier Egyptians called them 'ghul' – an Arabic word for desert ghosts which the

---

34 Steven Cohan and Linda M. Shires, *Telling stories: a theoretical analysis of narrative fiction* (London & New York: Routledge, 1988), p. 4. Though this had nothing to do with the Irish, it is of passing interest that there was actually a green golliwog produced by Bradford Dyers Association, according to Robert M. MacGregor in 'The golliwog: innocent doll to symbol of racism', *Advertising and popular culture: studies in variety and versatility*, ed. Sammy R. Danna (Bowling Green, Ohio: Bowling Green State U.P., 1992), p. 125.

British troops turned into 'golly'.[35] Whilst the *OED* finds no evidence for an acronymic origin, it confirms the term 'wog's' independent existence, noting that it is applied more to 'one of Arab extraction', only later becoming more generalized.

Fascinating though it is to speculate about origins, it would be naïve to think that an innocent etymology might rescue the golliwog. This would suggest an essentialist view of language, with meaning being somehow encoded in the signifiers, rather than, as argued earlier, meaning being socially negotiated by different social groups, in what Vološinov[36] saw as a struggle over the sign.[37] This certainly occurred in the case of the golliwog. It became an icon for racists and anti-racists alike, often with overlapping interests; thus innocent campaigns such as 'Save the Golliwog' themselves became associated with far right elements. Lady Birdwood, for example, who stood as a British National Party candidate for Dewsbury in the 1992 General Election, and who was prosecuted for distributing racially offensive literature, kept her golliwog prominently in view whenever she was interviewed.[38]

Enid Blyton's name was itself to become a signifier of racism in this struggle, in particular, thanks to an infamous episode in *Here comes Noddy again* 1951, where Noddy is effectively mugged by four golliwogs. By the 1960s and 70s, this was read by some as provocatively racist, and hastened the golliwog's demise. As I have commented elsewhere, the episode seems to me to be an intertext of a very similar scene in *Pinocchio,*[39] and it is certainly a powerful one, recapturing some of the ambivalence and threat that had been lacking in many golliwog representations. It was the only Noddy book I could remember from my own childhood – and this was probably because of this scene – but I have to say that I never saw golliwogs as representing black people, and neither, from my wide survey, did others. Some contemporary children I spoke to knew of the association, but of those that did not, none made it. Even their descriptions show how culturally loaded our interpretations are. Thus, one writer to the *Guardian* states that '[t]here is not much doubt in my mind that the golliwog... with its goggle eyes, spiky hair, and banana lips is in fact a distorted representation of a black person'.[40] However a six-year-old white girl who took part in my study described it as 'like a ... a sun shape, and it has, like, like cotton things sticking out of its head'.[41]

35 Davis, *Lark ascends,* p.11.   36 Valentin Vološinov, *Marxism and the philosophy of language* (New York: Seminar Press, 1973), p. 29.   37 John Fiske, for example, has written about the struggle over the word 'nigger', recently reappropriated by black rappers. John Fiske, 'British cultural studies and television', *Channels of discourse reassembled: television and contemporary criticism,* ed. Robert C. Allen (London: Routledge, 1992), p. 299.   38 Russell Davies, 'What makes someone a neo-fascist?' *Daily Telegraph,* 4 May 1994.   39 David Rudd, *Enid Blyton and the mystery of children's literature* (London: Macmillan, 2000), p. 146.   40 Cindy Matthews, 'Well, Golly bejabbers!', *Guardian,* 12 May 1984.   41 Interestingly, the back cover of Upton's original Golliwogg book features just such a sun shape, which obviously offers a daytime contrast to the midnight adventures of the characters concealed within the book.

Though I have not time to detail it here, the same pattern of an initial uneasiness about the golliwog character, shifting to a view of him as amusing and likeable, was evident in various groups of children studied. It replicated that noted earlier and served to emphasise golliwog's essential ambivalence.[42] In more recent editions of the Blyton story, the golliwog has been removed and been replaced by goblins. The children's reactions to this were interesting. It was noteworthy that even quite young children thought that the more recent emended book did not work as well – in that Noddy would be stupid to go off into a wood with goblins, who were always bad, whereas 'he'd trust a golliwog'.[43]

However, over the years critics have not been so generous, and have actually helped to shape a discourse of racism by their comments. They have done this firstly by reading racism as itself being only about blackness and whiteness.[44] Secondly, they have done it by assuming that the golliwog always did, and always would signify a black person in some essentialist way. In other words, they have failed to read the text adequately. Thus Robert Druce accuses Blyton of 'a deeper dislike of blackness' and unwarrantedly speaks of 'her frequent casting of golliwogs, along with monkeys, as the wrongdoers in the Noddy stories'.[45] George Greenfield, her literary agent, is perhaps even more surprising in saying that 'her naughty characters were almost always black in hue'.[46] Having done a count of golliwogs in this and other series, I can report that this is simply untrue (in fact, they are often ideas characters, as was Upton's original). However, in picking out isolated examples and exaggerating them, a racist discourse is all-too-easily constructed.

The children I spoke to generally expressed sadness that the golliwog had gone, but understood the reasons when explained to them. However, they often preferred alternative solutions to the problem, such as having 'half the black ones bad and half the white ones bad as well... and half the black ones good and half the white ones good ... so it's just they're equal', as one said. Others were more radical: 'you make Noddy black and the ... [gollies] white' – which brings to mind a line from Joe Orton: 'She's making white golliwogs for sale in colour-prejudice trouble-spots ... it might promote racial harmony'.[47] Realizing that the black–white

---

42 Rudd, *Enid Blyton*, pp 147–50.   43 Ibid., Nine-year-old girl.   44 Bob Dixon, *Catching them young, volume 1: sex, race and class in children's fiction* (London: Pluto Press, 1977), p. 70; see also Rudd *Enid Blyton*, p. 134.   45 Robert Druce, *This day our daily fictions: an enquiry into the multi-million bestseller status of Enid Blyton and Ian Fleming* (Amsterdam-Atlanta: Rudopi B.V., 1992), p. 230.   46 George Greenfield, 'The famous one', *A smattering of monsters: a kind of memoir* (London: Little, Brown, 1995), p. 113.   47 Joe Orton, *What the butler saw. The complete plays* (London: Eyre Methuen, 1976), p. 387. There was also a 'white-faced Gollie' called 'Mr Smith' produced by Deans of Sussex, England, in 1966. Unfortunately, his launch coincided with Ian Smith, prime minister of Rhodesia, making his unilateral declaration of independence for his racially separatist country – which damaged sales considerably. Only a few such dolls were ever produced (some 2,500) and it is very rare among collectors (Koontz). More recently, I found an undated children's book on the Internet by Frederick Covins entitled *Gladstone the white golliwog*, advertised as an 'anti-racist story'! Covins, Frederick, *Gladstone, the white golliwog*. URL: http://www.pipeelm.com/newworks. htm. Accessed 7 May 2003.

opposition was the problem, some children suggested other colours, 'like green or purple' as one put it, to which his colleague (both fourteen year-olds) perceptively responded, 'Seeing it's Toyland they could have done it as anything.'

This has been a necessarily brief look at the genealogy, the rise and fall of the golliwog. The character clearly had to go once discussion of him closed in on the issue of racism, around which both pro- and anti-racists organised themselves. However, what he represented was an unfortunate loss, given the power he clearly possessed as a grotesque, as a culturally indeterminate, mischievous and likeable icon. However, although erased from children's literature, it is of note that both the name, and the doll, live on. Most recently, a successful South African funk group, formed in 2001, which claims to represent 'freedom of expression', has called itself 'Golliwog'.[48] As for the doll, the English company, Dean, and the German, company Steiff, which produced the first golliwog dolls in 1908, continue to manufacture them. The latter introduced a centenary 'girliwog' in 1995, called 'Molly'; fittingly the doll was accompanied by its own miniature Dutch doll, called 'Peg', in explicit homage to Florence Upton. These limited editions, though, seem to be aimed at the adult market rather than children – just as were facsimile editions of the books, issued in the 1980s and 1990s.[49]

48 Online at URL: http://www.music.org.za/artists/golliwog/. They are not the first group to use this name, either. The American band, Creedence Clearwater Revival, was earlier known as 'Golliwog', emulating the British sixties groups and sporting blond [sic] 'moptop' wigs. 49 Beth Savino, 'New "Girliwog" from Steiff', *International Golliwog Collectors Club Newsletter* 3 (1999). URL: http://www.teddybears.com/golliwog/3gw3a.html. The sales of the original Golliwogg books were declining by the time of the publication of the last book, *The golliwogg in the African jungle* (1909).

Colonialization of food in children's literature: apple pie or Turkish delight?

ANN ALSTON

Children's literature entertains something of an obsession with food. This obsession is laden with ambiguity; food is both wholesome and poisonous, both magical and traditional. Mealtimes attempt to civilize but also illustrate power relations. Food is linked with sexuality, and extremes of size come under constant ridicule and attack. British children's literature practices an unhealthy attitude towards both food and size; these issues are so integral to the fiction, so expected, that they have been constantly overlooked in editions revised to fall in line with modern, politically correct conventions. The fat or skinny villain, in contrast to the lean hero or heroine, has come to be stereotypical; size in itself is taken as a reflection of character. In a somewhat fascist manner extremes of size have come to represent either a sense of sexuality and gluttony in the obese characters or sterility and unkindness in the skinny characters; varieties of figures are not accepted. This narrowness is also evident when considering different types of food, as only certain traditional national foods are promoted, while foreign influences are viewed as threatening; food has acquired a semiotic place representing far more than simple nourishment, for what and how much is eaten are open to constant scrutiny.

The majority of the texts focused on in this essay are from the 1930s to the 1950s, a time which included economic depression and the rationing of food due to the war. Food and body images in children's literature were increasingly linked with ideas of national loyalty, hence the emphasis on eating of traditional food, and perhaps even the emphasis on the sin of gluttony; to over-eat was not a patriotic activity. This complex issue of sizism continues into the twenty-first century. It is not simply a product of war-time rationing or xenophobia.

We may begin with a 1930s text which is an exception to the rule. André Maurois' *Fattypuffs and Thinifers* is a rare example of children's literature that brings to the fore conventional divisions between sizes. Two brothers, Edmund and Terry, discover an underground world where all characters are divided not by gender, religion or colour, but by weight. The illustrations in the British edition by Fritz Wegner emphasize the extremities of the two, for the Fattypuffs are not just chubby but obese, while the Thinifers look to be on the verge of anorexia. War breaks out between the two, but the Fattypuffs and Thinifers learn to like each other and they even interbreed. Tensions due to size have been resolved by the time of the text's conclusion:

The official approached a grille and cried:
'Two Surface-dwellers. Two!' He did not add as formerly:
'One Fatty. One Thinny.' Distinctions by weight had been abolished for-
ever in the countries of the Underground.[1]

While distinctions by weight may have been abolished in the Underground in
Maurois' book, such forward thinking is not widely evident in children's literature.
The distinction between English and non-English writing here is a significant one.
Fattypuffs and Thinifers was originally published as *Patapoufs et Filifers* in 1930, and
not translated into English until 1941. The moral emphasis that the text places on
understanding and embracing difference, both of size and country, is far more
sophisticated and advanced than that of much of English children's literature in
that period, although allegory obviously pushes at accepted, unquestioned, standards.

It is worth considering whether there are many fat heroes or heroines in English
children's literature. It seems that are very few, for these heroes and heroines tend
to be strong and slim. This pattern is apparently timeless as illustrations assume
thinness in texts from the slim children in *The story of the treasure seekers* (1899) to
Peter Pan and Wendy (1911), to the Fossils from *Ballet shoes* (1936), to Harry Potter
(1997–).[2] The chubbier characters are often dismissed as ugly, stupid, or villainous.
Consider the following: Billy Bunter, Cornelia Flower from Elinor M. Brent-
Dyer's *The head girl of the Chalet School* (1928), Augustus Gloop from *Charlie and
the chocolate factory* (1964), and more recently, Dudley from the Harry Potter series.
While there are exceptions to this pattern, it is nonetheless strong. Size is an important determining factor in whether the character is to be a hero or villain. Indeed,
before even meeting Cornelia Flower, the 'nice' girls at the Chalet school have
already labelled and dismissed her as obese and therefore other and bad:

'What is she like?' asked Klara. 'She has a pretty name.'
'Well, she doesn't live up to it – as far as looks go,' said Jo. 'She's nearly
square, and she has a jaw like – like – well, like a ramrod! About fourteen, I
think, and she's in the Yellow dorm. Who's Head there this term? Anyone
know?'
'Mary is, I think,' said Bianca.
'Well, she's got a handful in Cornelia, or I'm blind! What possessed
Matey to put two Americans in one dorm?'[3]

1 André Maurois, *Fattypuffs and thinifers* (London: Jane Nissen Books, 2000).   2 Edith
Nesbit, *The story of the treasure seekers* (Ware: Wordsworth Classics, 1995); J.M. Barrie, *Peter
Pan and Wendy* (Sevenoaks: Knight Books, 1993); Noel Streatfeild, *Ballet shoes* (London:
Puffin, 1994); J.K. Rowling, *Harry Potter and the philosopher's stone* (London: Bloomsbury,
1997).   3 Elinor M. Brent-Dyer, *The head girl of the Chalet School* (Edinburgh: Chambers,
1988), pp 127–8.

Cornelia's character and fate are decided on two factors: she has a large unattractive figure and she is foreign. It follows in a mythology of children's fiction that she will be a troublemaker, since she shows all the troublemaker's semiotic features. Similarly, the reader can tell by Dahl's description of Augustus Gloop, 'who was so enormously fat he looked as though he had been blown up with a powerful pump',[4] that he is Charlie's antithesis. The moral world of children's literature is simplified by archetypal signs. The slim 'normal' character will be good whereas the obese character will be *other* and thus bad, just as the foreign character may well be suspect. Indeed, to marry the foreign and the fat as in the case of Cornelia Flower is significant as it links concerns of the foreign with those of greed and obesity; the *other* comes to mean everyone that is not English, not slim and thus not normal.

Why are these obese characters portrayed in such a negative light? In order to answer this we must look at the wider connotations of food. Food is often associated with sexuality. One only has to refer to the sensual language used in restaurant menus, or consider the illustration on page 171 of a modern cookery book, Nigella Lawson's *Forever summer,* published in 2002, in which she consumes a phallic ice cream cone, to comprehend this. Food also signifies a certain sexuality[5] in children's fiction, for while on the one hand it can be good and wholesome, on the other hand it can be sensual, tempting and forbidden. Food penetrates the child's body and thus who feeds the child and what they feed him/her become important, for it appears that the child should only take good things into his/her body. The Queen in *The lion, the witch and the wardrobe* uses food in order to seduce Edmund, thus placing him firmly under her control:

> [H]e stepped on to the sledge and sat at her feet, and she put a fold of fur mantle round him and tucked it in well.
> 'Perhaps something hot to drink?' said the Queen ...
> Edmund felt much better as he began to sip the hot drink. It was something he had never tasted before, very sweet and foamy and creamy, and it warmed him right down to his toes.[6]

The actions of the Queen are somewhat ambiguous as she tucks him in. Offering a hot drink suggests that she is playing a motherly role. This role here also invokes power, for Edmund sits at her feet, powerless, while the Queen penetrates his body by feeding him the 'sweet, foamy, creamy' drink. This is the beginning of Edmund's fall. He has tasted the magical, the forbidden, the sexual, metaphorically speaking. After the drink, in order to complete the Queen's control, Edmund is given his greatest desire in food, Turkish delight. There are both sexual and for-

---

4 Roald Dahl, *Charlie and the chocolate factory* (London: Puffin, 1985), p. 33. 5 Wendy R. Katz, 'Some uses of food in children's literature', *Children's Literature in Education,* 11 (1990), pp 192–9, p. 191; Maria Nikolajeva, *From mythic to linear: time in children's literature* (London: The Children's Literature Association and Scarecrow Press, 2000). 6 C.S. Lewis, *The lion, the witch and the wardrobe the complete chronicles of Narnia* (London: Collins, 2000), pp 85–6.

eign signifiers here, in its sweet 'delicious' form it emphasizes the sensual, but by its name, Turkish it shows the eastern 'other'. It is exotic, foreign and this adds to its dangerous appeal. It is significant that sexuality and foreignness are linked since both are represented as potentially threatening and both are considered to be non-English.[7] The other, in this case the foreign, is often regarded as being sexually dangerous. Thus the double meaning of the foreignness and the sensuality of Turkish delight has come to represent a somewhat clichéd sign.[8] Indeed, having eaten the Turkish delight Edmund 'has the look of one who had eaten her food', he has lost his childhood purity, has been polluted by the foreign sexual influence, has taken on a look of a member of her regime as opposed to one of his own family/country. Having tasted the delights of the other, Edmund can no longer be satisfied by wholesome English food. His appetite for the foreign, the luxurious, and thus the sexual has been awakened. While his siblings eat fish, potatoes and tea at the Beavers', these are not sufficient to satisfy Edmund's appetite. Thus he betrays his family as he follows his desire for Turkish delight. Edmund has lost control over his own body. He has fallen into temptation, has become gluttonous and so has betrayed his family.

Considering the context of this story, its wartime setting, and the fact that food rationing that was still in force even when the text was published, this betrayal can be linked to that of a war-time traitor. Unable to satisfy his appetite, Edmund has reached beyond the ration book to the sweetness of Turkish delight. He has betrayed his nationality as he rejects traditional food for the foreign, a convention, as we shall also see in the case Arthur Ransome, well established in the English psyche. Edmund has broken the rules of childhood, and thus he is punished within the text and not allowed to become a hero in the same sense as his brother, Peter. Later, Edmund is purged but is not automatically given hero status. Instead he is made to earn it. Adult writers will only allow the civilized, strong characters to gain hero status.[9] Like Eve, Edmund has to be reprimanded and only the death of the messiah, Aslan, atones for his sin.

Children's literature demands not only that its heroes eat in a civilized manner, thus avoiding gluttony, but that they also eat the right sort of food. Like Edmund, Augustus Gloop, Billy Bunter and Dudley fail to control their appetites. Their desires outweigh the social etiquette that they should have learned. They are seen as threats and cannot be allowed to gain heroic status. Instead they are ridiculed.

It seems to be a paradox then that the heroes in Enid Blyton's *The famous five* series (1942–63) and Arthur Ransome's *Swallows and Amazons* series (1930–47) are

7 Interestingly, the word 'sexuality' is not listed in the index of Judy Giles and Tim Middleton (eds), *Writing Englishness, 1900–1950: an introductory sourcebook on national identity* (London: Routledge, 1995).   8 There exists a great deal of criticism that takes note of links between the foreign and sexual within English literature across the ages. For example, see R.I. Moore, *The formation of a persecuting society* (Oxford: Blackwell, 1987).   9 Nikolajeva in *From mythic* also makes interesting points regarding this passage in a discussion which concentrates on food as a marker of character, morality and enchantment, pp 129–31.

allowed to eat with such frequency and yet maintain their slim figures, as implied by Blyton's insistent descriptions of other fat characters and by Ransome's pictures. Explanations are, however, possible. Firstly, especially with regard to *The famous five* the children are often fighting wars of their own against criminals and thus, they, like the troops, need to be well fed. Secondly, through their continuous exercise in the healthy outdoors, the appetites of the children can be justified; they eat because of hunger rather than gluttony. Finally, the food provided tends to be traditional since the children drink tea and ginger beer, and eat sandwiches, fried breakfast and fruit pies, and there is no mention of anything foreign like Turkish delight. In consuming traditional English food the children are embracing their national heritage, for as Roland Barthes argues, food gives a feeling of belonging that adds to a sense of national identity.[10] It is significant that both *The famous five* and the *Swallows and Amazons* series continued to be written and published during the Second World War, for while both are essentially retreatist – the picnic baskets have certainly not been curtailed by rationing – the type of food consumed remains patriotic. Indeed, as Diane McGee points out,

> the choice of what is acceptable to eat plays a major role in defining the culture [...] one of the first things that a child learns is what is eaten in the group [...] accepting these strictures as absolute is a formative experience in childhood, both in terms of the development of the individual and of that individual's membership of the group.[11]

Blyton and Ransome's characters learn to respect the food rituals of their culture, to stay loyal as their country stands in danger of attack and invasion. The consumption of wholesome English food contributes to the children's hero status: they remain reliable and unpolluted as they consume their national inheritance; the foreign unknown never tempts them. Indeed, in Ransome's *We didn't mean to go to sea* (1937) English conservatism regarding food is illustrated to the full. Power relations are evident as Commander Walker takes over while he orders food on behalf of his children after they have sailed to Holland by themselves. They have no opportunity and, it seems, no wish to make their own choices. Commander Walker as father is trusted to keep the children's diets safe as he orders traditional food: ' Can't go far wrong with soup and steak," said Daddy. "You never know what you get when you try something with a fancy name.' Notwithstanding Commander Walker's dictum, the book's epigraph favours initiative: ' "Grab a chance and you won't be sorry for a might-have-been.'[12] However, with regards to food, it seems that no

10 Roland Barthes, 'Towards a psychosociology of contemporary food consumption', *Food and culture: a reader*, eds Carole Counihan and Penny Van Esterik (London: Routledge, 1997), pp 20–8. 11 Diane McGee, *Writing the meal: dinner in the fiction of the early twentieth-century women writers* (Toronto: U. Toronto P., 2002), p. 15. 12 Arthur Ransome, *We didn't mean to go to sea* (London: Red Fox, 1993), title page and p. 295.

chances should be taken. A different culture should not be embraced. Commander Walker ensures that the children remain faithful to their family and, by proxy, to England.

The adult demands that the child hero/heroine is slim and loyal, for the obese character embodies a lack of control, as he/she has bowed to temptation in the form of gluttony. In the mythology of children's fiction that has been created by these stereotypes, it follows that the obese character must be impure. In children's fiction the hero/heroine must always be pure, for to be impure renders him/her, in effect, adult, and thus excluded from a typical adult reading of children which tends to promote the innocent and naturally civilized child. We come again to the simplicity of the underlying basic structures and premises of much of children's literature: it is black or white, home or away, fat or slim, English or foreign, good or bad; there is no happy medium.[13]

A problem arises when considering the skinny adult character. In many ways one would expect this character to be the epitome of control. He/she has not fallen to temptation and has not committed the sin of gluttony and thus remains a virginal, even child-like, figure. This is true of characters who have been denied food due to their circumstances, for example Charlie's family in Roald Dahl's *Charlie and the chocolate factory*, or Miss Honey from his *Matilda*. In a well-off adult figure, however, skinniness (and there is a difference between being lean and slim, and being on the verge of anorexia) comes to represent a certain sterility, a refusal to consume wholesome national food, a defiance that prevents heritage from being reproduced. The skinny adult character is usually depicted as a villain, or a less than noble character. Consider the following: Scrooge from Charles Dickens's *A Christmas carol* (1843), Aunt Spiker from Dahl's *James and the giant peach* (1961), Mr Wormwood from Dahl's *Matilda* (1988), Aunt Petunia from Rowling's *Harry Potter and the philosopher's stone* (1997) and Count Olaf from Lemony Snicket's *A series of unfortunate events: the bad beginning* (1999). Their skinniness is, like the obesity of previous characters, extreme. Extremes are disparaged in children's literature, for they represent a lack of balance. Those adults who have failed to achieve a happy medium cannot be trusted to take charge of children. Appetite is something that must be controlled and civilized. Child heroes/heroines achieve this naturally. Those who have not achieved this as children are expected to do so by adulthood. It is part of the civilising, growing up process. To eat food at a table is a social activity. To refuse to do this is to break the rules of society in which the individual must be sociable and ready to exchange love, opinions and food. Wendy Katz argues that 'compulsive eating sometimes signifies a failed or strained relationship between parent and child'[14] and goes on to cite *Nobody's family is going to change*[15]

13 For further discussion on thematic structure and binary oppositions refer to Perry Nodelman, *The pleasures of children's literature* (London: Longman, 1996), pp 189–92.   14 Katz, 'Some uses of food', pp 192–9.   15 Louise Fitzhugh, *Nobody's family's going to change* (London: Gollancz, 1976).

as an example of this.[16] Katz emphasizes that on maturing and beginning to accept her parents, Emma begins to control her appetite, but what is important here is the fact that slimness is vital in representing maturity. Emma has to lose her excess weight to become civilized. She becomes neither too fat nor too thin. The adult who has failed to make this transition is constantly rebuked by children's fiction as he/she remains 'other'- firmly placed under a label of fat or thin. In *Swallows and Amazons*, the Amazons' Great Aunt is skinny and symbolizes unkindness, Captain Flint is on the chubby side and is untrustworthy, while Captain Walker is the epitome of the trustworthy figure, as when he reappears with the children in *We didn't mean to go to sea* his wife recognizes him first by the 'hand, a lean, brown hand' that comes up cradling a kitten before his head appears out of the forehatch.[17] Commander Walker is lean, strong and thus entirely dependable.

To a certain extent children's literature has its own vital statistics: heroes and heroines must comply with a figure that is 'normal', neither skinny nor obese. Adults who remain 'other' are deemed to be untrustworthy and unkind villains. It seems that children's literature has neglected political correctness with regard to both physical figures and the type of food consumed. There is little room for variety. It has, indeed, established its own mythology in making fat and thin synonymous with the villain, and normal and slim but not skinny synonymous with heroes and heroines. This is something rarely challenged in children's literature, which in common with teenage magazines and the contemporary world of multi media products, encourages a single normative body type. The same motifs continually reappear from the nineteenth to the twenty-first century. Children's literature values only the slim.

16 Katz, 'Some uses of food', pp 196–7.   17 Ransome, *We didn't mean*, p. 386.

Robert Frost and Edward Thomas: poets' stories

DEBORAH THACKER

This article discusses the prose stories for children of two writers, Robert Frost and Edward Thomas (Philip Edward Thomas), known primarily as influential twentieth-century poets. As is the case with many children's books which are written in the first instance to amuse the authors' own children, their stories are full of private jokes and family knowledge. This, together with their publication histories, has ensured that they are not well known. However, they are interesting because of their appreciation of a childlike sensibility and of the poetic power of children's language. They are also interesting as examples of writing about relationships between adult and child that reflect contemporaneous modernist concerns. An analysis of two collections of stories, Frost's *As told to a child: stories from the Derry notebook* and Thomas's *Four-and-twenty blackbirds* may contribute to wider discussions about the continuities between children's literature and the canon.

Robert Frost and Edward Thomas formed a friendship and a shared interest in the development of poetry in 1914, and continued their correspondence until Thomas's death at the battle of Arras in 1917. Each wrote stories based on tales that he had told to his children. In Frost's case, they were not intended for publication and did not appear in print until the Latham and Thompson collection of poetry and prose in 1972.[1] Although there is an edition entitled *Stories for Lesley* edited by Roger D. Sell in the Barrett Collection at the University of Virginia,[2] the first publication for the general reader was produced by the Cyder Press in 2000. This edition is illustrated with drawings by Frost's children.

Thomas struggled to find a publisher for his stories, to which he referred in his letters as 'proverbs', until Duckworth published them in 1915 (and for which Thomas received £10). It is clear from his correspondence that Thomas worked on stories he had told his children in order to make money, a factor that contributed to much of his writing and reviewing at the time. The volume was *Four-and-twenty blackbirds*, whose title was probably suggested by Eleanor Farjeon. Bodley Head published a second edition, with illustrations by Margery Gill in 1965, but in this edition the order of the stories was changed. The book then

1 Edward Connery Lathem and Lawrance Thompson (eds), *Robert Frost: poetry and prose* (New York: Holt, Rinehart and Winston, 1972).   2 Roger D. Sell, *Stories for Lesley, edited from the Derry Notebook* (University of Virginia and the Bibliographical Society of the University of Virginia, Charlottesville, 1984) (illus. Warren Chappell). I am grateful to Dr David Rudd for this full reference.

remained out of print until the Cyder Press published a facsimile edition in 2001. There is very little reference to these stories in any of the critical literature on either poet, although they contribute significantly to both men's poetic development.

While Robert Frost's poetry is frequently studied by children and appears in many children's poetry anthologies (there must be very few such anthologies without Edward Thomas's 'Adlestrop'), both poets are regarded as writing predominantly for an adult audience. In addition to writing poetry, both also wrote prose and, in fact, early in his career, Thomas published *The pocket book of songs and poems*, and versions of Celtic stories and Norse tales.[3] What is particularly noteworthy, however, is that both wrote stories for their own children over a period of time during the first and second decade of the twentieth century when they were struggling to find their own modern poetic voices.

The process of writing these stories, of engaging through the medium of prose with children as interlocutors, thinkers and listeners, was influential in the formation of a philosophy of poetry that they evolved together during the brief period of time that they shared in Gloucestershire before the start of the First World War. According to Eleanor Farjeon, Thomas discovered Frost for England and, having read Thomas's prose, Frost made him into a poet. It is clear that Frost read Thomas's 'proverbs' manuscript, but it is not clear whether he commented upon it. Neither has it been established whether Thomas read Frost's stories for his own children. Thomas responded positively to Frost's attempts to break away from the dominant early twentieth-century poetic styles and admired his 'revolutionary refusal to use overtly poetical constructions'.[4] The search for new voices led Frost away from the erudition that is one of the modernist hallmarks of the work of T.S. Eliot or W.B. Yeats. It was the cadences of the ordinary voice and the serendipitous quality of everyday language that was particularly attractive and inspiring to Thomas, who was continually frustrated in his attempts to find a distinctive poetic voice.[5]

Experimentation with childlike playfulness is not a phenomenon that is exclusive to these two poets. Gertrude Stein was similarly attracted to the possibilities of the child's voice and published a story, 'The world is round', in 1939[6] that reflected similar qualities. There are further examples of poets who use writing for children in comparable ways. Randall Jarrell wrote children's stories (*The bat-poet*,[7] for instance) to escape the writer's block that tortured him.

---

3 Edward Thomas, *The pocket book of songs and poems for the open air* (London: Grant Richards, 1907); *Norse tales* (Oxford: Clarendon Press, 1912); *Celtic tales* (Oxford: Clarendon Press, 1922).   4 Rennie Parker, *The Georgian poets* (Plymouth: Northcote House, 1999), p. 39.   5 For further detail, Andrew Motion, *The poetry of Edward Thomas* (London: Hogarth, 1991).   6 D. Thacker and J. Webb, *Introducing children's literature from romanticism to postmodernism* (London: Routledge, 2002).   7 Randall Jarrell, *The bat-poet* (New York: Macmillan, 1964).

While Frost's and Thomas's narratives do not contain such modernist characteristics as fragmentation of form, their stories reflect a willingness to stretch the
conventional boundaries of meaning to a degree that occasionally approaches the
surreal. Although play with language is unsurprising as a function of children's stories in general, Frost's adoption of a child's storytelling voice seems to anticipate a
challenge to the stable narrative voice of nineteenth-century children's stories.

> The baby went up the Berry road and saw a donkey. And the donkey said:
> 'Look out – I'm going to kick.' And the baby said: 'Well, kick the other way
> then.' And the donkey said: 'I won't.' And the baby said: 'Well, wait a
> minute.' And the donkey said: 'I won't wait!' And he gave an awful kick
> right into the air. But he didn't kick her bonnet off because she ran. She ran
> home and told her Mamma. And her Mamma said: 'Don't go up there
> then.' And the baby said: 'I wants to.' 'But you won't.' 'No, I won't.' And
> the Mamma said: 'Hear him snap and click, just like a rubber donkey.'
> (*Rubber donkey!*)[8]

This story not only reflects the qualities of a small child's conversation with her
mother, but also celebrates the spontaneity and flow of childlike language. The
final, italicized repetition of *'Rubber donkey!'* calls attention to a distinct narrative
voice which comments on the surprising phrase and leaves interpretation completely open. This recognition of the serendipitous qualities of child-like language
and, simultaneously, an adult sensibility observing it, parallels the dialectical voices in key modernist texts such as James Joyce's *A portrait of the artist as a young
man* or William Faulkner's *The sound and the fury*.[9]

Although his stories are more conventional, Thomas's transformation of familiar sayings and proverbs so as to subvert expectations and to highlight their literal
meanings can verge on the surreal. This process undermines the authority of a
moralising adult voice and enters into a playful relationship with the child-as-read-
er. Language as a socializing and controlling force is challenged in such ludic
encounters. The ostensibly 'low' culture of children's literature playfully and self-
consciously challenges meaning in a manner more often associated with sophisticated texts.

Many critics and literary historians remark on the poets' mutual understanding.
Rennie Parker, for instance, likens Frost's influence on Thomas to that of a 'guru',
claiming that 'Thomas was drawn to the older poet like the proverbial moth to the
flame'.[10] Anthony Thwaite[11] and Andrew Motion both acknowledge the encouragement and influence of the older poet on the younger, Motion maintaining that:

---

8 Robert Frost, *As told to a child: stories from the Derry Notebook* (Cheltenham: Cyder, 2000),
p. 49.   9 See, for instance, the opening episode of James Joyce's *A portrait of the artist as a
young man*.   10 Parker, *Georgian poets*, p. 42.   11 Anthony Thwaite, *Twentieth-century
English poetry* (London: Heinemann, 1978), p. 36

> The story of Frost's effect on Thomas's personality and work is well known. The instinctive understanding they were to show for each other's poetry had its origins in similarities between their backgrounds and temperaments. After Thomas's death, Frost called him 'the only brother I ever had'.[12]

It is possible that the childlike uses of language and the unstudied misapprehension or 'play' with language reflected in these children's stories contributed to, or influenced, what both Frost and Thomas were trying to achieve, namely, new poetic forms for a new age.

A modernist fascination with what has been termed the primitive, with stripping away surfaces to attempt to reveal meanings that may be prior to, or beyond, language, is also reflected in these stories. Juliet Dusinberre[13] calls attention to the shared shift in consciousness of children's writers and such adult writers as Henry James, Virginia Woolf and James Joyce. Some writers of the early twentieth century 'approached the task of writing for children as an attempt to find a language that rejects the rational and conventional in order to "make it new"'.[14] Although critics of high modernism rarely mention children's literature, Julie Kristeva's interpretation of modernist poetics,[15] for example, casts some light on these stories. Kristeva considers that the revolutionary possibilities of modernist texts were in some senses inspired by the uses of language prior to the socialisation process. The power of words and sound in the pre-symbolic imaginary 'bubbles up' from beneath the linguistic constraints imposed by the symbolic order. Out of this tension poetic language arises. Children negotiate the divide between the pre-symbolic imaginary and the symbolic order, and it is this process that Frost and Thomas draw upon. Not only is this relationship to language reflected in the stories they wrote for their children, but it is also a key to their poetic experimentation.

Although Thomas spent less time with his children and seemed less engaged with their upbringing than Frost was with his, Richard Emeny comments in his introduction to *Four-and-twenty blackbirds* that Thomas enjoyed the company of children, and his letters, particularly to Farjeon, make frequent reference to the odd and surprising things that his children said. 'Baba [Myfanwy]', he writes, 'rhymes verse regardless of sense and makes verse without rhyme and equally without sense for a long time on end nowadays'.[16]

---

12 Motion, *Edward Thomas*, p. 23.   13 J. Dusinberre, *Alice to the lighthouse: children's books and radical experiments in art* (London: Palgrave, 1999).   14 Thacker & Webb, *Introducing children's literature*, p. 105.   15 In Toril Moi, *Sexual/textual politics* (London: Routledge, 1985).   16 Eleanor Farjeon, *Edward Thomas: the last four years* (Oxford: O.U.P., 1979), p. 109. Thomas shared these observations with Farjeon because of her interest in children. Although she claimed that her work, specifically *Martin Pippin in the orchard* (London: Collins, 1921), was not intended exclusively for children, she was working on a similar project to the 'Proverbs' – *Nursery rhymes of London town* (London: Duckworth, 1916) – at the same time. Both works were based on the conceit of 'fantastic explanation[s] of well-known proverbs, sayings or nursery rhymes.' Richard Emeny, 'Introduction', Thomas, *Four-and-*

Frost was attuned to the less restrictive and authoritarian approaches to child-care and education that evinced shifts in the dominant constructions of childhood, and which were gaining acceptance at the beginning of the twentieth century. According to Dusinberre, Froebel's focus on 'child consciousness, instincts and relation to the world… anticipate[s] the early phenomenology of William James'.[17] Froebel's philosophy is reflected in Frost's notions of free expression and self-discovery through direct interaction with the natural world. Farjeon's memoir of the last four years of Thomas's life calls attention to the contrast between the American visitor's treatment of his children and the traditional, inhibiting British upbringing – something Thomas would also have witnessed. Both Frost and his wife believed that '[i]rregular hours for children meant an extension of experience for them; it was more important for a child to go for a walk in the dark than to have an unbroken night's rest'.[18] Frost's attitude to his children in some respects reflected an Emersonian – and indeed Wordsworthian, and therefore romantic – celebration of children as seers before they are clapped into jail by their consciousness. While a critic such as Oster is sufficiently aware of Frost's debt to Emerson to discuss it in some detail,[19] he does not advert to the parallels between Frost's approach to bringing up his children and Emerson's attitude.

Both Frost and Thomas referred in their stories to places and events familiar to their children, so emphasizing the local and the ordinary. Both included the voices of the children, and the ways in which children engage with language beyond conventional meaning, and it is this awareness that might be seen to have inspired the poetic voices of both Frost and Thomas. Frost's early work was marked by his desire to break away from what was then regarded as 'poetical' and to make poetry from ordinary language. The voices around him on the Derry farm (including those of his children) are echoed in his verse, and it is the power of the colloquial to praise common speech that sets Frost apart. This approach to poetry was attractive also to Thomas, whose interest in folklore and folk language Frost shared. (For instance, Thomas's writing on nature favours the colloquial or local over the formal Latin terminology for flora and fauna). In an interview, Frost stressed both the literariness of proverbs and the musicality of the folk idiom:

> [T]he beginning of literary form is in some turn given to the sentence in folk speech. Art is the amplification and sophistication of proverbial turns of speech … All folk speech is musical. In primitive conditions man has not as his aid reactions he can quickly and easily convey his ideas and emotions. Consequently, he has to think more deeply to call up the image for the communication of his meaning.[20]

twenty backbirds, p. iii.   **17** Dusinberre, *Alice*, p. 10.   **18** Farjeon, *The last four years*, p. 88. **19** Judith Oster, *Toward Robert Frost: the reader and the poet* (Athens: U. Georgia P. 1991). **20** E.C. Latham and L. Thompson (eds), *Robert Frost: poetry and prose* (New York: Henry Holt, 1972), p. 262.

There are marked similarities between Frost's analysis of the poetic power of 'folk' speech and the way that children create meanings from the limited vocabulary at their disposal at a young age.

Thomas had only been published as a writer of prose when he met Frost, yet Frost saw, in Thomas's prose, the appeal to ordinary cadences of the human voice, the primary ingredient of the poetry he was trying to create. Thomas indicated this fellow feeling when reviewing Frost's *North of Boston*:

> These poems are revolutionary because they lack the exaggeration of rhetoric, and even at first sight appear to lack the poetic intensity of which rhetoric is an imitation. Their language is free from the poetical words and forms that are the chief material of secondary poets.[21]

Frost's emphasis on the cadence of the human voice may make the poetry seem naive, and this may explain why Frost is so often taught to children (and sometimes mis-taught). The escape from the 'difficulty' of the erudition of poetry offered a new freedom, as well as a recognition of the flexibility of meaning that characterizes modern poetry. These qualities are also evident in the 'found' examples of his children's use of language in the stories from the Derry notebook. Take the case of 'The wrong side of a rabbit':

> When I went out to the raspberry patch to pick berries one day I got on the wrong side of a rabbit. The poor little fellow couldn't get home because I was in the way.
> He had to hide till I got through picking.
> He cuddled down in a dark place just like a little lost ball that won't tell you where it is.
> He trembled as if it was winter: but it was only raspberry time.
> He had to stay there two quarts.[22]

The construction of images here reflects the simplicity and surprising associations of children's language, and relates directly to Frost's desire to find a way to convey emotion and ideas in a more primitive way. The limited vocabulary that constrains also facilitates the creation of fresh, new images, perspectives and definitions.

Thomas's stories too call attention to the use of children's language in similar ways. His interest in folk language is reflected in his choice to use (or misuse) proverbs for his stories. 'A proverb', according to Gabriella Vöő,

> is a stereotype entity expressing a fixed idea. On the linguistic level it is the artistic picture, on the level of ideas a judgement. As a work of art of folk-

---

21 Quoted in Farjeon, *The last four years*, p. 77.   22 Frost, *As told to a child*, p. 61.

lore it belongs to the secondary semiotic systems. It is a communication system with a double code, a carrier of information at the level of language,
but at the same time the information carries another content, too, becoming an instrument of poetic expression.'[23]

In a sense, the proverb represents folk wisdom, that which exists beyond the for-
malised and authoritative language of the law and the state. At the same time, it is
authoritative as a speech act in Bakhtin's terms.[24] A proverb can have meaning as
advice or as a statement about how the world is and so has a part to play in the
communication of ideology from parent to child. However, as Bakhtin also suggests, the context of such an act (or phrase) can have multiple meanings (or,
indeed, none). Thomas, in a way that carnivalizes the authoritative power of proverbial speech, radically reinterprets the proverbs, so offering new meanings in stories. At the same time, the stories tell of events familiar to his own children and
their experience of the British countryside. Some of the stories play with fairy and
folk tale themes: the tale 'Too many cooks spoil the broth' involves a king who
prefers his broth after one of the cooks drowns in it. However, it ceases to be so
tasty when more cooks are added. By changing the meaning of the proverbs,
Thomas at once challenges their authority to offer advice and calls attention to
their potential for poetic expression. The power of the words beyond a direct
meaning is something that Thomas learned from his writing for children, claiming to Farjeon: 'something [Myfanwy] felt put me onto it'.[25]

Farjeon herself selects 'Birds of a feather' when discussing Thomas's work.
This story reflects most strongly both Thomas's awareness of the poetic power of
children's speech and the inherent darkness of many of these stories. The story
tells of a boy who makes up the phrase while being carried by a drover to meet his
father at Glastonbury. Within the story, and through the voice of the drover,
Thomas quotes something his daughter Myfanwy said at the age of two.

> Some people are born to make poetry. Now, I have a little lass just gone two
> years old, and one day she sees a sparrow hopping close to the door and says
> to me, 'What is it?' and says I; 'A little cock sparrow,' and what do you think
> she says? Well, she says: 'Sat on a sallow.' A little cock sparrow sat on a sal-
> low. That's poetry. But it isn't true. He wasn't on a sallow, and she doesn't
> know a sallow from an oak. But it's poetry and so is yours:
>
> > 'Birds of a feather
> > Flock together.'
> I like that. Besides, 'tis true.[26]

23 In Gabriella Vöő, 'Igaz ember Igazat szol' in G. Paczolay, *Some notes on the theory of proverbs*, http://www.mek.iif.hu/porta/szint/tarsad/nyelvtud/theory/html/theory.htm. Accessed 4 April 2003.   24 M.M. Bakhtin, *Speech genres and other late essays* (Austin: U. Texas P., 1991).   25 Farjeon, *The last four years*, p. 237.   26 Thomas, *Four-and-twenty black-*

This powerful childlike language and its ability to go beyond the restrictions of sense are particularly relevant to modernist poetry. Both Frost and Thomas, in their search to 'make it new', found in the process of writing for (and to some extent, *with*) their children a radical form of poetic expression.

As the study of children's literature continues to move beyond the boundaries of the classroom and the library, it becomes more important to investigate the ways in which it provides testing grounds for the boundaries of language. The status of children's literature as marginal or inferior to canonic literature belittles its artistic engagement with notions of power and freedom. This engagement is influenced by the tenor of the times. These stories by Frost and Thomas reflect and respond to the modernist aesthetic, demonstrating that 'the pursuit of writing for children [is] a complex and ambiguous pursuit, one that articulates the changing nature of authorship in the face of social change.'[27]

The significance for the writer of the process of writing for children is particularly relevant at a time when more and more publishing houses are publishing children's stories by established adult writers such as Sylvia Plath and Toni Morrison. While many of these efforts may be seen as cynical marketing ploys, the work of Frost and Thomas suggests that there is further work to be done. Not only do these stories entertain and amuse, but they testify to the power of children's language: always radical and experimental, continually drawing our attention to its flexibility and poetic qualities.

birds, p. 72.   **27** Thacker and Webb, *Introducing children's literature*, p. 5.

The development of Patricia Lynch's writing in the light of an exploration of new archival material

MARGARET BURKE

This paper will attend to the exploration of the sense of Ireland in Patricia Lynch's writing and also to developments in her writing that can be observed throughout her lifetime. The information in it is drawn principally from the as yet uncatalogued manuscript collection in the National Library. References to periodical articles are drawn mainly from the archive and many of the cuttings are undated. Where dates are available they are cited in the text.

The most interesting discoveries were the reviews of Patricia Lynch's children's books, correspondence and many short stories, some of them from very early in her career, along with a substantial piece of autobiography that is very different in tone from the well-known *A storyteller's childhood*. In a review of *Brogeen and the green shoes* in the *Irish Times* in December 1953, Lynch's world was described thus: 'Miss Lynch gives her material a universal appeal without sacrificing one whit of its native quality. Her magic sunlit world has great gaiety and charm: it is indeed the land where the rainbow ends.'[1] The most striking characteristic of all of Patricia Lynch's writings, either novels or short stories, books set in rural or urban Ireland or abroad, is her acute awareness and exploration of 'Irishness' as she perceives it or would like it to be. She played a key role in the definition and consolidation of Irishness for children not only in Ireland, but in Britain and especially in the United States. Most of the reviews of her novels remark upon this. In the Jesuit magazine *America*, for example, Thomas B. Feeney made a comparison between *The grey goose of Kilnevin* and Donald Duck. He comes down squarely in favour of the wholesome and gutsy character of Betsy in *The grey goose*. 'It is equally presentable to the big chief or the small child. It has four star Irish charm. It is a direct importation from Éire and is another definite sign to the sceptical that the Irish in their almost freedom are underway. You never met a goose like Betsy. Beside her, Donald Duck is a double ache in the neck.'[2] Again in *Smith's Trade News*, the distinctly Irish character of her writing is noted. 'With subtle strokes Patricia Lynch reveals the beauty and atmosphere of the Irish scene and creates a world that belongs to children.'[3] Patricia Lynch's role as a native writer, whose sto–

1 Archival material from the as yet uncatalogued Patricia Lynch/R.M. Fox papers in the National Library of Ireland, accession number N.L.I. 4937.   2 Ibid.   3 Ibid. *Smith's Trade News*, 18 August 1962.

ries are suffused with a sense of Irishness – however it manifests itself – is significant. As one of a small number of children's writers, writing during the early years of Irish independence, and one whose books were widely read in Ireland and abroad, she wielded a considerable influence over the minds of young people.

Her best-known book, *The turf-cutter's donkey*,[4] opens with a description of the cabin in which Eileen, Seamus and their parents live, and the surrounding landscape. They live in a cabin which 'was so low and the thatch so covered with grass and daisies, that a stranger would never have found it only that the walls were whitewashed.' For a people without any obvious racial distinction from their imperial neighbours and with a native language on the verge of extinction, images of rural Ireland such as the traditional thatched cottage, became potent cultural symbols. The fact that the cabin here merges into its natural setting reflects the period of relative cultural and political stagnation in which the country now found itself. Its whitewashed walls are a symbol perhaps of the traditional life of the countryside – one of the only things which distinguishes Ireland from its neighbour.

A change in Patricia Lynch's view of Ireland can be seen in *Brogeen follows the magic tune*.[5] The idea of the thatched cottage as a symbol of a stable Irish culture is interestingly subverted in the following episode, in which the roof of Mary Nale's thatched cottage is caught by the wind and blown clear off.

> The wind lifted the roof, let it fall with a crash, lifted it again in the air, so that they sat with their heads thrown back, watching in wonder until bits of thatch dropped on them and the roof, rising high, disappeared.
> 'I'll not be treated this way!' exclaimed Mary Nale. (51)

The cottage, which seemed so solid and permanent in *The turf-cutter's donkey*, published twenty years earlier, is vulnerable here to unpredictable and surprising outside forces. The inhabitants of the cottage are highly indignant at the injustice of the situation.

In an article for a series entitled 'Living Writers', Patricia Lynch made the following comment about her own writing: 'I wrote before I knew how books were published and if publishers had never been thought of I would write stories to please myself.'[6]

The success and popularity of Patricia Lynch's children's novels has led to the perception that this was the sole outlet for her creativity, and for the greater part of her life this was the case. She began her writing career as a journalist though, writing for Sylvia Pankhurst's paper *Worker's Dreadnought* and she also wrote short stories throughout her life.

The only extant example of her early journalistic writing is her account of the 1916 Rising, which she wrote for the *Worker's Dreadnought*. As an employee of the

---

4 Patricia Lynch, *The turf-cutter's donkey* (Leicester: Knight, 1968).   5 Patricia Lynch, *Brogeen follows the magic tune* (Leicester: Knight, 1972), p. 51.   6 N.L.I. 4937.

newspaper, her principal duty was to report on political meetings. With the out-
break of rebellion in Dublin in 1916, she was given the opportunity to expand her
boundaries. 'Scenes from the Rebellion' is a subversive piece of writing. In it,
Patricia Lynch reports conversations she had with various people in the direct
aftermath of the Rising. The so-called 'ordinary' people were given a chance to
recount what they saw, heard and did. Patricia Lynch had a political motivation
when she chose to write this account in this way. These people, living in a colonial
state, had no public voice, least of all on the international stage. The way she represents these characters is very much indicative of her own prejudices and preoccupations. She is scornful of people who fear for their own safety or that of their
friends, or of anyone concerned with the material deprivation that resulted from
the unrest. 'A red cross nurse had come over to seek for friends, from whom nothing had been heard for over a fortnight. These and the others I had met there were
solely occupied with their own grievances. I was glad to be rid of them.'[7] A woman
on holidays who was left with nowhere to stay is judged even more harshly:

> While I waited at the Town Hall in Kingstown for my pass to Dublin, a
> woman who had been detained there for more than a week told me she had
> seen nothing of the fighting. All the time that she and her family had heard
> firing, they had been so much occupied in trying to get food and a safe place
> to sleep in, and had succeeded so badly that she connected a revolution with
> hunger and personal discomfort and nothing more ... She was English and
> thought the Irish people were inconsiderate, as usual, to start their revolu-
> tion when other folk were beginning their holiday.[8]

There are also two collections of short stories for adults among the papers in the
National Library. In both collections, the stories have been cut from newspapers
and glued into copy-books. The style and subject matter is very different from
Patricia Lynch's later writing. By comparing examples of these very early stories
with a story from a later anthology I hope to show the development in Patricia
Lynch's thinking from these earliest stories to her mature work. One of the collections of stories in the archive is called 'Local colour'. Inside, there is a typed list
of all of the stories, and an extra copy of one story pinned in. This is the only story
on which the date and the name of the publication are visible. The story is called
'Charles Hussey's Homecoming', and it appeared in the *Christian Commonwealth*
on 5 December 1917. The stories in this collection are depictions of people and
places in the east end of London. They are concerned with the humdrum events
of everyday life. Just as in 'Scenes from the Rebellion', Patricia Lynch gave an air-
ing to the opinions and experiences of anonymous people, here she pauses to
notice ordinary life. These stories are the literary equivalent of a snapshot, an unas-

7 Patricia Lynch, 'Scenes from the Rebellion', N.L.I. 4937, p. 6.   8 Ibid.

suming picture of life being lived. 'Tramway Liz' is an imagining of the story of a wandering girl. 'She came along East India Dock Road, muddy, ragged, forlorn. The children picking up tram tickets in the gutter, barely raised their eyes as she passed them.'

The other collection of short stories is also glued into a copy, but in this case there is no date or name of publication on any of the stories. There is a list of titles on the cover and about half of the stories are missing from the copy. Interestingly, the American spelling of the word 'color' is used throughout, which would seem to point to an American readership.

The first story I will look at is called 'Kathleen and the Professor'. Kathleen is a young woman returned to Ireland from England who is forced to work as a hired help in a boarding house after her father dies. There she befriends a professor who has fallen on hard times. The story opens as Kathleen is shown the ropes by her employer. That this man intrigues her is clear from the very first sentence: 'And the professor at the top – doesn't he get any attendance?' The phrase 'at the top' is at once suggestive of the professor's isolation, and of the respect he is owed but not afforded here. This is a story with a strong sense of class and social position, masquerading as one that espouses egalitarian ideals. Kathleen's virtue in the story is that she sees the professor's dignity and status despite his lack of money. He, in return, admires Kathleen for her 'womanly' qualities. She takes it upon herself to make his rooms into a comfortable home for him.

> The professor smiled. It was a smile which expressed all he did not know how to say. For quite a long time, he had taken his own tray down and left it in the hall ... His eyes followed her rough capable little hands. He had always admired white slender fingers on a woman's hand, but now he awakened to a wider sense of beauty.
>
> 'What a little household fairy you are!' he said, speaking with the indulgent tone he would have used to a winning child.
>
> Kathleen flushed with pleasure. It was the most graceful compliment she had received since the day when, her father's death leaving her alone and penniless, she had screwed up her courage and entered service. Her pride had revolted every time she heard herself referred to as a 'slavey' or a 'skivvy'. 'Household fairy' was far more to her taste!

There are definite sexual undertones to the professor's appreciation of Kathleen's work, the focus of which is her hands, which he finds surprisingly beautiful. His eyes are described following them, again reinforcing the sense of his physical admiration. We are also told that 'Kathleen flushed with pleasure' at the compliment he paid her. That he speaks to her as he would to 'a winning child' indicates the inequality that is accepted in their relationship and leaves the reader with an uncomfortable feeling. Patricia Lynch's intention was probably to describe a paternal relationship here, and the fact that the impression she creates is quite different suggests that she did not always achieve what she set out to do. The story soon takes a more appropriate romantic turn with the arrival of the professor's nephew, Maurice. 'The professor', we are told 'was proud of his nephew's democratic ways: and an idea which would have greatly astonished the two people concerned rose dimly in his mind.' We too can only admire the nephew's condescension! This young man is involved in the Irish struggle for independence, again one of Patricia Lynch's lasting preoccupations. Tragically, it appears he has lost his life in the fighting. '"He will come no more!" sighed the old professor. "He has died for Ireland, my poor brave boy! Why should youth be taken and old age left?"' All is not lost though. Miraculously, Maurice returns, injured, but alive. 'One evening when the wind was blowing up from the sea and she thought how like it was to that night on which she had first heard of the professor, there came a knock at the door. It was a low, almost stealthy knock, but it was like – her heart stood still!' There are fairy-tale echoes of a Cinderella motif here as Kathleen, who has preserved her kind heart despite years of hardship, is rewarded with the safe return of her beloved.

The seventh pig and other Irish fairy tales[9] is a collection of nineteen short stories. It was first published in 1950. By this time Patricia Lynch was very well known as a children's writer, with a strong reputation and a loyal following. The book is dedicated to Mrs Hennessy, the *seanchaí* with whom Lynch stayed as a child and whose inspiration stayed with her throughout her life. The fact that the book is dedicated to her seems to signal the debt these stories owe to the oral tradition. The stories have the atmosphere of the small, intimate, vivid fireside tale. They belong to that part of Patricia Lynch's output that describes an Irish landscape that barely conceals the world of magic beneath the surface. There is a sense that she is describing the Irish psyche: an ultra-conservative conscious mind under which lies a wild and unruly sub-conscious. This world of the magical subconscious is one in which the injustices of the real world are put to rights. The restrictive world of rural Ireland opens out into a world of endless possibility. The magical world provides a way out or escape, a place where pent-up emotions can be released. That she appreciated a certain unruliness that she associated with the Irish fairies is clear from her comment in an untitled article dated 1946. 'We call them "Good People" for just the same reason that the harrassed mother tells her bold child that he is a "good little boy" even when he is being tiresome. She wants to flatter him into being good.'[10]

Garda Mick O'Halloran is frustrated by the lack of crime and excitement in the small town of Assaroe where he is stationed, in the story 'The Lost Garda'. The fact that his attention is absorbed by one falling snowflake indicates the lack of

---

9 Patricia Lynch, *The seventh pig and other Irish fairy tales* (London: Dent, 1967).   10 N.L.I. 4937.

excitement in the town. 'A flake of snow fluttered from the grey sky and settled on the toe of his boot. As it melted he waited for another, but the first snowflake he had seen that day seemed also to be the last.' Brought by a cunning leprechaun into the parallel world of Queen Maeve's court, where his fame as a law enforcer precedes him, he brings order to an unruly gathering. 'Go quietly in there and sit down at the tables like civilised Christians, instead of behaving like a parcel of heathen savages. Quiet now!' Garda O'Halloran, having escaped from the world of 'civilised Christians' into that of 'heathen savages' is suddenly the object of respect and esteem.

> The pushing ceased. The warriors stood back, and slowly, yet without a pause, the women and children filed in sitting on the inner side of the tables. The warriors followed. Garda O'Halloran was rubbing his hands with satisfaction and wishing the sergeant could see how he had settled the trouble.[11]

When Patricia Lynch first began to describe Ireland in her early adult stories, she did so in serious, moralistic terms. She continues to describe it thus but here there are overtones of light-hearted teasing.

Her sense of Irish identity is centrally important in her autobiographical writings. R.F. Foster discusses the extremes that are to be found in Irish memoirs, from the poles of the miserable Irish childhood described in *Angela's ashes*, to Alice Taylor's highly sentimental reminiscences. His juxtaposition of these two is dramatic and humorous. Of *Angela's ashes*, he says,

> Charity is cold, the kindness of strangers almost non-existent, and the remnants of the family end up living with a repulsive cousin, whom the passive and exhausted mother is forced to sleep with: a step for which her writer sons do not forgive her, then or – apparently – later. Simultaneously, in a parallel universe, little Alice Taylor is out there in the countryside saving the hay and milking the cows and quenching the lamps. It would all come as something of a surprise to her.[12]

Patricia Lynch's memoirs fall somewhere along the continuum between these two extremes. The Ireland she depicts is idealized in some respects; she has very traditionalist ideas about Ireland, and what it means to be Irish. In most of her books small, inward-looking communities are depicted against a rural backdrop. At the same time, though, she never shies away from describing the often harsh reality that was her early life. She remembers and describes vividly her upset at the cruelty she suffered at the hands of her frustrated and vindictive Aunt Hannah, but

11 Lynch, *The seventh pig*, pp 148, 155.   12 R.F. Foster, *The Irish story: telling tales and making it up in Ireland* (London: Penguin, 2001), p. 168.

no less vivid and evocative is the fond description of her Aunt Kattie: 'She was like a bright eager bird, with her sparkling eyes and the loose sleeves of her flowered dress flapping as if they were wings.'[13]

Although Patricia Lynch's childhood experiences preoccupied her throughout her life, and she used easily recognizable motifs and characters from her childhood again and again in her children's writing, it was not until shortly before her own death that she again began to write factually about her life. In the archive in the National Library, I found an unpublished draft of a continuation of her autobiography. It is called *A storyteller grows up*[14] and is seventy-two pages long. *A storyteller grows up* is a very different piece of writing from *A storyteller's childhood*. It was completed after Patricia Lynch's husband, R.M. Fox, had died. She was living in Monkstown with their friends, the Lamberts, at the time. It was written by a woman grieving at the death of her husband. The following comments which comes from the last page illustrates the contrast in the tone of her writing at this stage 'ever since R.M. died I see very little of [our friends]. I go so seldom into Dublin, but sit looking out on Dublin Bay, dreaming not thinking. The sea is quiet now – a background. I try to plan, but I have no future. I can't build.' (72) Here is a woman not far from death taking stock of her life, and the parts of her life she chooses to focus on at this stage are very interesting. As with the first part of the narrative, she places huge importance on certain characters she meets. She describes the Cadogans, an Irish couple living in London, with evident fondness.

> Pádraig, a small, thin man with wondering eyes and a timid smile, had been sacked from his job because he was always writing poetry when he should have been doing accounts. Philomena Cadogan, his wife, was even smaller and so dainty I thought what a wonderful doll she would make... My mother said they came from Tír na nÓg and for years I believed it. In a way, I still do. (14)

The Cadogans are the representatives of Irish tradition in London. They are not storytellers but singers and dreamers. Just as Patricia Lynch described people gathering to hear Mrs Hennessy, the *seanchaí*, telling stories in Cork, the Lynchs' Irish neighbours come to their house to hear the Cadogans' singing

> They both sang, and their sweet, small, clear voices could keep a crowd of Gaels quiet and enchanted. When they came visiting, it wasn't easy to confine the gathering to a few friends, for the moment the word went round that the Cadogans were at the Lynches', our place would be packed. (14)

In this continuation of her autobiography, Patricia Lynch also gives us a sense of the political sensibility that infused their life in London.

---

13 Patricia Lynch, *A storyteller's childhood* (Dublin: Children's Press, 1982), p. 2.   14 Patricia Lynch, *A storyteller grows up*, N.L.I. 4937.

> My mother would have been far more homesick for Cork only that the narrow street where Mary found rooms for us, was mainly inhabited by Irish exiles and friendly Jews. Many of our Irish neighbours belonged to the Gaelic League and soon we were going on Sunday nights to concerts, lectures and debates on the history, not only of Ireland and the Irish but of Israel and the Jewish people. (10)

There is the sense that these communities tried to recreate their homelands in London.

After the sudden death of her brother Henry Patrick, Patricia Lynch decided to take her mother home to Ireland. The train to Holyhead was described as being packed with Irish emigrants returning home. In the following quotation Lynch describes her experience of the train as a foretaste of what her life in Ireland would be like. She also considered it to be a microcosm of the whole of life. Earlier, I outlined how Patricia Lynch seems to describe Ireland every time she sets the scene in one of her stories, and perhaps this is one of the most self-conscious examples of this. She describes these Irish travellers being united by the stories they shared.

> It was a wonderful journey! Irish people are at their best on journeys, especially those which are taking them back 'home'. The histories that were told, the families that were brought up from the past, the hopes and fears for the future, blended us into one big family. We talked of the past, discovered dead forgotten friendships, even enmities served to unite us. But at every stop, for the odd one or two gained, we lost others. The train was like life itself – greetings and partings.[15]

Despite numerous entreaties from friends and admirers (evident in her correspondence) that she write a sequel to *A storyteller's childhood*, it was not until shortly before her own death that she attempted this task. She seems to have been more comfortable with the unselfconscious working out of childhood issues in her children's writing than overtly autobiographical writing. In *A storyteller grows up*, she describes her eyewitness report on the 1916 Rising, 'Scenes from the Rebellion', as her proudest achievement and, later notes that she began to write for children chiefly because of financial necessity. Despite her prolificacy and the apparent ease with which she wrote, she postponed writing about the later part of her life until her final months and in it she barely refers to her children's writing. Could this reticence point to a doubt as to the value of her children's writing in comparison with her early political material? Is there a sense of disappointment that her early and spirited political activism was not followed through in a more concrete way? The non-conformist instinct that lay at the root of this activism expressed itself in the

15 Lynch, *A storyteller grows up*, p. 64.

mischievous rebellion and dissatisfaction with their lot of some of the protagonists
in her children's books, but she never again wrote non-fiction in an overtly political vein.

In the closing lines of *A storyteller grows up*, some of the last lines Patricia Lynch
ever wrote, we are left with an image of a woman who had a grand vision of the
world and the possibilities it offered.

> I always dreamed of sitting, working at a window looking out on the sea.
> And here I am – with Howth Head in the immediate distance – grey sea,
> grey sky, grey hill of Howth, and I am still dreaming.[16]

16 Ibid. p. 72.

The Talbot Press and its
religious publications for children

MARY FLYNN

The year 1910 saw the formation of the Educational Company of Ireland and the launch of what John Dunne calls 'a new and vibrant era in educational and secular publishing and in supplying the astonishing range of material needed in Irish schools of Ireland. It was also the catalyst, that a few years later precipitated the birth of a sister firm, the Talbot Press, destined to be one of the most remarkable publishing enterprises in the history of the State'.[1] The two businessmen who spearheaded the foundation of both companies, W.G. Lyon and W. Fitzsimmons, 'recognized the need to modernize the schoolbook trade in Ireland'. Three years later, in 1913, having had extensive experience in the publishing business, they saw a niche in the market for a 'separate imprint to cover non-educational publications, fiction as well as non-fiction'.[2] So the Talbot Press was born. Its policy was to publish books about Ireland and books written by Irish authors.

Religious publications constituted a considerable proportion of the overall output of the Talbot Press. While these publications were mostly aimed at an adult readership, young people were also targeted. Religion and religious practices were an endemic feature of Irish life in the early 1900s and remained so, until the 1980s, as the rapturous welcome of Pope John Paul II to Ireland in 1979 confirms.

By the 1930s Catholicism had become a central characteristic of Irish nationalism. The Eucharistic Congress in 1932 demonstrated the central importance of Catholicism in the celebration of national identity. On that occasion faith and fatherland were as one.[3] Article 44 of the 1937 Constitution of Ireland, which was deleted in 1974, affirmed the dominant position of the Roman Catholic church and declared that '[t]he state recognizes the special position of the Holy Catholic and Roman church as the guardian of the faith professed by the great majority of its citizens'. The Catholic church has always attributed signal importance to its role in education, in particular in relation to the supervision of the instruction of the young. At the end of the nineteenth century when religious influence in education was declining in most European countries, Ireland proved to be an important

---

1 John G. Dunne, 'Talbot Press – sixty golden years of Dublin publishing', Dept of Early Printed Books, T.C.D., Dublin: unpublished, pp 1–2. 2 Dunne, 'Talbot Press', p. 2. 3 Dermot Keogh, 'Church, state and society', ed. Brian Farrell, *De Valera's constitution and ours: Thomas Davis lectures series* (Dublin: Gill and Macmillan, 1988), pp 103–22, p. 105.

exception.[4] The foundation of the Talbot Press, therefore, was a timely response to a religious and commercial need.

Ecclesiastical authority may be seen in the context of an Irish society in the early twentieth century that was rigidly structured along class and social lines. In the words of Finola Kennedy, '[i]t was a place where people appeared to know their place - masters and servants, teachers and pupils, parents and children, shepherds and flock'.[5] The authoritarian strain in Irish culture that permeated the religious sphere was evident in father-son relationships, in pupil-teacher relationships as well in priest-people relationships. The system helped to maintain the status of the family and reinforced class structures. The family farm was the economic base of Irish rural society, and keeping it intact was paramount among the beliefs and values of rural dwellers. This scenario was not uniquely Irish. Kennedy cites the French situation, 'where the fear of family decline was widespread among sociologists including Comte, Le Play, de Tocqueville and Durkheim. It was believed that parental authority was eroded by State intervention and the full restoration of patriarchal authority, which had been lost in the wake of the Revolution, was recommended'.[6] The drive to maintain the status quo in family farms combined with a belief in Catholic church tenets 'deeply embedded in historical tradition', because they were seen by several generations of countrymen 'as supreme intrinsic values and goods in their own right'[7] Most of the clergy were drawn from and had their roots in the rural agrarian background and were the sons of farmers and landowners. The church was also enabled in its drive for control and domination 'by the absence of an educated laity'.[8] The prevailing authoritarian system, Kennedy asserts, encouraged obedience to authority and snuffed out freedom of enquiry.

THE INVOLVEMENT OF THE CATHOLIC CHURCH IN THE EDUCATION OF THE YOUNG

In 1831, the British government sought to establish a national non-denominational system of education in Ireland. In time, each of the three main churches, Catholic, Presbyterian and Anglican, came to oppose vigorously the 'mixed' principle of the schools, and by the end of the century their struggle resulted in an education system that was 'de facto denominational'.[9] Traditional public support for the Catholic church combined with the 1916 rising and its nationalistic patriotic aftermath only served further to entrench the Catholic church's hold on the

4 Brian Titley, *Church, state and the control of schooling in Ireland, 1900–1944* (Dublin: Gill and Macmillan, 1983), p. x.   5 Finola Kennedy, *Cottage to creche: family change in Ireland,* (Dublin: I.P.A., 2001), p. 165.   6 Ibid., p. 165.   7 J.A. Humphreys, *New Dubliners: urbanization and the Irish family* (London: Routledge and Kegan Paul, 1966).   8 Kennedy, *Cottage,* p. 166.   9 Titley, *Church,* p. 6.

Irish education system. Brian Titley remarks that in 1922, as the new Irish state emerged, 'clerical power in the school system seemed as secure as ever'.[10] The importance that the Catholic church places on education is derived from the Thomist view of man.

> The ultimate happiness of man lies in the salvation of his soul, made possible through Christ's redemption. If education is to be in any way meaningful, it must constantly bear in mind this final destiny of man. As the Catholic church claims to be the body founded by Christ to bring the means of salvation to man, it follows that is must be accorded a special place in the education of youth.[11]

It follows therefore that in its efforts to educate children the church's aim was to exclude any ideas contrary to its faith system and morals. Its zeal resulted in a drive to exert control over the lives of young children under its care, such that parents were marginalized from the education of their children. The approach of the Catholic church was manifest in the well-known maxim attributed to Jesuit educators: 'Give me a child until he is seven and I will give you the man.' Its conservative approach disapproved of individualism or private conscience: children were to follow instructions and happiness and success would flow from that. Success was not measured in worldly achievements, but in the life after death. The Jesuit maxim corresponded with and pervaded much of the religious literature for children published by the Talbot Press. Many of its publications contained instructions on how they should be used in the classroom. In the preface to *Stories for children from the old testament*,[12] teachers were directed to use the book to instruct children up to the age of seven or eight orally, and thereafter to use it both orally and as a reader.

RELIGIOUS PUBLICATIONS: INFLUENCING THE LIFE OF
THE IRISH CHILD

Many religious publications sought in effect to instruct their child readers on how their lives should be lived. They included direction on unquestioning obedience to parents and adults, guidelines on Catholic morality and encouragement towards self-sacrifice and self-denial. The image most often portrayed was of a godhead, quite often stern and austere, who dispensed justice and some mercy, but whose love for his subjects was less apparent. In a story called 'After the flood', young readers were given a biblical lesson in unquestioning parental respect:

10 Ibid., p. 89.   11 Ibid., p. 5.   12 Anonymous, *The Saint Patrick's series of bible stories: stories for children from the Old Testament* (Dublin: Talbot Press, 1915), p. 4.

Noah, having planted a vineyard, made wine from the grapes. One day when he had drunk freely of this new wine, his son Cham mocked him but his other sons Sem and Japheth showed great respect to their father. Noah cursed Cham and gave Sem and Japheth his blessing ... This story teaches a great lesson to all children, who should honour and obey their parents; and they should always love them, even if they sometimes do things which are not right.[13]

One wonders how children dealt with the inherent ambivalence and confusion of that message. The image of the domineering, authoritarian father who, having made the wine and proceeded to get drunk on it, was not to be challenged. Gluttony is traditionally one of the 'seven deadly sins', yet in this case children were expected to see it as somehow acceptable. This respect for adults is also emphasized in relation to teachers. In George O'Neill's book *First steps to heaven*, Jesus is portrayed as telling the reader:

It is my will that you should be taught and guided in all things, now and through your life by men, by human beings like to yourself. I'm sometimes grievously offended by children who without any sufficient reason think and speak evil of their teachers. Such children besides often make very serious mistakes and do much harm to their companions. If your teacher punishes you, try to receive the punishment with the greatest possible patience, meekness and humility.[14]

There was little recognition of fair play on the part of the teacher, or of the rights of the child. Considering that the punishment referred to here was most likely corporal punishment, typical of that time, this prayer book appears to give it the sanction of the almighty. There seemed to be no redress for the child – he or she was destined to suffer and endure this suffering, with the knowledge and approval of God. By any standards the view of life for children portrayed in this prayer book was grim and joyless.

THE DIRECTIVE TEACHINGS OF RELIGIOUS LITERATURE

Children are also taught how to be 'good' through the teachings of another publication, *First steps to heaven*, which begins with Jesus assuring the readers that if they read this book diligently, they will find:

great truths that change and improve the heart. You will learn from it not only how to pray, but also to think, to talk and to act as a good child ought

13 Anon., *Saint Patrick's series*, p. 10   14 George O'Neill (ed.), *First steps to heaven* (Dublin: Talbot Press, 1912), p. 106.

to. The reason I wish you to learn and do all this, is that I want to bring you one day into my heavenly glory and to make you happy with myself forever ... You ought to think, pray, speak, work and live as I thought, prayed, spoke, worked and lived; now this book will help you to do all that.

While the child readers are assured of their potential to achieve their goals, they are also reminded that they may have to endure suffering and pain in the process:

> You will indeed have to overcome yourself in many things, but I will make these things seem sweet; you will have to fight with powerful enemies, but I will give you the strength you need; you must refuse yourself many things you would like, but in return I will fill your soul with an inward consolation and sometimes with great joy ... There have been children who for love of me have endured most bitter sufferings, even torments and death; and sometimes in the very height of their very pain and torment, I cause them to feel nothing but sweetness and delight.

The language and tone of the text is serious, even adult. If children understood it, which is questionable, the message it conveyed was in some way threatening and almost foreboding of damnation and ruin if children did not comply. It seemed to advocate an acceptance of adverse circumstances; there was no encouragement, affirmation or acknowledgement of self-worth. Young readers were constantly reminded of their imperfections, inadequacies and weaknesses. They were to disparage themselves in order to be saved and to achieve a place in heaven. Most prayer books provided readymade replies that were to be learnt by heart, a practice that literally put words into the mouth of the child:

> What could I wish for more earnestly than to make my soul pure and holy, to make my life good and great, to be eternally happy in heaven? But you know also (for you know me better than I know myself) how very weak I am in doing good and avoiding wrong.[15]

In the story 'Patrick',[16] when the daughters of the King of Connaught meet Patrick and his companions, the story goes that the princesses understood little of them, as they were only poor pagans. The message of Christianity was driven home and is implicit in a condescending reference to paganism. The girls were both baptized and we are told they were overcome with a longing to see Christ.

> They longed so much to be with Christ that they died of longing. We don't and we will never know until we die ourselves, why God took those young girls, but he must have loved them very much to have done so. (9)

15 O'Neill, *First steps*, pp 6–7.   **16** Alice Curtayne, *Irish saints for boys and girls* (Dublin: Talbot Press 1955), p. 6.

When Patrick baptized Aengus, the King of Munster, and inadvertently stuck the spike of his Crosier in Aengus's foot, the prince endured the pain and never faltered right through the ceremony. "'Christ' he said slowly, "shed his blood for me and I am glad to suffer a little pain at baptism to be like our lord.'" (10)

The message of God's love here and the question of how it was interpreted by young readers is ambivalent. It is difficult to see how children could find joy and excitement in such a strange sequence of events as befell the girls above. Again, it seems that the only happiness a Christian can hope for is in heaven. Even the behaviour of Aengus as shown above is marked with self-denial, self-sacrifice and self-deprecation.

RELIGIOUS PUBLICATIONS AND A SENSE OF GUILT

In many of the religious publications there was a strong emphasis on the guilt that the young people incurred and carried as a consequence of failing to comply with what was expected of them. *The angel of the Eucharist* is the biography of a French peasant girl, Marie Eustelle Harpain (1814–42),[17] who lived a life of exemplary holiness and self-denial. In her early years she was idolized by her parents and they lavished love and affection as well as material gifts on her. 'But all this adulation sowed the seed of self-conceit in the child, and began to poison the gifts of nature which adorned her, and to wither the work of grace in her awakening soul.' (12) Her conversion was brought about by her observance of a young girl in Mass rapt in prayer. (13) Struck by this model of piety and modesty, she resolved there and then to imitate her and thus to begin fervently to prepare for her first communion. Straight away she set about checking her pleasure-loving propensities and renounced certain village frolics, which, though harmless, she felt dulled her heart towards God. The practice of her religion meant that Marie Eustelle had to abandon the joyful, social, interactive pursuits of her youth because she believed they were evil.

> Truly I can say Father that I loved dancing as much as it is possible to love it. I counted the moments until the hour came for indulging in this amusement so full of peril to youth. I cannot calculate the number of thoughts, desires, looks and words, which on these unhappy occasions may have rendered me guilty in the sight of God. And I was but fourteen! (15)

She relinquished personal desires and lived out of the expectations of others. Her self-denial knew no bounds – even when her hair was taken away it was described thus: 'Her beautiful hair was cut off at this time because once it had fed her vani-

17 Sister Mary Bernard, *The angel of the Eucharist: Marie Eustelle Harpain, 1814–1842* (Dublin: Talbot Press, 1964).

ty. But far from disfiguring herself, her banded brow gave her a sort of regal distinction.' (12)

Looking at Marie Eustelle's situation through contemporary eyes, one perceives little more than adolescent behaviour of a young person involved in the normal process of growing up and achieving self-realisation. The normal progression to adulthood in her case was thwarted and supplanted by religion. The religion, or practice thereof, that is promoted in this story was stifling, and did nothing to enhance personal growth in the young.

One prayer book, *The little one's massbook*,[18] appears to have been hugely popular: it sold 750,000 copies. Decorated with attractive coloured pictures, it contained prayers of supplication that children are urged to use in the celebration of mass. 'Dear Lord, I give myself to you. Oh please make me your own little child. My God I know that if I am good all the days of my life, you will make me happy forever when I die.' (13) The language of the prayers is formal and lofty. There is little evidence of the child being encouraged to experience joy and excitement at life or at the world in which he or she is participating. The powerlessness of the child is emphasized: 'Oh my God I thank you for letting me come to mass today. May it help me to be a good child. Be with me all my life and at the hour of my death.' (31)

There is even a formula for the child reader to examine his or her conscience before confessing the sins: Did you talk or laugh in church? Was there a morning or night that you didn't say your prayers? Were you angry or sulky? Again it appears that there is an emphasis on the sense of guilt that the child reader should experience as a consequence of minor misdemeanours.

Come unto me, a prayer book for children, had coloured pictures and contained a more extensive variety of prayers for various occasions; grace before and after meals, dedications for the days of the week and months of the year, prayers to accompany the stations of the cross and prayers to a selection of saints including Maria Goretti: 'O Saint Maria Goretti, who strengthened by Divine Grace did not hesitate, though only twelve years of age, to shed thy blood and sacrifice thy life rather than commit sin, turn thine eyes compassionately towards the multitude of men and women who are wandering far from the real path of virtue.'[19]

As the representative excerpts above show, pious and formative reading matter was framed in a way that was rarely positive or indeed conducive to fostering a positive relationship with the God to whom the prayers were directed. Yet parents and schools widely supplied them to children as regular reading material.

18 Anonymous, *The little ones' massbook* (Dublin: Talbot Press, 1964).   19 Anonymous, *Come unto me* (Dublin: Talbot Press 1953), p. 21.

THE TALBOT PRESS: MARKETING CATHOLIC PUBLICATIONS

The willingness of the Talbot Press to reflect the status quo as dictated by the Catholic church is evident in the fact that they republished the book entitled *An alphabet of Irish saints*[20] in 1932, especially to mark the fifteen hundredth centenary of the coming of St Patrick. The book aspired to 'encourage the children of the new Ireland to seek their inspiration from the Saints and scholars of the old'.[21] The book is a bi-lingual collection of profiles of Irish saints, beginning with Adamnan (AD 624–705) from Donegal who later became abbot of Iona. Each profile contains a short account of a detail of the saint's life written in verse. Many exhort children to emulate the saints' lives and to look upon them as models or examples of holiness.

> B is for Brigid, who spread out her cloak,
> Which ran over the ground round her Cell of the Oak.
> A convent she built and its Abbess became,
> Many there joined her, so well known was her name.
> For Brigid was wise and in work did excel,
> Read Latin and wrote and cooked, scrubbed, sowed quite well.
> All Eire's daughters should as their model take,
> 'Mary of Ireland' and her ways ne'er forsake.

This Talbot Press publication differs from other early religious publications in that it is less overtly didactic and instructional. In harking back to ancient Ireland, in its adherence to a narrative form, in its artistic embellishment and in its English and Irish rhymes, it held an appeal for young readers. This more sympathetic approach is also evident in a book by Alice Curtayne, *Irish saints for boys and girls*, which was published in 1955 and which presents the reader with a human and fallible side of the saints described therein:

> We sometimes forget that Saints grow in size as well as in sanctity, for one of the most delightful things about the Saints (and one of the most comforting too) is that when they were young, they were as wayward and unpredictable as the rest of us. Alice Curtayne has picked many of her Saints and she shows them all young and old, not only as heroic figures, but as human and loveable people. These fine tales are part of our tradition. Some of them belong to the folklore of the fireside, and others have been gleaned from old manuscripts. Alice Curtayne's stories are rounded and fascinating, her writing had freshness and charm and in every story, the telling adds something to the tale.[22]

Despite this move towards a more realistic and relevant kind of religious story-telling, however, these books still perpetuated a complex and authoritarian view of

20 C. Dease (Torna), 'Introduction' in *An alphabet of Irish saints* (Dublin: Talbot Press, 1915), n.p. **21** Ibid. **22** Foreword to Curtayne, *Irish saints*, p. 1.

God. Furthermore, as the re-publication of *The angel of the Eucharist* as late as 1964 indicates, there was no clear linear progression towards a more child-centred or enlightened approach.

CONCLUSION

Some of the categories of literature outlined above have become obsolete as church teachings have evolved since the second Vatican Council of the early 1960s. Religious publications for children in the early part of the twentieth century were relentless in their pitch for the minds, hearts and souls of their young readers. That many of the stories and prayers the Talbot Press published, especially in its early decades, instilled fear, guilt and a sense of powerlessness is undeniable, and they undoubtedly had a deep and lasting influence on religious attitudes and the personal lives of the children who read them. Religion and the devotional exercises associated with the dominant Catholic faith were central to life in Ireland during the years of the publisher's operation. Demand for prayer books, missals, breviaries, hymnals and books that contained various religious exercises was considerable. The total output of religious publications was considerable. Its management saw the commercial opportunity and availed of it, and effectively preached to the converted.

Children's publications were strongly focused on the formation of mind, character and person. The catechism used in Catholic schools at that time taught that salvation was possible only as a member of the 'one holy Roman Catholic and apostolic church'.[23] Ninety eight per cent of that population belonged to that church and as such, were the obvious target of the religious publications of the Talbot Press. The power and influence of the Catholic church in Irish society reached its pinnacle in the 1940s and 1950s. Church influence on every aspect of life went largely unchallenged and in many cases was encouraged by secular authorities. The Censorship of Publications Act (1929) was another manifestation of that influence and its activities dovetailed with contemporary church policies. The mood and tone of religious publications were truly conservative. God was portrayed as remote, austere, and as a moral policeman, a God of justice and punishment to be feared. This image reflected the authoritarian attitudes to parenting then prevalent. The price to be paid for eternal happiness was perceived to be worldly suffering and self-denial. Children's prayer books, religious manuals and religious storybooks applauded suffering, self-denial and self-deprecation, and children were discouraged from celebrating their lives, gifts or talents. They reveal an overall drive to render children compliant and obedient, so that they might mature into compliant adults who would pose little threat to the authority of church or State. The legacy of the system may well have been a loss of creativity, independent thought and artistic endeavour.

23 'Everyone must belong to the Catholic Church, and no one can be saved who, through his own fault, remains outside it.' *A catechism of Catholic doctrine approved by the archbishops and bishops of Ireland* (Dublin: Gill, 1951), p. 41.

Forging national identity: the adventure stories of Eilís Dillon

CIARA NÍ BHROIN

In 1931 the critic, Daniel Corkery, described national consciousness in postcolonial Ireland as 'a quaking sod… not English, nor Irish, nor Anglo-Irish'.[1] Corkery drew particular attention to the debilitating effects on Irish children of the colonial mentality perpetuated by an imperial school curriculum and emphasized the need for an indigenous literature with which they could identify. Such a literature would decolonize the minds of Irish children by inculcating in them a distinctive Irish identity. Irish writers of children's literature in the English language faced a difficulty similar to that of their counterparts in adults' literature, expressed by Thomas Kinsella in his influential article, 'The Irish writer'. With no national tradition in the English language to draw upon, writers such as Patricia Lynch and Eilís Dillon were, in a sense, writing out of a literary vacuum, faced with the challenges of pioneering a new national children's literature. What the distinctive characteristics of such a literature should be was an important issue in a newly independent state anxious to establish a separate identity. While Corkery's aim was to replace a colonial notion of Irish identity with a narrowly essentialist one, Kinsella, three decades later, wrote that the very dislocation or duality of Irish experience was intrinsic to his identity. He argued that 'every writer has to make the imaginative grasp at identity for himself; and if he can find no means in his inheritance to suit him, then he will have to start from scratch'.[2]

The heroic image of Irish identity expressed in the literature of the Revival and emulated by Irish revolutionaries had dissipated in a post-revolutionary disillusionment exacerbated by the civil war of 1922 and postcolonial partition. 'Irishness' became increasingly associated with Catholicism, the Irish language and a traditional, rural way of life. The insularity and essentialist ideology of the new state in the early decades of independence were hugely significant in shaping Irish children's literature. While dissenting, critical voices were heard among those writing for adults, literature for children largely reflected the dominant ideology and indeed continued throughout much of the twentieth century, despite major changes in Irish society, to perpetuate an image of Ireland remarkably similar to

---

1 Daniel Corkery, *Synge and Anglo-Irish literature* (Cork: Cork UP, 1931), p. 14. 2 Thomas Kinsella, 'The Irish writer' (1966) in Seamus Deane (ed.), *The Field Day anthology of Irish writing*, vol. 3 (Derry: Field Day Publications, 1991), pp 625–9.

the over-simplified pastoral envisioned by de Valera in 1943.[3] The lack of a strong indigenous publishing industry for children's books until the 1980s was an influential factor. The need to satisfy the expectations of English and American publishers contributed to the continued emphasis in children's literature on Irish exceptionalism. The western island has been a predominant image in literature for both adults and children and is the setting for most of the adventure stories of Eilís Dillon. Most of the stories discussed here were published in the late 1950s and 60s, when the Irish Republic was opening up economically and culturally to the outside world, due largely to the innovative economic policy of Sean Lemass, who succeeded de Valera in 1959. Lemass' economic nationalism and Ireland's increased participation in European politics resulted in a modernizing drive that was to radically change Irish society.

Dillon's adventure stories have many of the usual characteristics of the genre – heroic boy protagonists, dangerous adversaries, an island, and sometimes a sea voyage and hidden treasure. What is particularly noteworthy, however, is Dillon's use of a genre more typically associated with the British imperial adventure to create a decolonizing, distinctively Irish literature. Kiberd's comment that 'Irish writers sometimes had to pour their thoughts and feelings into incongruous containers'[4] echoes Fanon's depiction of the decolonizing writer attempting to stamp imperial forms with a native hallmark.[5] Dillon, however, appropriates the form and succeeds in recreating it. Her adventure stories evoke the heroic tales of the Revival and, though set specifically in the West, reflect many of the issues that faced the wider national community. There is, as Suzanne Rahn has observed, a development apparent from Dillon's depiction of the remote, quasi-mythical island of *The lost island*[6] with its Crusoe-like castaway, Jim Farrell, and its treasure of pearls and white sealskins, to her more complex portrayal of island life in a later story such as *The Coriander*,[7] which is narrated from within the island community.[8] Unlike the exotic island representing 'otherness' in imperial adventures, the island in Dillon's stories can be seen as a metaphor for Ireland and the community as a microcosm of the larger Irish community.

The Gaeltacht setting of these stories has particular resonance. From Revival times the west of Ireland had symbolic significance and represented the authentic, uncontaminated heroic Ireland, which would redeem the rest of the nation. After independence, and despite its continual decline due to poverty and emigration,[9]

3 Eamon de Valera, 'The undeserted village, Ireland', in Seamus Deane (ed.), *The Field Day anthology of Irish writing*, vol. 3 (Derry: Field Day Publications 1991), pp 747–50. 4 Declan Kiberd, *Inventing Ireland: the literature of the modern nation* (London: Vintage, 1996), p. 299. 5 Frantz Fanon, *The wretched of the earth* (London: Penguin, 2001), pp 180–1. 6 Eilís Dillon, *The lost island* (London: Faber, 1963, 1952). 7 Eilís Dillon, *The Coriander* (Dublin: Poolbeg, 1971, 1963). 8 Suzanne Rahn, '"Inishrone is our island": rediscovering the Irish novels of Eilís Dillon' in *The Lion and the Unicorn* (1997), pp 349–59 9 Caoimhín Ó Danachair, 'The Gaeltacht', in Brian Ó Cuív (ed.), *A view of the Irish language* (Dublin: Stationery Office, 1969), pp 112–21.

the Gaeltacht continued to absorb the Irish literary imagination, with autobiographical accounts of island life coming from within the communities themselves.
Interestingly, Kiberd suggests that 'the very construction of a *Gaeltacht*, a zone of
pristine nativism, might itself be an effect of colonialism rather than an obvious
answer to it'.[10] Dillon's first books for children were written in Irish and although
these adventure stories are written in English, in most of them we are given to
understand that Irish is the spoken language of the community. Indeed, in *A family of foxes* Dillon deliberately estranges the English language in which she writes
and establishes Irish as the norm. Referring to the arrival of a letter from a Galway
lawyer, the narrator Patsy says: 'the letter was written in English, and the men were
never quite happy in that strange language, though they knew it was useful for
writing letters in and for people who went to school'.[11]

Each of the islands in these stories has a distinct identity and culture; its own
patron saint, after whom it is sometimes named, its historical ruins, its particular
lore, superstitions and traditions. In an article entitled 'Irish oral tradition', Seán
Ó Suilleabháin expressed concern that the traditional lore of the countryside was
dying with the Irish language.[12] Dillon, writing at a time of economic and social
transition in postcolonial Ireland, incorporates such lore into her own storytelling
to invoke an ancient oral tradition for a new generation. Fanon's theory of decolonization illustrates the role of native folklore and myth in recovering a pre-colonial
past.[13] Equally, Said emphasizes the primacy of the geographical in the nationalist
imagination and links it to repossession of the land, which is at first only imaginary.[14] The history and geography of the islands in Dillon's stories are closely integrated and intimately known to the islanders, enriched by pagan and Christian
lore. Yeats's dream that Ireland, through myth and folklore, would be a 'Holy
Land' to her people is true of Dillon's island.[15]

The island, especially the western island, is a strong geographical image. Its
extremity and its exposure to the elements endow the islanders, particularly the
boy protagonists themselves, with heroic qualities, further highlighted by Dillon's
frequent reference to Celtic and Greek mythology. Even more significantly, the
island is a powerful image of geographical unity, an effective antidote to the rav-
ages of colonialism and its legacies of civil war and partition. Joe Cleary outlines
how culture can be used either to consolidate or to challenge partitionist identities
and, in the case of Ireland, he emphasizes the significance for nationalists of its status as an island. Interestingly, he points out that while logo-maps of the Republic
usually represent the island as a whole, logo-maps of Northern Ireland usually represent the six-county state as if it were a separate island altogether.[16] That the

10 Kiberd, *Inventing*, p. 336. 11 Eilís Dillon, *A family of foxes* (London: Faber, 1991), p. 102.
12 Seán Ó Súilleabháin, 'Irish oral tradition', in ed. Ó Cuív, *A View*, pp 47–57. 13 Fanon,
Wretched, pp 168–70. 14 Edward Said, 'Yeats and decolonization', in Dennis Walder (ed.),
Literature in the modern world (Oxford: OUP, 1990), p. 36. 15 W.B. Yeats, Preface to Augusta
Gregory, *Cuchulainn of Muirthemne* (Gerrards Cross: Colin Smythe, 1960, 1902), p. 17. 16
Joe Cleary, *Literature, partition and the nation state* (Cambridge: CUP, 2002), p. 98.

island is an aspirational image of unity for Dillon is emphasized by her characters' frequent use of the phrase 'for Ireland free'. In *The Coriander*, Roddy says; 'Inishgillan is as much part of Ireland as Galway or Dublin or Belfast. If it weren't, why would they let us vote in the elections and pay rates and taxes?'[17] In her desire to incorporate imaginatively the Northern State into a unified Ireland, Dillon denies the political border and overlooks the fact that the people of Belfast do not pay rates and taxes to the Republic, nor do they vote in its elections. Indeed, Dillon's stories could be read as allegories of union in much the same way as those of nineteenth-century author Maria Edgeworth, except that Dillon depicts a distinctive, homogeneous Gaelic community while Edgeworth tries to assimilate Irish difference into an all-embracing British imperialism.

The rugged landscape and the perils of storm and sea, vividly depicted by Dillon, contrast with cosy domestic interiors and the warmth of a closely-knit community. The versatility that Synge noted in the Aran islanders is evident in Dillon's islanders and especially in the boy protagonists themselves, whose many skills include sailing, fishing, turf cutting and thatching as well as problem solving and diplomacy. Island life is precarious but the islanders demonstrate resourcefulness, skill and, above all, cooperation. The needs of the community often take priority over those of the individual, as Pat explains to the reader in *The fort of gold*:

> We all knew that no matter how exciting our private business might turn out to be, the work that we had been given to do must be carried out. The whole economy of our island depended on each person having a sense of his part in it, from the four-years old boy minding a goose to the great-grandmother of ninety left in charge of the cradle.[18]

Dillon's emphasis on social cohesion and the continuity of tradition renders the island in these stories a strong image of cultural unity. The islanders are distinctive even in their style of dress. Pat and John in *The sea wall* are easily recognizable to the mainlanders in Galway by their island tweed. Traditional music, song, dance and storytelling bind the community together.[19] Wisdom and skill is passed down from generation to generation. The first scene of *A family of foxes* depicts the island men sitting in cottage doorways in the sun, cutting the seed potatoes and instructing the children in the proper way to do it. In *The fort of gold*, Pat attributes much of his knowledge to the teaching and example of his father. 'I learned a great deal about the good sense and the reasons behind our ancient traditions, and the dangers of not taking heed of my ancestors' wisdom. "Never make a custom, never break a custom," was one of my father's favourite proverbs'.[20]

It emerges, however, that the younger generation, represented by the boy protagonists, have much to teach their elders. Indeed, it is on them that the continued

---

17 Dillon, *The Coriander*, p. 106. 18 Eilís Dillon, *The fort of gold* (London: Faber, 1961), p. 53. 19 Eilís Dillon, *The sea wall* (Dublin: Poolbeg, 1994, 1965). 20 Dillon, *Foxes*, p. 7.

survival of the community depends. Emigration, modernization and potential conflict threaten to tear the community apart and the young protagonists demonstrate
heroism in leading the way forward. The difficulties they face generally involve the
resolution of old feuds and innovating change in order to survive, a mirroring of
the challenges facing the larger national community at the time. Rapid economic
and social change, due to a newly opened economy and foreign investment, rendered even more complex the already ambivalent dialectic between tradition and
modernity in a republic whose cultural ideology was grounded in the revival of an
ancient Gaelic heritage. Central to Dillon's stories is the struggle to achieve a harmonious balance between tradition and modernity. In this respect they reflect the
wider national attempt to marry romantic conceptions of Ireland with a more
practical economic nationalism. Over-adherence to tradition by the men of the
community in particular, along with superstition and suspicion of outsiders, are
frequent obstacles to modernization.

Often it is through partnership between the protagonists and an old woman of
the island that progress is initiated. While the absence of girls in these stories is
notable, each story has a strong, usually elderly, female character. The heroic youth
and the old woman were popular Revival figures and are particularly evocative of
Cuchulainn and Cathleen Ni Houlihan. In her use of such figures, Dillon draws
on the heroic tradition of the Revival as an inspiration for the new nation-building
project. In *The sea wall* it is John, Pat and Pat's grandmother, Sally, who secretly
take the initiative in bringing an engineer from the mainland to mend the old sea
wall on Inisharcain. They conspire to overcome the resistance of the island men
whose suspicion of outsiders has blinded them to the need to protect Inisharcain
from tidal waves. John explains to the chairman of Galway county council that it
would be important to have the work done by the islanders themselves under the
supervision of an engineer as 'the men on Inisharcain did not like strangers and
were prepared to risk their island's safety rather than admit them'. (107) While initially hostile to the engineer, Mr Lynch, the men of Inisharcain are eventually won
over. 'The months during which the sea wall was being prepared' we are told 'were
like one long, wonderful party'. (117)

Tradition and modernity are reconciled and, indeed, in this case progress
ensures the survival of tradition. Sally's wish to die in the cottage in which she was
born will now be fulfilled and she expresses her gratitude to the two boys: 'There's
an old wish that you often hear: "Long life to you and death in Ireland". Death in
my own house I wanted, and now I'll have my wish'. (119) That Dillon's books were
published in England and America and were intended for the wider diaspora is evident in these lines, which are evocative of the nostalgia of an emigrant towards the
homeland. Indeed, elements of nativism in Dillon's writing fed into romanticized,
essentialist notions of Irish identity commonly felt by emigrants, wishing to 'pre-
serve' an idealized image of a traditional community in contrast to the modernized
societies in which they found themselves. That the Republic of Ireland was under-

going rapid modernizaton made its writers for children all the more anxious to pre-
serve traditional values perceived to be under threat. A sense of nostalgia pervades
the romantic descriptions of cosy homesteads throughout these stories, with the
result that the heroic is often reduced to the pastoral. Fanon, who draws a distinction between custom and culture and warns against over-valuing native traditions
at the expense of a living evolving culture, derides such nostalgia.[21]

   Beneath the apparently romantic surface of idyllic thatched cottages and tradi-
tional community values in these stories, however, the threat of violence simmers.
This is particularly evident in the description of Jim O'Malley's arrival at the
Faherty's cottage in *The house on the shore*:

> My first sight of the warm lights from a cottage came like a comforting arm
> around my shoulders. Its little boreen led down to mine. The lamplight
> showed up a pattern of flowers on the curtains and while I stood there
> watching, a woman's shadow moved between.[22]

Jim decides to seek shelter in a shed at the back of the cottage. Noticing a hard
object in the warm hay beneath him, he discovers, to his astonishment, a little pile
of long-barrelled guns. The men of Cloghanmore plan to enact revenge on Jim's
greedy uncle Martin Walsh and his two foreign accomplices, Pietro and Miguel,
who have stolen the profits from the community's lobster fishing venture. Jim and
his new friend Roddy Faherty eventually succeed in recovering the stolen money
and, with the help of the local women, prevent the shedding of blood. Martin is reconciled to his neighbours and even the foreign pirates go unpunished. The over-
whelming emphasis is on reconciliation rather than on the perpetration of justice.

   The need for peaceful resolution of conflict appears to be Dillon's message in
all of the stories, with the exception of *The seals*, which is set during the War of
Independence. Published in 1968, it is overtly and militantly nationalist and
romanticizes Irish history in a way that became unacceptable after the eruption of
'The Troubles' in the North. The interpretation of Irish history in terms of colonialism or imperialism, particularly any glorification of militant nationalism,
became increasingly associated with support for the militant republican campaign
in the North. In *The seals* Dillon attempts to transcend the divisive legacy of the
Civil War by invoking the heroic unity of the struggle for independence as an
inspiration for postcolonial national reconstruction. Even here, therefore, Dillon's
emphasis is on unity – the unity of the island community and, by implication,
national unity. The heroism of Jerry Lynskey, whose grandfather had been an
informer, earns him the admiration of the islanders who no longer bear a grudge
against the Lynskey family. The enemy has been externalized and the community
(nation) is united in a common cause.[23]

21 Fanon, *Wretched*, pp 175–89. 22 Eilís Dillon, *The house on the shore* (Dublin: O'Brien
Press, 2000, 1995), p. 51. 23 Eilís Dillon, *The seals* (London: Faber, 1968).

Fear of civil strife due to the resurfacing of old antagonisms is palpable in these stories in which the men are easily incited to violence. Sometimes bad blood exists between islands, between islanders and the mainland or between local inhabitants and strangers. Often tension is rooted in some event in the distant past. The alleged betrayal of a priest in the rebellion of 1798 still causes bitterness between the men of Rossmore and those of Inishrone in *The island of horses*. It is the young protagonists who lead the way in healing antagonisms and averting violence. Dillon clearly believes that it is with the younger generation, who bear no historical grudges or memories of civil war, that hopes for peace lie.

In some stories rifts exist between or even within families. In *The cruise of the Santa Maria*, John, Jim and Ciarán sail to Commillas in Spain in search of Colman Flaherty's daughter, Sarah. Sarah was the last of Colman's six children to leave Flaherty's Island and he has never forgiven her for marrying a Spaniard, instead of the local man whom he had chosen for her. Flaherty's Island, with its abandoned, ruined cottages and its lonely sole inhabitant, is a stark reminder of the devastation of emigration. After a heroic voyage across the sea, the boys succeed in re-uniting Colman with Sarah and her Spanish husband and children.[24]

The story is a comment on the wider national problems of emigration and former separatism and on the importance of closer cooperation with Europe. Again, the younger generation acts as a bridge between the past and the future and between the Irish and their European neighbours. That the protagonists make their voyage in a hooker of new design is significant. The people of Rossmore had initially disapproved of the *Santa Maria*, which seemed to them more foreign than native in design and, worse still, had been partially built by a red-haired woman. The boys' voyage proves not only its seaworthiness but also its superiority over traditional vessels. Superstition is overcome and the community finally acknowledges the benefit of modernization. However, while Dillon condemns blind nativism, the changes initiated by the boys are not as radical as they may appear. John's grandfather initially conceived the novel design of the *Santa Maria*. In helping to complete the boat and in taking it on its maiden voyage, John is actually continuing a family tradition. Similarly, in initiating contact with Colman's Spanish relatives the boys are rekindling a tradition. The references to the Spanish Armada, which permeate Dillon's stories, remind the reader of the historical alliance between the Irish and the Spanish. Progress, in Dillon's stories does not involve a complete break with tradition, rather the evolution of tradition to facilitate change. While Dillon's adolescent heroes are at a transitional stage of life, living at a transitional time in post-independent Ireland, Dillon's aim is clearly to facilitate as smooth a transition as possible. As Robert Dunbar points out '(w)hat emerges forcibly in Dillon's fiction is a sense of, in many aspects of the word, transition, though without, perhaps, a full acceptance of the upheaval which that state generally involves'.[25]

24 Eilís Dillon, *The cruise of the Santa Maria* (Dublin: O'Brien, 1991, 1967). 25 Robert Dunbar, 'Rarely pure and never simple: the world of Irish children's literature' in *The Lion*

The boy protagonists of Dillon's adventure stories demonstrate heroism in venturing into the unknown, facing danger and acquiring through their experiences valuable skills and education. These are ultimately used to sustain and strengthen the community to which they invariably return. Such emphasis on community was at odds with trends in teen fiction in Britain and America in the late 1970s, which emphasized the autonomy of the individual and increasingly portrayed adolescent alienation and the disintegration of community. In contrast with Britain, whose empire was crumbling, postcolonial Ireland was in the relatively early stages of nation building, a project that is clearly reflected in Dillon's work. Her adventure stories can be read as allegories of national unity, which attempt to heal the divisions caused by colonialism, civil war and partition. Their emphasis on community is understandable in this context. However, considering that the protagonists of these stories are all teenagers, the lack of emphasis on more specific adolescent concerns such as individuality and developing sexuality is notable. Indeed, the lack of privacy is a difficulty often facing the protagonists whose every move on the island is noticed and open to questioning by their neighbours. Kiberd argues that:

> The colonialist crime was the violation of traditional community; the nationalist crime was often a denial of the autonomy of the individual. Liberation would come only with forms that stressed the interdependence of community and individual, rather than canvassing the claims of one at the expense of the other.[27]

Undoubtedly, Dillon attempts to marry both, allowing her heroes personal adventure and autonomy in the service of their community. However, it is finally on the needs of the community that the greater emphasis is placed. While the distinctiveness of the community is emphasized in these stories, and by implication national distinctiveness, individual difference is not. In their emphasis on native tradition, custom and folklore, and in their tendency to romanticize the past, Dillon's adventure stories belong largely to the 'nativist' stage of Fanon's model of decolonization. However, they can be seen as transitional in their advocacy of moving forward, albeit as part of a traditional, homogeneous community, to a future of peace, opportunity and economic prosperity.

and the Unicorn, vol. 21 (1997), p. 317. **27** Declan Kiberd, *Inventing*, p. 292.

Wars of independence: the construction of Irish histories in the work of Gerard Whelan and Siobhán Parkinson

PÁDRAIC WHYTE

In their book *Reinventing Ireland*, Peadar Kirby, Luke Gibbons and Michael Cronin describe Irish culture in the 1990s as 'characterized by an adulatory and uncritical tone, and which often fails to trace its historical development or to identify the forces that have shaped it. Instead it is seen as marking a break with the past and the coming of age of an enlightened tolerant and liberal Ireland'.[1] The essentializing of national historiographies to suit elements of contemporary culture presents problems when the forces that have shaped modern society are explored.

Kirby, Gibbons and Cronin propose that in attempting to validate a pedigree and promote an image of a tolerant and welcoming nation, Ireland produced a distinct view of history in the1990s. They believe that Irish nationalist history is fashioned into a category of a *distant past* 'that massages conflict out of representation'; thus distancing itself from nationalist violence in Northern Ireland, while simultaneously providing an acceptable cultural commodity in the heritage industry.[2] Viewing the past in such a way thus creates a sense of historical continuity for Ireland. As a result, the fragmentary and antagonistic nature of Irish history is often blurred or overlooked in support of the ruling order. Such a rejection of the Irish past as an area of study ignores many of the unfinished debates within Irish history that may aid in our understanding of contemporary issues.

The beginning of Gerard Whelan's *The guns of Easter*, a novel set in Dublin during the insurrection of 1916, attempts to cater for this neo-liberal, cosmopolitan culture. Whelan includes several political movements that were present in the cultural climate of 1916, with various adult characters reflecting different and often conflicting ideals and philosophies in Irish society at the time. The character of Mr Conway is fighting in the British army during World War I, while on the other side of the divide is the voice of uncle Mick, a member of the Citizen Army.[3] (The

---

1 Peadar Kirby, Luke Gibbons and Michael Cronin, *Reinventing Ireland: culture, society and global economy* (London: Pluto Press, 2002), p. 2. 2 Kirby et al., *Reinventing Ireland*, p. 6. 3 The character of Mr Conway joined the British army and is fighting for the empire, not in defence of queen and country but because he is unable to get work in Dublin as a result of being involved in the 1913 lockout. Although he wonders 'why should I fight their damned wars?' he blames the bosses for Ireland's problems rather than the English, while Mick views the English as the cause of Ireland's economic and social woes. Gerard Whelan, *The guns of Easter* (Dublin;

Irish Citizen Army was established during the labour disputes of 1913 to protect workers during marches and meetings. James Connolly later became leader of the I.C.A., which mainly consisted of socialist workers. They participated in the 1916 rising.) This offers a more intricate account of events rather than simply rooting the Rising in a simplistic dichotomy of the Irish people versus the Empire. As a result, it appears that any sense of Irish historical continuity is complicated from the outset. The multifaceted nature of the events of 1916, however, is subsequently reduced and retold by the character of Jimmy as he pieces together fragments of arguments that he has overheard in adult conversations. As a result, the narrative form itself problematizes the reception process involved in the construction of dominant historiographies.

Initially through Jimmy's idiolect, the Irish Volunteers and the Citizen Army are not seen as 'real soldiers' in comparison to the Georgius Rex (or Gorgeous Wrecks, as the British soldiers were sometimes known), since Jimmy is clearly in awe of these soldiers, attaching a lot of prestige to them. He believes that 'At least the wrecks had once been real soldiers – not like the Irish Volunteers who wanted Ireland to be a separate country ...' In this description of the legacy of the British, Whelan raises concerns in relation to the writing of history. The tone of the text and the narratorial control of the author are unclear in references to the accomplishments and victories of the Georgius Rex:

> Some of them had fought the Boers in the African war that had ended a few years before Jimmy was born. Others had battled the savage Zulus, or the wild Dervish hordes of the Mahdi, who had killed the saintly General Gordon in Khartoum.[4]

While Whelan is satirizing the methods of historical writing in many British colonial histories, most notably empire adventure stories aimed at a young male readership, it is possible that the irony is lost on the implied child reader.[5] There is no change in tone for the reader and no indication that the passage should be read as ironic. This section is of particular importance when questioning the modes of historical representation and the reception processes that construct the individual's perception of history. Perhaps this is only the character's view of British colonial history that he has acquired through reading various newspaper reports and by listening to adult conversations. But this is also how his perception of Irish history is

O'Brien Press, 1996), p. 11.   **4** Whelan, *Guns*, p. 21.   **5** The implied reader is a term used by Wolfgang Iser to describe a hypothetical reader of a text. The implied reader 'embodies all those predispositions necessary for a literary work to exercise its effect – predispositions laid down, not by an empirical outside reality, but by the text itself. Consequently, the implied reader as a concept has his roots firmly planted in the structure of the text; he is a construct and in no way to be identified with any real reader.' Wolfgang Iser in Greig E. Henderson and Christopher Brown, 'Glossary of Literary Theory', http://www.library.utoronto.ca/utel/glossary/Implied_reader.html. Accessed 20 September 2003.

established. This has implications for the reception of the entire novel, as Whelan is possibly assuming that his implied reader shares his set of values and knowledge. If Whelan has not structured an implied reader into the text, then the narrative functions to perpetuate racial stereotypes and representations inherent to the colonial project, despite it being a postcolonial text.

This language of imperial adventure stories is mirrored in the immediate glorification of the rebels as Jimmy witnesses the Citizen Army and the Irish Volunteers marching toward the GPO. (The Irish Volunteers were a nationalist organization established in 1913 that aimed to fight for the liberty and rights of Irish people. They joined forces with the Citizen Army during Easter 1916.) It is at this point that the complexities of histories outlined above are lost and the rebels are romantically glorified as the British soldiers descend to the level of brutes. As Jimmy recognises the leaders of the rebellion, he comments that 'It was almost as though the three men were surrounded by a light that came from inside them, that had nothing to do with the real Dublin that they were walking through'.[6] They are no longer described as 'lunatics' or 'would-be-heroes', but are firmly mythologized as deliverers of Irish freedom. From this point onward, the acknowledgement of contradictions in Irish history and society is limited, apart from a momentary thought that his mother will be unable to get her separation allowance from the GPO. (The separation allowance was a payment given by the British Government to the families of soldiers who were fighting for the British army during World War I.)

Within the development of the narrative, the depiction of Jimmy's private struggle must fight for space against the public national struggle. The depiction of the stereotypes of history overshadows Jimmy's original battle to find food. He appears to float from historical landmark to historical landmark, as the novel transforms itself from the adventures of a boy during 1916 to a version of 1916 for young children. However, at one point, Jimmy's private moral dilemma eclipses the public history, as he considers stealing the basket of food. He strives to do the right thing, vacillating between becoming a looter and letting his family starve. At home, he explains his confusion to his mother. In response, she begins:

> 'You know it is wrong to shoot at people'. Jimmy was puzzled. 'Yeh', he said. 'But your father is in the army and he shoots at people. And now Mick is out fighting, and maybe he'll have to shoot at people too.'
>
> 'But that's different…' He stopped. It was a complicated matter. He didn't have the words to express himself.
>
> 'Sometimes', his mother said, 'Taking things that aren't yours is the same. It's wrong. But you know it would be more wrong to leave us with no food while this lay thrown away in the street.'[7]

6 Whelan, *Guns*, p. 54.   7 Ibid., p. 88.

What may be deduced from this exchange is that in order to feed the starving, sometimes stealing is the only option; in order to achieve freedom from an oppressive situation, sometimes shooting the opposition or oppressor is the only option. In this manner, violence is established for the child reader as the only means of liberation and in turn war is justified. Whelan glosses over the complex arguments and contradictions (such as the role of the women's movement, and the differing ideals and philosophies of the Volunteers and the Citizen Army) found within the various movements in favour of establishing these absolutes.

This justification of violence may also be understood through an analysis of images of childhood in the novel. The construction of childhood as a period of innocence devoid of responsibility is represented, not through the child characters, but through Uncle Mick and the rebels. Whelan constantly likens Mick to a child, using the analogy of rebels as children, found in much of the writing of W.B. Yeats and Pádraic Pearse. In *Inventing Ireland*, Declan Kiberd notes this obsession with metaphors of childhood at the time of the uprising. He believes that there was a conscious effort to invent an image of childhood at the time similar to the conscious effort to construct or invent Ireland.[8]

Kiberd continues by discussing Yeats's use of childhood, particularly in his poem 'Easter 1916', in which the dead heroes are likened to stolen children: 'the rebels being children were not full moral agents, he seems to say, and so, even when they seem to have done wrong, they can be forgiven'.[9] This would concur with Whelan's image of nationalist violence. I argue that it is this romantic depiction of childhood that Whelan perpetuates throughout his novel. This image of childhood innocence is transferred to the rebels, particularly uncle Mick as his 'boyishness' seems to call for forgiveness for his actions and it is indicated to the implied reader that sometimes it is right to do the wrong thing. In this way, violent conflict is not massaged out of Irish history (as proposed above). There does, however, appear to be a definite legitimisation of a violent national history, possibly supporting the current social order's image of a mythical Irish past.[10] Although violent, the Irish Rising is represented as the only means to freedom. Drawing on Kirby's idea, it is in the *distant* past, the present distanced from violence, yet functioning as a vital strand in the pedigree of the current social order.

In the sequel, *A winter of spies*, Sarah's family home is dominated by the intrusion of public events in the private world, primarily through the family's close links with Michael Collins.[11] Sarah wants to be directly involved in a war against the Black and Tans (the irregular members of the Royal Irish Constabulary recruited to patrol an increasingly hostile Ireland), while Jimmy, Da, and Mick reveal their

8 Declan Kiberd, *Inventing Ireland* (London: Cape, 1995), p. 10.   9 Ibid., p. 114.   10 See Kirby, *Reinventing Ireland*.   11 Following his involvement in the Rising, Collins created an intelligence network and employed guerrilla tactics using 'flying columns' to assassinate British troops during the War of Independence. He later became Minister for Finance in the new Irish parliament. Collins was assassinated in 1922.

weariness with killing and violence. The representation of Collins as hero unearths unresolved debates in Irish society. He is in one sense seen as a hero, as in the novel, leading Ireland's war against the Empire.[12] However, he may also be viewed as the signatory of the 1922 Anglo-Irish Treaty, cause of Ireland's partition into two political entities (the then Irish Free State, now the Irish Republic, and the six counties of Northern Ireland) and possibly of the continuing conflict in Northern Ireland. The celebrity status of Collins is interesting in that the novel was released only two years after Neil Jordan's 1996 film *Michael Collins*. At the time, the Irish film censor Sheamus Smith acknowledged that the film contained scenes depicting explicit cruelty and violence. However, he gave the film a Parental Guidance (PG) certificate and recommended that all Irish people, including children, should see the film because of its national importance. The implied readership of *A winter of spies* was therefore already familiar with the figure of Michael Collins. Again, there is a commodification of history in a very postmodernist sense.[13] The audience's knowledge of a previous historical fiction is called upon in order to sustain the narrative of another historical fiction, in an attempt to create historical fact; an imitation of an imitation of history.

The construction of history is also questioned in *A winter of spies*. As Sarah transgresses the boundaries that separate her from the adult world, she analyses her own perception of history. She begins by reflecting that: 'In school she learned of history as something made by Kings and Queens and armies', but then she realizes that these official histories are not the only histories that have created society. Sarah grasps that 'History was, for that matter, her Ma baking in the kitchen'.[14] There is a recognition, as in the closing pages of *The guns of Easter*, that both public and private histories have shaped Irish society. However, Whelan primarily documents the public history rather than the private struggle of a family during the Rising and the War of Independence. Within this public history, he assumes a shared set of values and knowledge for his implied readers, presenting a historical narrative as tradition. There is a development in his use of the Irish past in *A winter of spies*, as the narrative focuses on Sarah's predicament during the War of Independence. However, the Conway's history is firmly rooted in the public events of the war, particularly through their close links with Michael Collins. These principally public histories of the novels often gloss over the complexities of the Irish past and subsequently adhere to versions of history that serve to marginalise certain contemporary struggles while promoting others. In contrast, Siobhán Parkinson's exploration of private histories influenced by the public sphere is aligned with contemporary cultural debates. Her narrative calls into question the process of writing history and invites the child reader to question the very idea of a unified notion of history.

12 See Tim Pat Coogan, *Michael Collins: a biography* (London: Arrow Books, 1991).   13 For a further discussion on *Michael Collins* and postmodernism, see Ruth Barton, 'From history to heritage: representations of the past in Irish cinema 1970–2000'. Unpublished thesis, University College Dublin, 2000. M0120407UD.   14 Gerard Whelan, *A winter of spies* (Dublin: O'Brien Press, 1998), p. 118.

In her novels, Parkinson uses the Irish past to scrutinise local and contemporary issues in order to make sense of universal issues, working through and exploring narratives of the past in order to create solidarities in the present. This idea of interrogating dominant Irish historiographies can be found in the work of Luke Gibbons.[15] He believes it is important 'to give a belated hearing to voices or patterns of experience that have escaped the nets of official knowledge or have been muted by the dominant ideologies of the day', and to continue to explore the forces that have shaped contemporary society.[16] *Amelia* and *No peace for Amelia* attempt to create a more balanced historical memory, with such an investigation of Irish history revealing some of the marginalized dimensions of the Irish Renaissance.

In *Amelia*, set in Dublin in 1914, we are presented with a version of Irish history that differs from dominant national historiographies. Parkinson centres the narrative around the protagonist Amelia and her private struggles within her family home. It is these private struggles that are of great concern in the public sphere of the time as issues such as class, gender, nationalism, religion and violence are raised through various social and ideological movements of the period. In the novel, many of these public debates are explored through the private struggles and concerns of the Pim household.

The fact that the family are Quakers, members of the egalitarian, non-conformist Religious Society of Friends, is an important narrative construct, as it allows the author to explore the issues of the time from an unconventional and perhaps more objective viewpoint. It evades the traditional binaries found in many accounts such as English versus Irish, or Catholic versus Protestant, avoiding the simplification of ideological movements. It also is the Quakers' belief in pacifism that complicates the use of violence to achieve freedom. The depiction of such a history is also related to Michel Foucault's idea of popular memory, in that it deploys the memory of popular struggles that were suppressed by dominant historiographies. Popular memory is a means of deconstructing the forces at work in the production of official history and recognising the validity of those predominantly undocumented histories of marginalized groups.[17]

Amelia and *No peace for Amelia* challenge some of the dominant or received histories in Irish society; particularly history that acknowledges events of the public but not the private sphere.[18] Amelia is overtly concerned with material wealth and frivolity, while her mother is equally passionate about issues of equality and women's rights. However, the complexities of the debates are revealed through the characters of Amelia, Mrs Pim and the servant, Mary Ann. The view that

15 Luke Gibbons, *Transformations in Irish culture* (Cork: Cork U.P. in association with Field Day, 1996). Also see his editorial work in *The Field Day anthology of Irish writing*: 'Constructing the canon: versions of national identity', vol. 2, pp 950–1020, and 'Challenging the canon: revisionism and cultural criticism', vol. 3, pp 561–680.   **16** Luke Gibbons, *Transformations*, p. 16.   **17** See Keith Tribe, 'History and the production of popular memory', *Screen*, vol. 18, no. 4 (Winter 1977–8), pp 9–23.   **18** Luke Gibbons notes the suppression of Irish struggles in the construction of dominant historiographies.

women's rights are of any significance is strongly linked to issues of social class. Mrs Pim sees it as a matter of natural justice that women should be allowed to vote. Amelia complicates the matter by asking why some people get to be 'ladies' and others 'women', and wondering whether that should be a case of natural justice also. Meanwhile Mary Ann, a member of the lower classes, is so preoccupied with her day-to-day concerns and keeping her family alive that she cannot see the difference a vote will make to her immediate circumstances.

Throughout the novel, Parkinson maintains a pacifist undertone, mainly through the character of Mrs Pim, while simultaneously creating a forum for the debate of various ideological viewpoints. It is not until her mother is sent to jail that Amelia realizes the true value of the women's struggle. Her father, revered up to this point, remarks:

> 'They've done it before, you know, arrested these suffragettes with their chains and their stones and their ridiculous placards. Votes for women, indeed! If they stayed at home and looked after their families they wouldn't need votes. They'd be happy doing the work God intended them to do. They shouldn't be out on the street disrupting the natural order.' Amelia gaped at Papa. She had never heard him express opinions like this.[19]

When presented with such an extreme viewpoint, Amelia slowly begins to change her opinion. Although she cannot quite articulate the reason behind this change and is still confused by feminist issues, she believes in her mother's cause.

However, the true value of the suffragette movement is revealed to Amelia through her own private experience as she tends to her sick brother. Her father laments the possible loss of his son by saying 'Ah, a daughter. Daughters are well and fine, but what is a man without his son?'(143) Amelia, flabbergasted, is not angry with her father or with Edmund, but with society, for she believes that 'He was only saying what was true. That boys were more valuable than girls. That was what made her angry, that bare fact.' (144) It is now that Amelia begins to comprehend her mother's plight and the importance of the women's struggle. Through her own private history and experience, she realizes the relevance of the public history of the women's movement.

The continuing struggle for gender equality is aligned with the suffragette movement in the early part of the century, which in turn is linked back to the work of Mary Wollstonecraft. Amelia packs two books for her mother in gaol, the bible and Wollstonecraft's *A vindication of the rights of women.* (128) Parkinson thus emphasizes the importance of the women's movement to Irish history, in that it offers a model for present struggles against oppression. However, this historical continuity is problematized and contradicted. As Amelia supports her mother's cause, she con-

19 Siobhán Parkinson, *Amelia* (Dublin: O'Brien Press, 1993), p. 127.

tinues to send her washing to the Magdalen laundry (as laundries run by convents and staffed mainly by ostracized unmarried mothers – the Magdalens – were known. The last of these was finally closed in the early 1990s).[20] In this way, Parkinson reveals a subtle irony in the multifaceted fight for women's rights.

Despite Mary Ann declaring herself a socialist, issues of class, workers' rights and poverty are explored through the characters of Amelia and Mrs Pim, while Amelia's friend Lucinda represents the conservative views of the upper classes. Mrs Pim lays the blame with the broader social structure as Lucinda accuses the poor of inflicting poverty upon themselves. Social inequality is explored from both a public and private perspective, raising debates about the roots of poverty within society. The subject is further developed through the character of the unfriendly dressmaker who blames Dublin's problems on the 'foreign ideas'[21] that labour leader James Larkin and Constance Markievicz, revolutionary and suffragette, had imported. The portrayal of history is never reduced or simplified, as Parkinson reveals the worthy ideals of Larkin and Markievicz, while simultaneously representing the harsher social realities that accompanied the implementation of such ideals.

In *No peace for Amelia*, Parkinson continues to explore the trials and tribulations of Amelia Pim, now fifteen years old. The private history of a young Quaker girl is set against the backdrop of the public histories of Britain and Ireland. Amelia is aware of World War I but is more concerned with her hair staying up on a Sunday afternoon than with investigating the complexities of war. As a pacifist, Amelia does not engage directly with the ethics of war, but firmly maintains an anti-war opinion. That is, until the character of Frederick signs up to prove his manhood (44), and then Amelia calls her anti-war stance into question. She begins by adopting a mythical view of war and starts to see Frederick's fight as magnificent. This romantic account of war echoes many of the public histories that promote an image of brave young men fighting to protect those at home. This often acts as a justification of events and to support the ruling order that follows. This is also similar to mythical views of the Rising that created martyrs of the leaders of the rebellion. Amelia's attempts to romanticize events reach a climax as she waves to Frederick's ship. Her poetic language takes over as she comments 'Oh look, there's a definite glow in the east', mirroring many of the poetic histories of both Ireland and England.[22] The harsh realities of the private histories are transformed into public histories of valour and sacrifice. This romantic ideal is undercut by Mary Ann's response, reminding the implied reader of the brutality and suffering of war: 'Glow in the east, yer granny ... It's not a poem we're in.' (62)

Parkinson emphasizes the cruelty of war in Frederick's private account in his letter to Amelia. She reveals a private history that is often overshadowed by the

---

20 For a further discussion on the place of the Magdalen laundries in Irish history, see Francis Finnegan's *Do penance or perish* (Kilkenny: Pilltown Publishing, 2002).   21 Parkinson, *Amelia*, p. 52.   22 Siobhán Parkinson, *No peace for Amelia* (Dublin: O'Brien Press, 1994), p. 62.

public and official histories. Similarly, Amelia's exposure to the lives of Mary Ann
and Patrick force her to recognize the futility of war and return to her pacifist ideology with a greater understanding of the principles in which they are rooted, and
the true meaning of being a pacifist: ' "It means", she said firmly, "that you have to
work for peace, not just have a distaste for war".' (176) Although an important philosophy to keep in mind during any conflict, perhaps Parkinson is alluding to the
Northern Ireland conflict and the peace process that was developing at the time of
writing. As a result, historical events are not firmly positioned within a *distant past*
but are used to help understand contemporary issues.

As Amelia's personal ideologies are called into question, so too is the nationalist stance of Mary Ann. Similar to Sarah in *A winter of spies*, Mary Ann wants to
play a role in Irish history and become a heroine of sorts. Parkinson draws upon
famous Irish historical figures that are often mythologized within Irish historiographies as Mary Ann (in a melodramatic outburst) aligns herself to Ireland's
mythical heroes, believing that she would be:

> a modern warrior-woman, like Queen Maeve or Granuaile. She'd be part
> of the ancient struggle against the English oppressor and vital to the upris-
> ing that would finally rid Ireland of English rule and allow Robert Emmet's
> epitaph be written when his country took her place amongst the nations of
> the earth. (36)[23]

Mary Ann attempts to write a poetic history of Ireland, linking the current nationalist struggle to Ireland's legendary heroes, ignoring the complexities of Irish history.

The contradictory nature of the Rising is represented through Mary Ann's
inner struggle and the Pims' general and ideological support. Mary Ann can only
see a valid participation in the country's history as occurring in the public sphere
of history, negating the private history in which she is currently involved.
However, it is to her own private sphere that she constantly returns. Following her
romantic outbursts, the reality returns to her as she remembers Patrick and the
life-threatening events of the public sphere. On reading Patrick's letter, Mary Ann
can only comprehend elements of it as a result of his bad handwriting. She notes
the 'confusion in its construction and tone' and that 'It was full of sentences
repeated from things that Mr Pearse, the leader of the rebels, had said, and bits of
a poem by somebody else all about blood and roses, which was half like a prayer
and half not.' (35) The messages of Pearse as only half-understood may epitomize
the manner in which many of the goals and ideologies of the rebels were lost or
forgotten after the rebellion. The new leaders of the country did not bring the type
of freedom promised by many of the rebels, but took the form of a conservative

---

23 For this melodramatic outburst, Parkinson draws upon famous Irish historical figures that
are often mythologized within Irish historiography.

neo–colonialism. Many of the ideologies for which the rebels had died (in the belief that their ideals would live on in a new Ireland) were simply forgotten or ignored to suit the needs of the new ruling and social order.[24] The novels of Gerard Whelan and Siobhan Parkinson demonstrate two contrasting approaches to the writing of Irish history. Parkinson's re-writing appears to be much more self-conscious, as the past is used to challenge received 'official' history and highlight cultural debates in the 1990s. In comparison to Whelan's texts which ultimately depict a linear, public history, *Amelia* and *No peace for Amelia*, document a private struggle in Irish history around 1916, presenting the readers with conflicting historical narratives and allowing them to draw their own conclusions. The novels highlight the impact that the public history of the women's movement has had on the private history of Amelia Pim, simultaneously exploring an often-marginalized public history through a private sphere and exposing many forgotten ideals that have yet to be realized in Irish society.

24 For a further discussion, see Richard Kearney, *Postnationalist Ireland: politics, culture, philosophy* (London: Routledge, 1997); and Kirby, *Reinventing Ireland.*

A theory without a centre: developing childist criticism

SEBASTIEN CHAPLEAU

[C]hildren's fiction is impossible, not in the sense that it cannot be written (that would be nonsense), but in that it hangs on an impossibility, one which it rarely ventures to speak. This is the impossible relation between adult and child.
Jacqueline Rose

[I]f children's literature criticism depends on, and is defined by, its claim to the existence of the 'real child', [...] then it is [...] dead. [...] In making judgements and criticisms on behalf of a 'real child' who does not exist, its writings are useless to the fulfilment of its own professed aims.
Karín Lesnik-Oberstein

Notre question, c'est toujours l'identité. Qu'est-ce que l'identité, ce concept dont la transparente identité à elle-même est toujours dogmatiquement présupposée par tant de débats sur le monoculturalisme ou sur le multiculturalisme, sur la nationalité, la citoyenneté, l'appartenance en général?
[Our question is still identity. What is identity, this concept of which the transparent identity to itself is always dogmatically presupposed by so many debates on monoculturalism or multiculturalism, nationality, citizenship, and, in general, belonging?]
Jacques Derrida[1]

The writing of children's literature gives rise to a fundamental *aporia*, or insoluble contradiction, and so does its criticism. The adult writes the child, and the child reads the adult. As Jacqueline Rose insists very early in *The case of Peter Pan or the impossibility of children's fiction*, '[t]here is, in one sense, no body of literature which rests so openly on an acknowledged difference, a rupture almost, between writer and addressee.'[2] This essential dichotomy, this unavoidable rupture that separates the adult writer from the child reader, has compelled some critics to maintain that if the writers and critics of children's books do not manage to bridge the gap between themselves and the child for whom they write, then the writing of children's fiction is impossible[3] and its criticism dead.[4] The challenge facing critics and

---

1 Jacqueline Rose, *The case of Peter Pan or the impossibility of children's fiction* (London: Macmillan, 1984), p. 1; Karín Lesnik-Oberstein, *Children's literature: criticism and the fictional child* (Oxford: Clarendon Press, 1994), p. 163; Derrida, Jacques, *Le monolinguisme de l'autre* (Paris: Editions Galilée, 1996), pp 31–2. 2 Rose, *Peter Pan*, p. 2. 3 Ibid., p. 1. 4 Lesnik-

writers, therefore, seems to rest on dismantling the *aporia* with which I started, which implies that the child and the adult must become one, and that there must be a *competent* understanding of the child on the part of the adult. This, Lesnik-Oberstein suggests in *Children's literature: criticism and the fictional child*, can only be achieved through the use of psychoanalytic psychotherapy,[5] and it is this suggestion that I wish to address, contrasting it with what Peter Hunt called 'childist criticism'.[6] In weaving my argument through Rose, Lesnik-Oberstein and Hunt, I want to ponder the notions of production (writing) and individuality (reading), in an attempt to see whether or not criticism can claim to be capable of relating them to each other, and whether it can claim really to know or understand what criticism so often refers to as the 'real child'.

Before I start to examine Lesnik-Oberstein's psychotherapeutic suggestions, let us stay for a while with Jacqueline Rose who, in many ways, initiated and influenced Lesnik-Oberstein's somewhat pessimistic argument. Rose, as she takes *Peter Pan* (not only J.M. Barrie's original version, but also later re-interpretations) as a basic example to support her thoughts, claims that the 'constructed' child within children's literature represents adults' desires in relation to childhood. Therefore, she refers to the writing of children's books by adults as a 'form of investment by the adult in the child, and [as a] demand made by the adult on the child as the effect of that investment, a demand which fixes the child and then holds it in place.'[7] Similarly, as we will see, Lesnik-Oberstein, following Rose, extends this argument to the way critics of children's literature also tend to create versions of the 'real' child that differ from reality. Both Rose and Lesnik-Oberstein point to and concentrate on this dichotomy between fiction and reality, in order to argue that the actual, 'real' child is absent from children's literature and its criticism, and if adults do not manage to come to terms with this problem, then 'children's fiction is impossible, not in the sense that it cannot be written (that would be nonsense), but insofar as it hangs on an impossibility, one which it rarely ventures to speak. This is the impossible relation between adult and child.'[8] And not only children's fiction, but also its criticism, because, as Lesnik-Oberstein puts it, 'if children's literature criticism depends on, and is defined by, its claims to the existence of the "real child" […] then it is […] dead'.[9]

Children's literature rests on a rupture that keeps the adult writing away from the child reading, and as Rose develops, '[c]hildren's fiction sets up the child as an outsider to its own process, and then aims, unashamedly, to take the child in.' And she insists that to 'say that the ['real'] child is inside the book […] is to fall straight into a trap';[10] a trap, because, she believes, adults do not write for children but for themselves. They write for the child they *wish to believe* is there or want to see there, outside fiction. When books are approached in this way, it seems that Peter

Oberstein, *Children's literature*, p. 163.   5 Ibid., pp 168, 163–225.   6 Peter Hunt, *Criticism, theory, and children's literature* (Oxford: Blackwell, 1991), pp 189–201.   7 Rose, *Peter Pan*, pp 3–4.   8 Ibid., p. 1.   9 Lesnik-Oberstein, *Children's literature*, p. 163.   10 Rose, *Peter Pan*, p. 2.

Pan, the only child that does not grow up, is a very appropriate representative of adults' desires. Rose writes: 'Suppose, therefore, that Peter Pan is a little boy who does not grow up, not because he doesn't want to, but because someone else prefers that he shouldn't. Suppose, therefore, that what is at stake in *Peter Pan* is the adult's desire for the child.'[11] Children's fiction, Rose goes on, simply serves as an excuse for adults' writing, enabling them to fictionalise their wishes and desires as regards childhood. In other words, '[t]here is no child behind the category "children's fiction", (3) other than the one which the category itself sets for its own purposes.' Thus, children's literature becomes a myth, a sort of camouflage, for it creates a childhood that is controlled, shaped, constructed according to adults' wishes. And this, Rose insists, is 'a fraud', (10) by which she means that children's literature 'gives us the child, [without speaking] *to* the child.' (1)

Jacqueline Rose's entire argument centres itself around and departs from this idea of the constructed child within children's fiction, a constructed child whom she constantly equates with the adult writer's desires. This argument, she insists, implies that 'despite the possessive apostrophe in the phrase 'children's literature', [children's literature] has never really been owned by children',[12] and, as a direct consequence, that a sense of didacticism will always permeate children's fiction. By writing for themselves, by projecting/writing their wishes into the book, adults wish to make childhood what they wish it to be, so trying to equate reality and fiction. This was an overt and essential trait of most evangelical tales given to children during the nineteenth century, for instance, but, as Rose's argument claims, this didacticism is still present under different guises in more recent fiction for children. So, even though there has been 'an increasing 'narrativisation' of children's fiction, and a gradual dropping of the conspicuous narrating voice – that voice which in the very earliest books revealed itself as so explicitly didactic and repressive'[13] – that adult voice is still there, somewhere, lurking at the back, controlling and shaping the book, *writing* the book. Rudd refers to Hunt, as well as to Knowles and Malmkjær, whose stylistic analyses of children's literature often stress the 'ever-present speech tags, the instances of telling rather than showing, the intrusive narrators [...], the "have to" tone that Rose detects'.[14]

Writing for children, Philippe Romanski comments, is something 'adult', it 'is a gesture that can only be made from a distance, [...] every written word being the constantly reasserted confession of the distance that separates *here* [adulthood] from *there* [childhood].'[15] Writing for children can only be the result of an approx-

---

11 Rose, *Peter Pan*, p. 2.   12 David Rudd, 'The conditions of possibility of children's literature' *The international companion encyclopedia of children's literature, second edition*, ed. Peter Hunt (London: Routledge, forthcoming).   13 Rose, *Peter Pan*, p. 59; see also 137–44.   14 Rudd, 'Conditions' n.p.; see Hunt, *Criticism*, pp 100–17; and Murray Knowles and Kirsten Malmkjær, *Language and control in children's literature* (London: Routledge, 1996), pp 41–80.   15 Philippe Romanski, 'D'ailleurs, l'enfance – simulacre de babil préliminaire', *D'enfance, d'en face*, Philippe Romanski (dir.) (Rouen: Université de Rouen, 2002), pp 1–2, p. 1.

imation, an approximate *re*-construction of childhood as the adult writer may try to re-approach his/her own childhood, or approach the 'real' child; an approach which, like an asymptote,[16] maintains the writer at a distance, an irreducible distance, from its audience. Thus, writing for children *is*, first and foremost, writing childhood; and writing childhood is writing for oneself. This approximation resides in the writer, the adult. And as it is most commonly acknowledged, the writing of children's books is done on behalf of the child, as a kind of *gift* to the child. So pleasing the child means, or implies, pleasing the adult giver. This is where lies the fundamental and essential didacticism of children's literature. The adult writer, by sharing the book, can only please the child reader by pleasing himself/herself *first*. But, whether or not the child is actually pleased when reading it is another matter.

Lesnik-Oberstein, following Rose, takes the argument of the 'constructed child' somewhat further, not limiting it to the writing of children's books only, but extending it to the criticism of children's literature as well. According to her, critics approaching children's books also construct versions of the child that essentially differ from reality.[17] To avoid that, and in order to keep criticism of children's literature alive, she claims that one should approach the child through a psychotherapeutic lens in the sense that, if critics really wish to consider the individual 'real child', then they do need to work with that 'real child'. Taking Lesnik-Oberstein's argument to its logical conclusion implies working with the child on one-to-one bases, thus avoiding issues of categorisations and problematic re-constructions (164). As criticism tries to find the good book for the child – this being its professed purpose (3) – Lesnik-Oberstein's psychoanalytical, psychotherapeutic argument makes it clear that critics cannot, or, rather, should not, make categorical assumptions which are essentially wrong in relation to the individual child. *'Un autre n'est pas moi, et je ne suis pas un autre'* [Someone else is not me, and I am not someone else], as Roland Barthes would say.[18] This argument, positing the 'real/individual child' at the fore of criticism is, I believe, interesting in principle, and I certainly agree with Lesnik-Oberstein's position, *in principle*.

But, as she develops her thesis, I become less enthusiastic. She insists that the criticism of children's literature is based on false claims as regards the 'real child'. A few illustrative quotations will suffice to summarise her argument. She writes that

> [t]o children's literature criticism, and many other areas concerned with children [this includes the writing of children's books], children are more

16 An asymptote is a straight line that is closely approached by a plane curve so that the perpendicular distance between them decreases to zero as the distance from the origin increases to infinity (C17: from Greek *asumptotos*, not falling together).   17 Lesnik-Oberstein, *Children's literature*, pp 1–164, especially pp 131–64.   18 Roland Barthes, *Fragments d'un discours amoureux* (Paris: Editions du Seuil, 1977), p. 142.

'children' [i.e. children as constructed categories] than they are 'individuals'. We have also seen that children's literature repeatedly refutes this,
claiming that 'individuality' is its priority above all else. I have argued that
this is precisely the claim which cannot be sustained [...]. To children's literature criticism, the 'child' is an 'individual' *within* the category of 'childhood', but its 'individuality' cannot transcend the category of 'childhood'.
In fact, we can reformulate our conclusion with respect to the impossibility of children's literature criticism by saying that this field is torn apart by
the paradox of, on the one hand, involuntarily reflecting the disruption of
'childhood' by 'individuality', while on the other hand maintaining an
unfailing devotion to the claim that 'childhood' encompasses 'individuality'. Indeed, the paradox within children's literature may be said to reflect
the paradox present within our society in a much broader sense, and that is
the difficulty of simultaneously placing a high value on the notion of individuality while also being greatly attached to categorization.

And as she starts advocating her own critical method, she insists that

> [t]he belief in the ability to 'know' the 'real child' requires a conviction that
> levels of empathy, sympathy, identification, perception, or communication
> exist between persons – between 'selves' and 'others' – as the means of
> attaining communal knowledge and meanings.[19]

Psychoanalytical psychotherapy, Lesnik-Oberstein strongly holds, is therefore
the answer to the problems that arise in relation to criticism of children's literature.
She says:

> There are two reasons why psychoanalysis suggests itself as the discipline
> which may be helpful to us: first [...], children's literature criticism relies
> on random, loosely formulated ideas about emotional meaning and com-
> munication (*sic*) [...], the very processes and characteristics of which are the
> object of study of psychoanalysis. Secondly, there is a version of psycho-
> analysis which not only lends support to my claim that *all* 'children' are
> constructions and inventions, but which also concentrates on ways to work
> with the idea of the constructed 'individual' ('child' and 'adult') – this
> despite the fact that to many people the autonomous 'child' will seem to be
> even more unavoidably present in a therapy session than in children's liter-
> ature criticism.[20]

What makes me dubious as regards the way Lesnik-Oberstein's argument
develops is the sort of one-to-one relationships or individual therapeutic sessions

19 Lesnik-Oberstein, *Children*, p. 166.   20 Ibid., p. 168.

that she wishes to establish between the adult and the child. What her argument seems to imply is that this sort of relationship should also govern the writing of children's books, and that the provision of psychoanalytical apparatuses should enable writers to transcend problems of categorisation. But, as things are, and as things will undoubtedly – I feel adventurously tempted to say *surely* – always be, a situation in which we would have an adult writing single books for an individual child will never replace the way children's literature is produced, that is, on a non-individualistic basis. And not only the writing of children's literature, but also its criticism. What Lesnik-Oberstein calls for is an impossible change, in that what she seems to say is that the *categories* 'children's literature' and 'children's literature criticism' should lose their plural form and immediately become 'a child's literature' and 'a child's literature criticism'; otherwise, she implies, we may dispense with these categories. Perry Nodelman, in his review of *Children's literature, criticism and the fictional child*, points towards the same ambiguity, saying that:

> assuming that the children of children's fiction are constructed does not lead 'by implication' or in any way at all to the inevitability that the criticism of that fiction will be similarly flawed.
>   Indeed, quite the opposite. The flaw can exist only so long as that aspect of children's fiction remains unnoticed by critics. Alternately [...] useful and insightful criticism does emerge exactly at the point at which the constructedness of the children of children's fiction (indeed, the unavoidable constructedness of all our views of each other as human beings) becomes apparent. That constructedness, and an analysis of how it works and what it means (particularly in terms of the ideological dimensions of literature for children), can be the subject of criticism rather than a counterproductive feature of it. [...] Somehow, [...] I am not persuaded [by Lesnik-Oberstein's argument].[21]

Neither am I, for writing and criticizing will always be permeated by what Nodelman calls 'the unavoidable constructedness' of the writers and critics of children's literature. This, the sort of negotiation between fiction and reality, is the context in which criticism takes place. So we are back to the fundamental *aporia* with which I started, and this takes me on to childist criticism.

Childist criticism, a critical approach developed by Peter Hunt, asks adults to read children's literature *as if* they were children. But an adult is not a child, or, at least, not in any socio-categorical sense. That is why reading and writing, as I outlined above, can only be asymptotic approximations. Hunt bases his argument upon this difficulty when he notes that childist criticism is there to 'challenge all our assumptions, question every reaction, and ask what reading as a child actually

21 Perry Nodelman, 'Hatchet job', *Children's Literature Association Quarterly*, vol. 21, no. 1 (1996), pp 42–5, p. 45.

means, *given the complexities of the cultural interaction*.'[22] The writing of children's literature, in this sense, needs to rely on empirical investigations and both acknowledge and reflect the diversity that constitutes childhood. There needs to be a compromise between the adult and the child or, rather, between the adult and *children*. *Children* because, as we have seen, the production of children's literature does not happen within the sort of one-to-one structure that Lesnik-Oberstein's argument promotes, but on a large scale. Two cultures need to interact. This interaction, due to the context within which it is bound to take place, that of a power-relationship positing the adult as the one who dictates his/her wisdom on to the child – we are back to Jacqueline Rose and Peter Pan – should take both a critical form, as Nodelman argues, and a cultural form.[23] The writing of the children's book is therefore caught in the double helix of didacticism and cultural awareness[24]. The adult must work *with* the child, and for this to occur, the child must be given a voice.[25] Here lies the ideological agenda of childist criticism.

Similarly, the criticism of children's books should also happen within this same frame of thought, this empirico-critical frame: empirical, because children's literature criticism cannot work without the 'real child', and critical, because the adult needs to work on behalf of the child, *for* the child. Very often critics do work in this way with children and books. Margaret Meek, in another review of Lesnik-Oberstein's *Children's literature – criticism and the fictional child*, writes that 'as a teacher [...], I simply cannot imagine how I can *not* learn about children from children [...].' Here the 'real child' *is* present and Meek insists that '[m]y understandings come out of many years of study of what children *seem* to think and do. I read with them, listen to them, discuss books with them'.[26] By approaching children and their literature from such a childist angle, one can get closer to what happens when a child reads. One cannot, however, get to what actually happens in the mind of the reading child. Childist criticism does not construct a version of the 'real child', it constructs *versions* of the 'real child' that differ from one child to another, for one can only *pretend* to be someone else by constructing this someone else. Childist criticism approaches the 'real child' from an individual perspective, and by maintaining this individuality, it finds itself caught in problems of cultural approximation, essential problems when facing childhood from our adult position. Childist criticism is without a centre. It focuses on the uniqueness of the 'real

22 Hunt, *Criticism*, p. 191, emphasis added. The notion of 'culture' is essentially problematic. Within the scope of my argument, I restrict my definition of culture to 'the shared characteristics, practices and customs of a group'.   23 See Peter Hunt, 'Passing on the past: the problem of books that are for children and that were for children', *Children's Literature Association Quarterly* vol. 21, no. 4 (1997), pp. 200–2.   24 I use 'awareness' for lack of a better term. Nevertheless, it must be noted that the notion of 'cultural awareness' is also a problematic one within cultural studies.   25 See Barbara Wall, *The narrator's voice – the dilemma of children's fiction* (London: Macmillan, 1991), pp 198–9.   26 Margaret Meek, 'The constructedness of children' in *Signal* no. 76 (Stroud: Thimble Press, 1995), pp 5–19, pp 11, 15, emphasis added.

child' by working *with* the child. And it does the same with the text. Confronting both the text and the child, critics must work backwards towards what constitutes the individuality of both the text and the child. Critics must try to understand the mechanics of texts, the way texts work. They must do the same with the child and see *how* and *where* the text and the child *can* interact.[27] The book, to adopt a Bakhtinian terminology, is therefore a dialogical place where both the adult and the child must be allowed to communicate. The book, this dialogical place, is where children's literature is constructed, but *also* where it constructs itself.[28] Trying to understand the *place* and the role of this place is the challenge of children's literature and its criticism, an everlasting challenge that keeps the writer and the critic alive, contrary to Lesnik-Oberstein and Rose's pessimistic prophecies.

27 I develop this argument in 'The secrets of childhood – criticism and children's literature', forthcoming).   28 Rudd, 'Conditions', n.p.

Alchemy and alco pops: breaking the ideology trap

KIMBERLEY REYNOLDS

Shakespeare's *Henry V* begins with the bishops of Canterbury and Ely discussing the remarkable change that has come over Prince Hal since the death of his father. In one of the few descriptions Shakespeare has left us of adolescence, the two men compare their new paragon of a king with the young man he was when, as Canterbury observes,

> ... his addiction was to courses vain;
> His companions unlettr'd, rude, and shallow;
> His hours fill'd up with riots, banquets, sports;
> And never noted in him any study,
> Any retirement, any sequestration
> From open haunts and popularity.[1]

This description probably sums up how many adults today think about the teenagers they see around them, so it is worth remembering Ely's explanation, that 'under the veil of wildness' Hal has been metamorphozing so that when the time is right he is ready to take up the responsibilities that come with maturity.

It is the relationship between the books now created for adolescents and the kind of self-fashioning Hal undergoes that concerns me here, because I am concerned that the fiction of adolescence tends to be overly preoccupied with reflecting and appealing to negative aspects of adolescence. The effect of this can be likened to the alco-pops currently so popular with the young: seemingly harmless and pleasurable but when taken in excess, both intoxicating and incapacitating. Before looking at this problem in detail, it is useful to think back over how we came to hold our current view of adolescence and how the fiction of adolescence – young adult or YA fiction – has evolved.

Perhaps surprisingly in 2003, our constructions of adolescence still owe much to the pioneering work begun in 1904 by G. Stanley Hall and even more to Erik Erikson's model, developed in the 1950s, in which adolescence was presented as a time of heroic struggle and alienation. Their influence can be seen in the descriptions of YA fiction found in standard reference works[2] which agree that it features characters caught up in the turbulent and complex emotions associated with the teenage years; that it is addressed to readers presumed to be in this state of turmoil

---

1 *Henry V*, I. i, 54–59.

and that it acknowledges a division between an 'authentic' inner self and a 'false' public self.

One further attribute is usually ascribed to this kind of writing. It is usually assumed that its central characters and readers are critical of the world created by adults and struggle to resist and change that world. This final characteristic seems to me to be suppressed and/or contorted in much contemporary YA fiction, and I am concerned that as a result, adolescent fiction colludes with other forces at work in western society to depoliticize and emasculate many aspects of youth culture.

Initially, the adolescent critique of social organisation and interaction as dramatized in adolescent fiction was invested with meaning. The hero of J.D. Salinger's novel *Catcher in the rye*, Holden Caulfield, and his successors pointed a finger at the world and cried 'PHONEY', and the world appeared to listen. As we moved into and through the 1960s and 70s, undoubtedly in response to Erikson's work, adolescence was imbued with romantic qualities and typified by its struggles with authority, alienation from mainstream society, and its need to make problematic choices. Significantly too, adolescence at this time was tinged with a sense of moral and ethical superiority. By the 1970s, youth culture – the culture of adolescence – was acknowledged to be vibrant, political and highly creative. New kinds of music, new fashion statements, and new forms of writing proliferated. Society at large became juvenocentric, and the impact of youth movements was widely felt.

Ironically for those of us professionally involved with children's literature, one reason for this seems to be that many young people were reading *outside* juvenile literature, which had yet to develop the rich body of YA novels to which teenagers can now turn. Their reading, from Herman Hesse's *Siddhartha* and the works of Carlos Casteneda to *Zen and the art of motorcycle maintenance*, encouraged teenagers to take on board philosophical, political, spiritual and literary works so that, as the German critic Winfred Kaminski noted when writing about youth culture as late as the 1980s, young people 'were linguistically competent and, therefore, able to attack adult abuses of language'.[3] They could not only use and deconstruct language to expose what, in typically adolescent mode they identified as the hypocrisy of adult society, but they also had the ability to create alternative, often highly developed and sophisticated, forms of speech and art with which to contest and replace them.

The glory days of youth culture faded during the 1980s, and with the coming of Thatcherism and Reganism seemed to many if not to disappear, then to become less visible and proactive; meanwhile increasing numbers of teenagers lined up to join

2 See, for instance, H. Carpenter and M. Prichard, *The Oxford companion to children's literature* (Oxford: O.U.P., 1984); B.E. Culliman and D.G. Person (eds), *The Continuum encyclopedia of children's literature* (New York and London: Continuum, 2001); R. McCallum, *Ideologies of identity in adolescent fiction: the dialogic construction of subjectivity* (New York and London: Garland Publishing, 1999); V. Watson (ed.), *The Cambridge guide to children's books in English* (Cambridge: Cambridge University Press, 2001).   3 Winfred Kaminski, 'Literature for young people between liberation and suppression' in *Children's Literature Association Quarterly*, vol. 11, no. 4 (Winter 1986–7), p. 202.

corporate culture – in many ways young people seem to have replaced the activity of *creating* a self with *shopping* for a ready-made, brand-name image and lifestyle.

My purpose here is not to apportion blame: this behaviour is a[n] (intentional?) by-product of globalization driven by corporate culture. Consumer capitalism *depends* on young people's desire to buy themselves a place in society, and so constructs them as consumers. In the metanarrative of every day life, many young people feel themselves susceptible to exclusion if they do not wear brand name clothes and trainers – and this understanding of how social interactions work is vital to the success of corporate culture. Of course, this absorption into consumerism is not unique to the young – like Prince Hal, most of us who demonstrated in the 1970s became the establishment in the 1980s, by which time we were also consumers of life-style products. But it is in marked contrast to the anti-establishment, anti-materialist ideology of mid-twentieth century youth culture.

This is a sweeping generalization which should not be taken as an indictment of contemporary youth culture; however, the constraints of space preclude a more detailed analysis. Moreover, there is bound to be something askew with my analysis since I am not the implied reader of adolescent fiction and so to some extent I inevitably read it in the 'wrong' way. Bourdieu has pointed out that how texts are consumed is more important than what is read.[4] Perhaps if I could read like a fifteen-year old again, I would find different and more liberating meanings in these texts. But I think it unlikely. Bourdieu is concerned with opposition, with, for instance, remaking a text by reading across the grain of the narrative. YA novels tend to employ strategies of identification and collusion, and though it is undoubtedly true that an adolescent reader will bring different things to such texts, strategies of resistance are unlikely to be galvanized by them.

If I, with perhaps others of my generation, am inclined to look back to what I have presented as a time of *gilded* youth – when flower power and protests against the military industrial complex took place in an endless succession of Woodstock moments – it is largely because I fear that youth today is in danger of being *gelded*. Most campaigns in the public eye are largely led by the middle-aged; the same group protests against cruelty to animals, environmental issues, and the range of activities that once would have been the provenance of youth. We have retro fashion, remixed music, and a seemingly endless and deeply barren recycling of American television programmes of forty years ago on television and film.

Much of this ossification stems from the reluctance of the middle-aged to 'hang up our rock 'n roll shoes'. Whatever the reasons, it is a worrying situation, and I suggest that to some extent YA fiction contributes to it. Much of what is currently being produced for this sector of the publishing market veers between two constructions of adolescents: either they are dismissed as trivial entities given over to hedonism, or they are treated as damaged products of a damaging society. It is the

---

4 See Pierre Bourdieu, *Distinction: a social critique of the judgement of taste*, trans. R. Nice (London, Routledge, 1984).

latter tendency that bothers me most, since it is also in this strain of writing that we get some of the best and most profound YA fiction. Certainly there is a need for the dark books, and I would never want to see a return to the days when we had to fight to get Robert Cormier's 1974 novel *The chocolate war* published in the UK.[5] However, a great deal of the literature now produced for young people is potentially enervating and narcissistic, promoting passivity in rather than empowering their implied readers.

My reading of a large number of texts currently being produced for the adolescent market shows that many left the reader feeling atomized, lacking in political purpose, and sometimes self-destructive. If, as Judith Butler argues, 'agency is always and only a political prerogative',[6] the apathetic, unengaged turning away from issues results in at best the loss of agency, and at worst, metaphoric erasure from society.[7] While I do not agree with many aspects of his argument, it is worth mentioning Joseph Zornado's thesis,[8] that the books we give our young people to read can work for ill as well as good. Zornado's argument can rests on the premise that '[i]f adults are telling stories to children to acculturate them into social understanding, it is more than possible that these adults are using stories to coerce young minds into convenient ways of thinking'.[9] While writers do not set out to harm their young readers, it is worth considering whether cumulatively, the literature produced for adolescent readers may encourage them to capitulate to corporate culture, to retreat into privatized and narcissistic preoccupations, and to think of adolescence as a time when it is 'normal' to self-harm. These are the qualities in adolescent fiction that I feel may contribute to the gelding of youth.

GELDED YOUTH

A text that typifies the enervating side of YA fiction is *The beet fields* by Gary Paulsen.[10] Paulsen is a writer whose work I admire, and *The beet fields* is a well-written and intelligent book – it is certainly not an extreme example of nihilistic or dystopian YA fiction; however, like many other 'problem' novels aimed at adolescents, *The beet fields* has the potential to de-motivate readers.

5 Critic Nicholas Tucker recalls the debates that raged about the publication of *The chocolate war*. He told this author that publishers were afraid that the inclusion of swear words, sex and violence would have a detrimental effect on young readers and upset children's literature professionals.   6 Judith Butler, 'Contingent foundations, feminism and the question of postmodernism', in J. Butler and J. Scott (eds), *Feminists theorize the political* (New York: Routledge, 1992), pp 3–21, quoted in K. Mallan and S. Pearce (eds), *Youth cultures: texts images, identities* (Westport, Ct.: Praeger, 2003), p. xvi.   7 Ibid.   8 Joseph L. Zornado, *Inventing the child; culture, ideology and the story of childhood* (London: Garland, 2000).   9 Margaret Mackey usefully summarizes Zornado's argument in a probing review of the book that appeared in *Signal* 97, January 2002, p. 50.   10 Gary Paulsen, *The beet fields* (London: Random House, 2000).

This is the story of 'the boy', a nameless figure[11] who runs away from a sexually abusive mother at sixteen, learns to support himself under the instruction of a group of itinerant Mexican farm labourers, has his first sexual experience while doing manual work in a carnival, and enlists in the army in the closing pages of the book. The events take place in the American mid-west in the year 1955, making 'the boy' an adolescent contemporary of Holden Caulfield's.

Like many of Paulsen's books, this is a male survival story. The boy finds a succession of surrogate families, learns some basic ways of supporting himself, and has a sexual rite of passage into manhood with the wife of his employer. Despite a desperate preoccupation with escaping his original life and creating himself anew, the self the boy constructs is not offered to the reader as admirable. With his ducktail hairstyle and his pack of cigarettes rolled up in his sleeve, he may look the part of the rebel, but his actions go no further than the fashion statement. His aspirations are banal, his values increasingly questionable; he is uneducated and the knowledge he has acquired has made him cunning and self-protective rather than quick or sympathetic. His limitations are fully exposed in an interview with a recruiting officer, which forms an epilogue to the book. The interview shows that the boy knows no more about the army than he did about hoeing beet fields or working in a carnival. His ability to anticipate and manage events has not developed in the course of the text.

> The recruiter sat like a smug pimp. [The boy may not know much, but he does know what a pimp is, how one looks and how he operates.] ... The recruiter studied him. He was a sergeant. Impossibly neat. Impossibly clean. [The staccato thoughts, moving between omniscient narration and free indirect discourse, convey the boy's evaluation – 'impossible' indicates that there is no identification with the sergeant; certainly, he does not relate to him as a role model, so the reader is left wondering why the boy is enlisting.]
>   'What branch?'
>   'I don't know what you mean. I thought I was enlisting in the army.' [Again, it is clear that the boy knows no more about the army than he did about hoeing beet fields or working in a carnival. His ability to anticipate and manage events has not developed in the course of the text.]
>   'Yes, but in the army there are the cavalry and the artillery and the signal corps and the infantry. Which one do you want?'
>   The boy shrugged. 'I don't know.' [Still helpless, and though he despises the sergeant, he is now both in his power and despised by the sergeant.]
>   The tight smile, the pimp smile. 'Can you shoot a rifle?'
>   'Yes.'

11 In a brief introduction Paulsen indicates that this text is based on events from his own life; for readers who decide that the book is autobiographical, the ending could be read as less determinedly bleak than I suggest. However, the distancing techniques used by Paulsen, notably the use of third-person narration and the refusal to give the boy a name, suggest that he has an ambivalent attitude towards him(self) at this stage.

'Good. I'll put you down for the infantry. That's the best branch – all the promotions go for the infantry.' [The boy cannot judge, but the reader, who accepts the sergeant as having a pimp's smile, is encouraged to assume this is a trick. If the reader knows anything about the army, it is obvious that the boy has been evaluated as no more than canon fodder.]

'Fine.' [Does he acquiesce because he does not care? Because he can do nothing else?]

'You'll like the infantry.' [The pimp seals the bargain.]

'Fine.' [Again – no conviction, commitment, self-regard. His limited goal was to join the army and he has.]

'It will do you the world of good.' [This sentence closes the novel, but leaves the reader with no strong sense of impending doom, or outrage at the way fate has dealt with the boy, or even disgust at the boy's apathy.][12]

Ultimately, this is a story about cycles of deprivation repeating themselves – at the start of the novel, when the boy's mother makes her unwanted advances, the book offers just one piece of information about his father, which is that he is away in the army. If the reader can be bothered to speculate further about this unfortunate boy's dismal life, it will probably be to conclude that to all intents and purposes, the boy has become his father, and may well be joining the army to get away from a young woman he has made pregnant. The cycle will begin again.

For me, *The beet fields* is an example of the ideology trap Robyn McCallum associates with children's literature and impoverished adolescent fiction.[13] It fails to empower the reader, but rather promotes a cathartic – thank-God-it's-not-me - effect, which dispels energy and emotion rather than propelling the reader into action.

WE CAN CHANGE THE WORLD

Not all texts construct adolescence as negatively as the books I have used *The beet fields* to represent: YA fiction also includes some energising and empowering works. A sense of the breadth and variety of these is given by three recent texts. First is Judd Winick's *Pedro and me*,[14] based on a relationship formed during an American reality TV series in which it was revealed that one of the participants was HIV positive. *Pedro and me* relates the events leading up to Pedro's death from AIDS, including his effective campaigning for greater knowledge about HIV/AIDS and his determination to use all the life he had.

AIDS activism is one forum for political expression; Lesley Howarth's *Ultraviolet*[15] encourages young people to become politically active on behalf of the envi-

12 Paulsen, *The beet fields*, pp 153–4.   13 Robyn McCallum, *Ideologies of identities in adolescent fiction: the dialogic construction of subjectivity* (London: Garland, 1999), ch. 7.   14 Judd Winnick, *Pedro and me: friendship, loss and what I learned* (New York: Holt, 2000).   15 Lesley Howarth, *Ultraviolet* (London: Puffin, 2001).

ronment, using the Internet to subvert corporate capitalism. Finally, in Beverly Naidoo's award-winning *The other side of truth*,[16] readers encounter British ambivalence towards refugees. Naidoo's novel functions more like children's literature than YA fiction, but in its recognition that society is many-layered and contradictory, it can also speak powerfully to adolescent readers. It is a text that works well with other, more realistic, probing and possibly bleaker novels, to counteract feelings of helplessness in the face of manifest injustice.

All of these texts seek to enable at the level of plot. According to Robyn McCallum, the most empowering works for adolescent readers need also to function at the level of language.[17] McCallum cites Aidan Chambers's *Breaktime*[18] as exemplifying the best kind of adolescent fiction because it makes readers aware of the kinds of pre-existing systems and assumptions into which they are born. If they are going to be able to grasp both how the world works and how texts function, they need to be able to recognize that they are not the unique and autonomous individuals that children's literature, in tandem with many other forces, encourages them to think they are. Central to such awareness is becoming alert to how language functions and how texts work to massage readers' responses. A playful, witty, intellectual text such as *Breaktime* does just this – and is sexy and entertaining to boot. But it is also a quarter of a century old, and a small but significant body of texts have joined Chambers' works in bringing linguistic and other kinds of textual awareness to the adolescent novel.

This trend is exemplified by four pleasingly innovative texts that attempt to celebrate the creative potential of youth culture and its ability to reshape social attitudes and behaviour. Of particular interest to me is that each includes and appeals to the kind of adolescent male given so little attention and credence in modern British society (it is notable that none of the books is British and most are by women): boys who are intelligent, able, ambitious and engaged. Perhaps in the reciprocal dynamics of literature and culture, novelising such boys will also normalize them by giving them a more visible place in our often restrictive versions of masculinity.

In Ellen Wittlinger's *Hard love*,[19] the central character, John, uses writing to help him understand his feelings about sex, sexuality, his parents' divorce, his mother's new partner – and many other aspects of his life. The narrative progresses through first-person summary of events, told directly to the reader, and creative writing efforts such as play scripts in which he provides the various characters in his life with dialogue. John discovers the world of fanzines – several of these are incorporated in the text – and through them he enters a new world of slightly older, more sophisticated young people who use language, texts and writing (including lyrics) to explore themselves and to act on those around them. The

16 Beverly Naidoo, *The other side of truth* (London: Puffin, 2000).   17 McCallum, *Ideologies*, ch. 7.   18 Aidan Chambers, *Breaktime* (London: Bodley Head, 1978).   19 Ellen Wittlinger, *Hard love* (New York; Simon and Schuster, 1999).

young woman who introduces him to fanzines is lesbian, and much of the text involves John coming to terms with his feelings for her and his own sexuality.

As an artistic character who communicates primarily with girls, John initially seems to exemplify what Australian critic Sharyn Pearce calls the 'wussy boy',[20] but in fact, *Hard love* turns out to be just that - hard. John is tested in the conventional way, and is shown to have the strength required of an adolescent hero, but his strength does not come from discovering a true self and sticking to it. Instead, he recognizes that the self is a life-long project. Selves, including sexual selves, are shown to be complex, flexible and in process. What's satisfying about this novel is that *Hard love* celebrates both the value and creativity of self-fashioning. In this way, it is an empowering and energizing work, and through its emphasis on writing, reminds readers that language is at the heart of identity; therefore, exercising your linguistic skill develops your ability to be a player in the game of life.

Janet Tashjian's *The gospel according to Larry*[21] also features a teenage boy who explores relationships and ethical issues through writing; in this case, in the form of a website. Unexpectedly, the site becomes a cult phenomenon. The power of the internet to communicate instantly with the masses is explored, as are the rampant nature of consumerism, the lack of self-awareness of the current curriculum, and infatuation with the media and celebrities. This is a self-reflexive text, which regularly comments on and adjusts its narrative through footnotes, photographs, and additional remarks. It foregrounds the subjectivity of truth, the manipulative dimension to love, and the ethical complications of even the most day-to-day relationships and events.

The gospel according to Larry and *Hard love* do not presuppose that young people have stopped being creative just because the internet, computer games, satellite television and the whole panoply of electronic gadgetry occupy their time and attention more than conventional texts and activities. Rather, they show the possibility for fusion and invention between old and new forms of expression, and in doing so, they offer ways forward through narrative to their readers.

A text that takes the consequences of rampant capitalism to its logical conclusion in a bid to make readers think about its effects is M.T. Anderson's *Feed*.[22] Adolescents in this book belong to the first generation to have a chip inserted in their heads at birth which hooks them up to the version of the internet (called the Feed) that has evolved since it has been harnessed by multinational corporations to serve their own ends (they've also taken over schools, where young people study logos, brand names and shopping while being served the latest fast food in the cafeterias).

While the rest of the world struggles to survive the effects of exploitation and pollution resulting from the need to service western consumers, the young people

---

20 Sharyn Pearce, 'Today's boys: new millenium guides to masculinity and sexuality', in *CREArTA*, vol. 2, no. 1 (Southern Winter 2001), pp 61–70. **21** Janet Tashjian, *The gospel according to Larry* (New York: Holt, 2001). **22** M.T. Anderson, *Feed* (London: Walker, 2003).

we meet are literally fed a constant barrage of advertisements and soap operas that keep them fulfilling their one purpose in life – to shop.

The book culminates in the death of the main character's girl friend, who, because her parents were academics and so both suspicious of and unable to afford to have her chip fitted when she was born (this is not a culture that values academia), cannot manage the connection and eventually dies. Standing by her bedside the boy, who through her has gained some insight into the global situation, has his emotions read by the feed which instantly sends him a personalized message:

> *Feeling blue? Then dress blue! It's the Blue-Jean*
> > *Warehouse's Final Sales Event! Stock is just flying off the shelves at*
> *prices so low you won't believe your feed!*
> > *Everything must go!*
> > *Everything must go.*
> > *Everything must go.*
> > > *Everything must go.* [Page turn]

> > Everything must go.[23]
> > [The numbered last page is blank.]

Feed is verbally and stylistically innovative; it is also deliberately challenging, and spookily prophetic in its depiction of the American President. It certainly encourages readers to break the ideology trap.

My final example is, at the level of language and structure, less innovative than the other texts discussed, but Margaret Mahy's *Alchemy*[24] is notable for being the only joyful and optimistic of the books I've read. It gives boy readers the same opportunity to embrace and enjoy the transformations that come with adolescence as her novel *The changeover* offers girls.

While each of the previous examples has been concerned with evoking contemporary culture and showing adolescence as a time of endurance and compromize, Mahy makes her protagonist, Roland, a rather traditional boy. He cares about school and family, and experiences adolescence as a time of power, insight and excitement. As we have come to expect from Margaret Mahy, this is a magic realist text in which the inexplicable elements function metonymically: the subjective reality of the thinking adolescent is that the world and the self are simultaneously bizarre and banal; known and unknowable; alluring and alienating. What is important, Roland discovers, is not to turn away from the possibilities growing up offers but to go for them and to learn about yourself in relation to them. Among the opportunities on offer are sexual desire, which is shown as natural and pleasurable, and changes in the power dynamics in relationships with adults.

23 Ibid., pp 235–7.   24 Margaret Mahy, *Alchemy* (London: Collins Flamingo, 2002).

Mahy equates alchemy (defined in the text as 'a magical or mysterious power of transforming one thing into another') and adolescence. The book acknowledges the ambivalence associated with change, and the adolescent tendency to withdraw into the self (for brief moments Roland becomes a cosmic Sleeping Beauty, recalling Bettelheim's[25] reading of that tale and its relevance to the adolescent), but ultimately it is the opposite of a nihilistic text. Roland does dare to eat a peach; he learns that the things he does do make a difference (hugely important to political engagement), and as the book draws to a close, he is able to evaluate his strengths and weaknesses and decide that he is both strong enough and ready to act.

The qualities that Mahy's text values are precisely those that I feel are too often absent in adolescent fiction today. I am not advocating naïve optimism. However if children's literature fails to offer young people ways of thinking about themselves and their world that suggest that they can make a difference, and help them construct a discourse of their own to empower them as political subjects,[26] it cannot be excluded from the other social forces implicated in the gelding of youth and youth culture.

25 Bruno Bettelheim, *The uses of enchantment* (London: Peregrine Books, 1978), pp 225–36.   26 Karen Brooks, 'Nothing sells like teen spirit: the commodification of youth culture' in Mallan and Pearce, p. 9.

The hero in the twenty-first century: transgressing the heroic gender construct

JANE O'HANLON

Books written for children are created by adults who, consciously or not, work within their own ideological systems, which may support dominant cultural values, or resist them.[1]

With the meteoric rise in the popularity of fantasy fiction and the literary attention that the form is currently enjoying (of which the award of the Whitbread prize to Philip Pullman's *His dark materials* is evidence), it is timely to interrogate the ideologies at work in key texts, and especially their constructions of gender. This essay examines both the impact of gendering and the contemporary revisions of the hero character, and, working on the assumption that readers still need or welcome heroes in the twenty-first century, speculates on possible forms of gendered heroism.

Gender, 'the deepest foundation of the order of oppression',[2] is a social construction, which posits masculine as the norm and feminine as 'other'. It might be read as the 'difference as deviance' model of binary oppositional thinking. 'The sex-gender system [...] is both a sociocultural construct and a semiotic apparatus, a system of representation which assigns meaning (identity, value, prestige, location in kinship, status in the social hierarchy, etc) to individuals in that society'.[3] This in turn leads to 'the common belief that girls and women are inferior to boys and men'.[4] Gayatri Spivak tells us that this belief has powerful antecedents, and may be found in the work of such respected thinkers as Immanuel Kant, for whom 'the uneducated' are specifically 'the child and the poor, and the naturally uneducable' is woman'.[5]

Much standard horror and high fantasy reinforce and re-inscribe standard gender stereotypes both in their depiction of character and in 'relentlessly re-inscrib-

1 Claire Bradford, *Reading race: aboriginality in Australian children's literature* (Carlton, Vict.: Melbourne UP, 2001), p. 3.   2 Ursula Le Guin, '*Earthsea revisioned': a lecture delivered under the title Children, women, men and dragons at Worlds Apart, an institute sponsored by Children's Literature New England and held from August 2–8, 1992 at Keble College, Oxford University, England* (Cambridge: Green Bay, 1993), pp 23–4.   3 Teresa de Lauretis, 'The technology of gender', *Literary theory: an anthology*, Julie Rivkin and Michael Ryan (eds) (Oxford: Blackwell, 1998), pp 716–7.   4 Terry Eagleton, *Literary theory* (Oxford: Blackwell, 1996), p. 142.   5 Gayatri Chakravorty Spivak, *A critique of postcolonial reason: toward a history of the vanishing pre-*

ing the heterosexual paradigm'.[6] According to Margery Hourihan,[7] in the hero quest we are dealing with *the* master narrative form of Western civilization, particularly ubiquitous in children's literature, a totalizing discourse'[8] that is dangerous because 'Thou shalt not is soon forgotten but once upon a time lasts forever'.[9]

FANTASY: A GENDERED GENRE

The world of high fantasy is a gendered world. Typically, its plots adhere to what Susanne Kappeler calls the 'cultural archplot .. [where] [t]here is power on the side of the agent (hero), and [...] powerlessness incarnated in the victim-object.'[10] Predicated upon the totalling discourses of 'dead, white, European males' (DWEMs),[11] it poses a particular problem in that the gendered nature of the hero's role 'inscribes and naturalizes the ancillary role of females.'[12] Agency is gendered, and action and authority originate and rest with the male.

The corollary of this is that powerful female figures are depicted as dangerous and threatening, especially to the hero. One such instance is Tolkien's Shelob, whom Hourihan describes as 'the most striking instance of a devouring female in twentieth-century young adult or children's literature'.[13] 'The establishment of manhood in heroic terms involves the absolute devaluation of woman'.[14] Absence of sexuality, present by its very absence according to Jacqueline Rose, involves the 'denial of relationship',[15] which is replaced by continence, abstinence and male bonding. Questioning what this says about sexuality is important when reading fantasies for children written by adults, according to Kimberley Reynolds.[16]

Fantasy is concerned with testing and eventually establishing an identity. In high fantasy this identity has been unequivocally male. Nicholas Tucker tells us that Tolkien himself was 'concerned with crises and identity and men testing themselves out against evil.'[17] Subject positions offered to readers have been male, so that, in Carolyn Heilbrun's words 'we [...] have always read as men'.[18] Texts, then, both produce and are the product of this framing because 'the standards themselves [...] are gendered'.[19]

sent (London: Harvard UP, 1999), p. 13.   **6** Kimberley Reynolds, Geraldine Brennan, and Kevin McCarron (eds), *Frightening fiction* (London: Continuum, 2001).   **7** Margery Hourihan, *Deconstructing the hero: literary theory and children's literature* (London: Routledge, 1997).   **8** Lissa Paul, *Reading otherways* (Stroud: Thimble Press, 1998), p. 16.   **9** Philip Pullman, 'Carnegie Medal Acceptance Speech.' 1995. Accessed 28 September 2003. http://www.randomhouse.com/features/pullman/philippullman/speech.html.   **10** Susanne Kappeler, *The pornography of representation* (Cambridge: Polity, 1986), p. 105.   **11** Kimberley Reynolds, *Children's literature in the 1890s and the 1990s* (Plymouth: Northcote House, 1994), p. 76.   **12** Hourihan, *Heroes*, p. 206.   **13** Ibid., p. 191.   **14** Le Guin, '*Earthsea revisioned*', p. 11.   **15** Ibid., p. 16.   **16** Reynolds, *Children's literature*, p. 24.   **17** Nicholas Tucker, 'How children respond to fiction', in Geoff Fox, Graham Hammond, Terry Jones, Frederick Smith and Kenneth Sterck (eds) *Writers, children and critics* (London: Heinemann, 1976), p. 183.   **18** Judith Fetterley, 'On the politics of literature', Julie Rivkin and Michael Ryan (eds) *Literary theory: an anthology*, (Oxford: Blackwell, 1998), p. 565.   **19** Le Guin, '*Earthsea revisioned*', p. 6.

All of this has several implications for the genre of high fantasy. Sexuality and sexual relations are absent from the texts and the hero has no equal relationships. Stories are event-driven and the action takes place solely in the public sphere, ignoring and even denying the existence of the domestic realm. As a consequence, female characters exist on the periphery of the texts and are there only as representatives or evidence of events that take place primarily within the hero's psyche. For example, the bride functions as the physical manifestation of the prize won by the hero on completion of the quest. Children rarely appear in the texts, and then only as extras. Powerful magic, it seems, belongs to men and, Le Guin specifies, to celibate men. Therefore, magic itself is gendered. When Le Guin wants to use a trope to represent weakness, she seizes on women's magic: 'Weak as women's magic [...] Wicked as women's magic', her narrator remarks in *A wizard of Earthsea*, without a hint of irony.[20] Further, on completion of the quest the hero is redundant and, like Carroll's white knight, no longer serves any useful function. In psychological and political terms therefore, high fantasy re-inscribes the dominant western paradigm of power and control, perpetuating the powerful, interrelated dualisms of western culture - action and maleness. This has given rise to what I have termed 'the heroic gender construct' in the literature of high fantasy.

RE-PRESENTING THE HERO

> The idea that images of hero and heroine are culturally constructed and can be influenced positively by appropriate experiences is one that is believed by storytellers the world over.[21]

Jacqueline Rose[22] problematizes the notion of 'children's fiction', drawing attention to the power imbalance implicit in its usual definition, fiction produced by the child, or fiction produced or given by adults to children. The issue is further complicated by current constructions of childhood that say less about children than about adults whose projections they carry.[23] Francis Spufford in *The child that books built*[24] graphically illustrates the formative influence of children's literature on the young reader, showing how children's literature is not only a product of, but is also implicated in, the production of constructions of childhood.

High fantasy, with its belief in ultimate good and in the hope of eventually achieving that good, provides, in the words of Adrienne Rich, an ideal site for 'revi-

20 Ursula Le Guin, *A wizard of Earthsea* (London: Penguin, 1968), p. 16.   21 Hugh Gash and Paul Conway, 'Images of heroes and heroines: how stable?', *Journal of Applied Developmental Psychology*, vol. 18 (1997), pp 349–72, p. 369.   22 Jacqueline Rose, *The case of Peter Pan: or the impossibility of children's fiction* (London: Macmillan, rev. ed. 1994).   23 Joseph Dunne and James Kelly (eds), *Childhood and its discontents* (Dublin: Liffey Press, 2002), p. 6.   24 Francis Spufford, *The child that books built: a memoir of childhood and reading* (London: Faber and Faber, 2002).   25 Tony Watkins, 'Fantastic kingdoms: lands of hope?', *Inis*, no. 2, Autumn 2002, pp

sioning' the hero for the twenty-first century. Dealing with large themes, such as death, good, evil, morality, loyalty and betrayal, through a panoply of archetypes, these worlds can become 'lands of hope'.[25] Fantasy, whose etymological roots are in the Latin term *phantasticus*, to make visible or manifest, can hold a mirror up to the dominant cultural order and 'fracture […] it from within or below.'[26] This can be done by working to subvert that order, as the American writer Ursula Le Guin has done in her *Earthsea* series, comprising *The tombs of Atuan*, *The farthest shore*, *Tehanu* and *The other wind*.[27] Between 1968 and 2001 Le Guin systematically dismantled the heroic gender construct and began to revision the hero for the twenty-first century.

It is possible to trace a developing feminist consciousness throughout the thirty-year period of the series. Having begun by writing in the great tradition of high fantasy, in the style of Tolkien, Le Guin tells us that she abandoned 'the pseudo-genderless male viewpoint of the heroic tradition' with her fourth book *Tehanu*, in 1990.[28] *Tehanu* introduces a post-heroic character, Ged, who is an ex-wizard, ex-archmage and ex-hero. Le Guin here transgresses the received heroic gender construct by having her hero return home, 'done with doing',[29] no longer preoccupied with heroic deeds, at the end of the third book, *The farthest shore*. Had Le Guin faithfully reproduced the template of the traditional gendered hero within its established conventions, Ged would have died, never returning from the world of the dead. Indeed, had he been a traditional hero, Ged would have preferred this. Instead, he must 'learn to be what I am now.'[30] Significantly, this entails learning to be afraid. Fear is antithetical to the heroic gender construct and draws attention to the changed gender perspective, in *Tehanu*.

This book recounts the concerns of women in Earthsea, unspoken until now in the high fantasy tale. A sign that we are encountering a different type of text and an Earthsea no longer insulated by magic and the heroic gender construct, it opens with Therru, a child who has been beaten, raped and almost burned to death. The differing experiences of gender are graphically depicted in the characters of Ged and Tenar as Le Guin interrogates the heroic gender construct in the text. Disliking the constraints of traditional fantasy, she adopts a writing style that is more realistic and a tone that is decidedly more sombre.

URSULA LE GUIN AND THE 'REVISIONED' HERO

It is Tenar in *Tehanu*, however, who is the key to the re-presentation of the hero in high fantasy. She is the focalizing character, 'a woman dragons would talk to',[31]

18–20, p. 19.   **26** Rosemary Jackson, *Fantasy: the literature of subversion* (London: Routledge, 1981), p. 36.   **27** Ursula Le Guin, *The tombs of Atuan* (London: Penguin, 1972); *The farthest shore* (London: Penguin, 1973); *Tehanu* (London: Penguin, 1990); *The other wind* (London: Orion, 2001).   **28** Le Guin, '*Earthsea revisioned*', p. 23.   **29** Le Guin, *Farthest shore*, p. 477.   **30** Le Guin, *Tehanu*, p. 558.   **31** Ibid., p. 538.

because she has chosen freedom over power. Le Guin has Tenar make the journey from heroine to 'female hero': 'the two English words (hero and heroine) are enormously different in their implications and value, they are indeed a wonderful exhibition of how gender expectations are reflected/created by linguistic usage'.[32]

Set in a place that is itself a metaphor for the denial of sexuality, *The tombs of Atuan* sees Tenar and Ged escape this sterile environment, both literally and metaphorically, through mutual interdependence, a state that transgresses the heroic gender construct. Le Guin makes possible this escape by reclaiming the age-old device of the labyrinth that, in this case, only Tenar can navigate. She also underpins the last book *The other wind*, published in 2001, with a number of love stories that are antithetical to the heroic tradition and place adult sexual relationships, including that of Ged and Tenar, at the heart of the text.

The characteristics of the 'revisioned' hero as delineated by Le Guin in *Tehanu* and *The other wind* indicate that she or he – for the new hero could be either, and the connotations of the term 'heroine' make it a redundant and outmoded term – would grow up and grow older, instead of remaining a perpetual adolescent; would be interdependent rather than ruggedly individualistic; would be as likely to be located in the domestic as the public sphere; as likely be female as male; would have ordinary, unheroic attributes as opposed to or as well as extraordinary ones; would be sexual and would have relationships predicated upon equality and mutuality.

In radically departing from, and yet building upon the tradition, Le Guin successfully dismantles the traditional heroic gender construct. Her tales are dark and difficult, and her heroes are not yet sure into what forms they will metamorphose. This uncertainty coincides perfectly with her logic, because her heroes must always be open to change and it is precisely this that makes the transgressive Tenar and Ged the models for twenty-first century heroism as envisaged by Philip Pullman in *His dark materials*.[33]

PHILIP PULLMAN'S 'LYRA' AND THE PARTNERSHIP QUEST

In Lyra Belacqua and Will Parry in *His dark materials*, Pullman has created a pair of dauntless twenty-first century heroes. Foregrounding sexuality, knowledge and partnership as their chief attributes, Pullman has gone beyond Le Guin and has re-visioned the heroic gender construct in terms not only of interdependence, but of partnership. In what Riane Eisler might call 'a partnership quest', the male and female share equally, sometimes assuming non-traditional gender roles, as they 'both seek to free themselves from the perverted cultures of their respective worlds'.[34]

---

32 Le Guin, *'Earthsea revisioned'*, p. 9.   **33** Philip Pullman, *Northern lights* (London: Scholastic Press, 1995); *The subtle knife* (London: Scholastic Press 1997); *The amber spyglass* (London: Scholastic Press, 2001).   **34** Millicent Lenz, 'Philip Pullman', in *Alternative worlds in fantasy fiction*, Peter Hunt and Millicent Lenz (eds) (London: Continuum, 2001), pp 122–69, p. 136.

Pullman celebrates diversity, presenting the traditional male/female and matter/spirit dichotomies as complementary rather than oppositional. 'By envisaging everything as connected with everything else, Pullman effectively upsets and transforms the antitheses between conventionally divided entities, rendering them as two halves of a more complex and integrated whole'.[35] With the advent of Lyra, the heroic gender construct is definitively revised for the twenty-first century. Lyra, a female character, is the hero and she frames the text. Her name is the first word and the last word in the texts.

In its exploration of the themes of the death of God and the end of the kingdom of heaven, the trilogy contains the extended metaphor of Lyra as a new Eve, and re-frames the fall as the essential human journey from innocence to experience, necessary for the growth in self-awareness. By foregrounding sexuality in this way, Pullman creates a female hero who, in *succumbing to temptation*, fulfils her destiny and *saves* the world. Yet the tale is situated firmly within the heroic tradition and conforms to a number of features of the heroic quest pattern, among them its main protagonist having orphan status; being the subject of a prophecy; having a special gift; being apprenticed to a mentor who gives her a new name; having a weapon of supernatural power, and suffering temptation. At the heart of the text, both thematically and structurally, is her descent into the underworld. However, Pullman pushes the boundaries of the traditional quest tale even further, in that he gives his hero Lyra a partner in her heroic exploits.

Metaphorically orphaned, Will Parry also displays heroic attributes; he acquires a knife with magical properties that allows movement between worlds, and he is identified as the mythical 'bearer'. Significantly, however, he also differs from the traditional, gendered hero in that he lacks hubris and resists heroism and a 'warrior' destiny. Most of all, he longs for home, for the private, domestic arena. His sensitive and caring nature is established early on in the second book in the description of the way in which he cares for his mother and at the same time, he paradoxically inspires fear, being described as 'implacable.'[36] Nor, does not kill easily or with any pleasure, a characteristic highly transgressive of the heroic gender construct: 'Will did not want this. His body revolted at what his instinct had made him do [...] his stomach and his heart were empty.'[37] Wise beyond his years, compassionate and courageous, he articulates a breadth of understanding which throws traditional heroism into sharp relief: 'Maybe sometimes, we don't do the right thing because the wrong thing looks more dangerous. We're more concerned with not looking scared than with judging right.'[38]

With the advent of Will Parry, Lyra's model of heroism becomes a partnership model, where 'neither is subordinate to the other: by complementing one another,

35 Ann-Marie Bird, '"Without contraries is no progression": dust as an all-inclusive multifunctional metaphor in Philip Pullman's *His dark materials*', *Children's Literature in Education*, vol. 32, no. 2 (2001), pp 111–22, p. 122.   36 Pullman, *Subtle knife*, p. 4.   37 Pullman, *Amber spyglass*, p. 171.   38 Ibid., p. 204.

their power is doubled'.[39] Their combined actions and their 'unforgettable love story'[40] are the key to the salvation of both their worlds. Like Le Guin, Pullman also includes as a central motif in his last book, *The amber spyglass*, a number of love stories, in particular that of the 'two forever-bonded hearts'[41] of Lyra Belacqua and Will Parry. In this way, both writers affirm human love as, in the end, the greatest and most heroic endeavour of all.

ALICE, LYRA AND TENAR: TWENTY-FIRST CENTURY HEROES

Lyra is an intrepid twenty-first century Alice, in the tradition of Le Guin's Tenar. Her weapons are knowledge tempered with compassion and hope in the future of 'the republic of heaven'.[42] Will is the child of Ged, a male hero no longer seduced by the ultimately hollow tradition of the heroic gender construct. Allowing his protagonists to choose their own future/s and seeing in them 'lands of hope', Pullman opens up a whole range of possible futures for his heroes, and possible subject positions for his readers. As Serrafina Pekkala, that wonderful witch, tells Lyra, 'you cannot change what you are, only what you do'.[43]

In revisioning the heroic gender construct within the genre of high fantasy, while remaining firmly rooted in literary and mythical tradition, Le Guin and Pullman have given us the partnership quest as a model for the twenty-first century. They present us with male and female heroes who are relational rather than solitary, sexual rather than celibate, and interdependent rather than individualistic. Possessing ordinary as well as extraordinary attributes they are as comfortable in the domestic as in the public sphere. With the capacity to caste off the shackles of adolescence and borne, like Le Guin's *dragons*, on the winds of change, they emerge as powerfully attractive heroes for the twenty-first century.

39 Riane Eisler, 'The chalice and the blade: our history, our future', *The vintage book of feminism: the essential writings of the contemporary women's movement*, ed. Miriam Schneir (London: Vintage, 1995), pp 439–53, p. 451.   **40** Lenz, 'Alternative worlds', p. 165.   **41** Ibid.   **42** Pullman, *Amber spyglass*, p. 548.   **43** Pullman, *Northern lights*, p. 315.

Crocodiles and naked pigs: motifs and motives in Max Velthuijs's picturebooks

HOWARD HOLLANDS AND VICTORIA DE RIJKE

Picture the sound of John Cage's infamous musical composition in three movements, *4'33"* (1952), which consists of four minutes and thirty-three seconds during which the performer plays nothing. No sound is added, even by the pianist, to that of the environment in which it is performed. Cage said of *4'33"*:

> In the anechoic chamber at Harvard University I heard that silence was not the absence of sound but the unintended operation of my nervous system and the circulation of my blood. It was this experience and the white paintings of Rauschenberg that led me to compose *4'33"*.[1]

Though it is often called a 'silent piece', it is one in which the absence of sound acquires a conceptual resonance, within whose time frame of *4'33"*, all everyday, chance noise, can be considered music.[2] What difference might be made by reading whilst listening to John Cage's *4'33"*? And in particular, by reading the picture books of Dutch artist Max Velthuijs?

Frog and the other animal series of picture books by Max Velthuijs have won him international awards and have been praised for their 'rousing good humour', their 'quiet blend of curiosity, respect, and joy' and the 'inspired creation [and] graphic simplicity'[3] of his illustrations. However, his work has also been criticized for its plainly moralistic or didactic positions. Is the denial or invisibility of any ideological position a prevalent, twenty-first century form of political correctness? What are Velthuijs's motives in these books? Does he lay

---

1 John Cage, 'An Autobiographical Statement', written for the Inamori Foundation and delivered in Kyoto as a commemorative lecture after Cage received the Kyoto Prize in November 1989. It first appeared in print in the *Southwest Review*, 1991. Reprinted at http://www.newalbion.com/artists/cagej/autobiog.html. Accessed 22 September 2003.   2 When Mike Batt, creator of the Wombles, included a minute's silence in homage to Cage's *4'33"* on his *Classical graffiti* album, he was accused by the John Cage Trust of infringing copyright, and paid a six-figure sum out-of-court settlement in 2002.   3 http://www.amazon.com/exec/obidos/ASIN/0374376751/antiimperialiint/103-6159474-6937433; http://www.enovel.com/ search.html?cat=children& start=300; from *The Guardian*, cited at http://www.andersenpress.co.uk/Biogs/max-velthuijs/maxvelthuijs.htm. Accessed 28 September 2003.

these bare in the text? What might be the motives of teachers in using them, children in reading them, and researchers in studying them? This paper analyzes a selection of Velthuijs's works, and examines two picture books, *Crocodile's masterpiece* and *Frog in love,* from two metaphoric perspectives, namely, those of visual and verbal motifs. Absence is a motif.

MOTIF AND MOTIVE

The etymology of 'motif' and 'motive' indicates that these words are variants of one another, that both can be traced to French usage in the fourteenth century, and from the Latin *motivus*, meaning moving. In current usage, 'motif' describes a distinctive idea or theme found in a piece of music or literature, whereas 'motive' can mean a recurring form or shape in a design or pattern, as well as the reason (conscious or unconscious) for a certain course of action or decision.

Absence, or lack, is a common motif in children's literature. Countless stories begin with the death, absence or neglect of parent figures, and with a lack of certainty in the child protagonist's prospect of happiness. In *Frog in love,* Frog is sitting on a boulder looking into space, not knowing what it is he is feeling, not 'knowing if he was happy or sad … He was worried.' *Crocodile's masterpiece* begins with nobody ever coming to the eponymous artist's studio, while Elephant, Crocodile's neighbour, looks at the bare walls of his house and feels that 'something was missing.' In the original Dutch, it is Elephant's happiness that is described as incomplete. '*Het is bij mij zo'n kale boel*' he sighs, which translates directly as: 'There's loads of bare at my house'. In other words, there's a whole lot of nothing going on. The popularity of numerous television make-over programmes urging us to change or fill indoor and outdoor spaces reinforces the notion that if we do not give space personalized meaning, then there is a lack or absence in our character. Underlying this compulsion to fill empty spaces is a fear of absence.

Velthuijs is playing with a familiar motif, given all the empty precedents in masterpieces of literature and the visual arts. These range from the deliberately blank pages in Laurence Sterne's *Tristram Shandy* (1759) and Jon Scieszka's *The stinky cheeseman* (1992), to an empty volume called *The nothing book* which ran to several editions in 1974, but not before the publisher of an earlier book of blank pages took action for breach of copyright. *The nothing book*[4] is, in fact, one of numerous publications involving blank pages that are described in *The book of*

4 Cited in John D. Barrow, *The book of nothing* (London: Cape, 2000), p. 7.   5 Barrow, *Nothing.*   6 The entry in the United States Library of Congress catalogue reads as follows: 'Elbert Hubbard's essay on silence. A new ed. / done here by Fra. Robertus. *Essay on silence* Okemos, Mich. (2411 Indian Hills Dr., Okemos 48864): Rob Run Press, 1988. [17] leaves ; 53 mm'.

nothing[5] (2000) by mathematician and cosmologist, John Barrow. Among these, Barrow mentions 'Elbert Hubbard's elegantly bound *Essay on silence*[6] [which] contains only blank pages, as does a chapter in the autobiography of the English footballer Len Shackleton,[7] which bears the title 'What the average director knows about football'.

The white canvases of Robert Ryman, a New York-based painter who uses white paint to obliterate, create yet another precedent for inscribed blankness. By using white paint, which erases in Tipp-Ex fashion, always leaving a visible sign of what was erased, Ryman, like Crocodile, draws attention to the metaphorical characteristics of the all-white painting, just as Cage does in sound.

Like Sterne or Scieszka, Velthuijs follows over-determined text with empty space. Once Frog has been given a lecture by the well-read Hare on how his symptoms must mean he is in love, he jumps with joy into the void, demonstrating that words are not the same as feelings, so evoking that surreal motif of faith in the unknown, a giant leap into his future.

Frog lands on Pig, who is picking strawberries, naked, as is usual in Velthuijs stories. While it may seem odd to point to an animal figure without clothes as 'naked', all the other animals in Velthuijs's books - bar birds - wear clothes, even if they are minimal, like Frog's swimming trunks. Pig is an exceptional case, and the recurring motif of his nudity seems again to refer to creative motive: deliberate absence, a pointed, meaningful lack.

In *Crocodile's masterpiece,* the leap of faith occurs when Elephant accepts a canvas from the artist which has 'nothing on it. It's blank!'[8] Crocodile has told Elephant: 'It seems blank […] but close your eyes and think of what you'd like to see'. In this way, Elephant finds he can picture whatever he pleases, clothing the blank canvas, giving form to his desires. Crucially, Elephant creates pictures with speech bubbles.

Velthuijs rarely draws on comic strip or cartoon conventions, so it would seem that this 'one-off' work, like Satoshi Kitamura's speech-bubble conversation between a boy and a tiger *In the attic*[9] conducted in visual imagery, is similar to, but in key ways, beyond, speech. Such motifs attempt to 'clothe' what we cannot articulate. Slavoj Zizek's comments, made in the first instance about Hitchcock's films, are equally applicable to Kitamura and Velthuijs's picture books:

> How are we to interpret such extended motifs? If we search in them for a common core of meaning […] we *say too much* … if, on the other hand, we reduce them to an empty signifier's hull filled out in each of the films by specific content, we *don't say enough*, the force which makes them persist

7 Len Shackleton, *Return of the clown prince: a personal, retrospective anthology* (Rosemount: GHKN Publishing, 2000).   8 No page numbers are cited in Velthuijs' books.   9 Hiawyn Oram (text) and Satoshi Kitamura (pictures), *In the attic* (London: Andersen 1984).

from one film to another eludes us. The right balance is attained when we conceive them as *sinthoms* in the Lacanian sense, as a signifier's constellation (formula) which fixes a certain core of enjoyment, like mannerisms in painting - characteristic details which persist and repeat themselves without implying a common meaning (this persistence offers perhaps a clue to what Freud meant by the compulsion to repeat).[10]

The boy and tiger literally speak in one another's clothing as the stripes of the boy's jumper and the tiger's fur are metaphorically contiguous, even logical equivalents. Expression creates being, and the speech bubble-as-picture illustrates what Gaston Bachelard in *The poetics of reverie* defines as metaphor: 'a new being in language', 'a growth of being'. The combined power of the imagination of the author, illustrator and reader bring this into being. For Bachelard, for Kitamura, for the boy and the tiger, for Elephant, for Velthuijs, and for us, 'Yes, words [and pictures] really do dream'.[11] The speech bubble in this context makes an ironic gesture towards the 'talking cure' of psychoanalysis. If motifs, as metaphoric tropes, are linked to the psychoanalytic theories of condensation and displacement found in dream work, then are Velthuijs, Elephant and Frog only dreaming, after all? Are they implying that we are dreaming as we read, that all is pretence, a dressed-up surface invented by humans to 'prepare the face to meet the faces that we meet'?

In Hans Christian Andersen's tale 'The emperor's new clothes' (1838), swindlers posing as weavers tell the emperor that their clothes are invisible to any fool not fit for the office he holds. Finally the emperor is dressed up in the invisible clothes for a grand procession, and walks the streets naked. The crowd cheers until a little child says: 'But he has got nothing on', and one person whispers to the other what the child had said. The emperor winces but thinks to himself: 'I must go through with the procession now.' And he draws himself up more proudly than ever, while the chamberlain walks walked behind him bearing the train that is not there.[12]

This story lays political correctness bare. People see the facts for what they are, but out of fear of self-exposure, they nevertheless conform. Bear in mind that it is the child who has the 'bare-faced cheek' to reveal the truth about the Emperor; a child who strips him of his vain pretensions. Faced with uninhibited, new modes of engaging with art, Elephant knows he can close his eyes and make art come alive, and Frog knows he's in love. The problem is that Elephant feels he's been cheated of 'real art' that a proper artist has given form to (the classic dismissal of modernist art is that 'a child of six could do it!'), whereas Frog has Pig telling him

10 Slavoj Zizek (ed.), *Everything you always wanted to know about Lacan (but were afraid to ask Hitchcock)* (London: Verso 1992), p. 126.   11 Gaston Bachelard, *The poetics of reverie*, trans. Daniel Russell (New York: Orion 1969), pp 3–6, p. 18.   12 According to Jackie Wullschlager's biography, Andersen took the outline of 'The emperor's new clothes' from a medieval Spanish collection of stories based on Arab and Jewish sources called *Libro de patrino*, by Infante don Juan Manuel: J. Wullschlager, *Hans Christian Andersen: the life of a storyteller* (London: Penguin 2000), pp 170–1.

he cannot love a duck (because she's white and he's green) and anyway, that he does not know how to express his feelings.

Velthuijs makes it clear that giving form to silent thought is a creative struggle, both for the maker and receiver. Elephant tries to choose a single painting from Crocodile's enormous range, but ends up going home with the blank canvas again. There was no other picture with so much going on in it as in that masterpiece.

> 'What did I tell you? Said Crocodile modestly.
>> 'It's a very special work.'
>> 'Yes, you're right,' answered Elephant. 'Now I understand that your masterpiece has enriched my life.'
>> He took the white canvas under his arm and hurried home.

The Dutch text translates more literally as: 'But on no other painting was there so much to be seen as on the white masterpiece.'

WHITE PAINTING

Rauschenberg requested that Willem de Kooning, his mentor and renowned abstract expressionist painter, give him one of his drawings in order that he could erase it and claim it as his own. It took Rauschenberg one month and forty erasers to rub out most of the thick crayon, grease pencil, ink and charcoal pencil markings. This action has been described as 'parodying the act of effacing as a primary act of art making', in that Rauschenberg 'does not go on to use the ground he has cleared and levelled. He rests his case in a negative position'. Yet digital artist Sawad Brooks, using the processes of rubbing out on computer interfaces, says: 'Knowledge is predicated on the necessity of its erasure'.[13] When the critic Leo Steinberg telephoned Rauschenberg to discuss the erased de Kooning drawing, he asked if he would appreciate it more if he actually saw it. Rauschenberg thought not.[14]

Rauschenberg had also at this time been making white paintings. Realising that they would get dirty (a case of environmental erasure of his own work!), he arranged for assistants in later years to paint them over in white, effectively blanking out his original blank paintings. Rauschenberg says of these works that it was not important how they were painted, but what they revealed, in that 'they had to do with shadows and projections of things onto the blank whiteness'. John Cage referred to them as 'airports for lights, shadows and particles'.[15] The term 'projection' especially links to Frog and Elephant and their quest(ion).

13 Sawad Brooks, 'Digital Erasure' (1998), http://www.thing.net/ ~sawad/erase/trait/text.html. Accessed 25 September 2003. **14** Tony Godfrey, *Conceptual art* (London: Phaidon, 1998), pp 63–4. **15** John Cage, 'On Rauschenberg, Artist, and his Work', *Metro*, vol. 2, May (1961); in *Art in theory 1900–1990: an anthology of changing ideas*, Charles Harrison and Paul Wood (eds) (Cambridge: Blackwell, 1992).

Elephant goes back to Crocodile to get a real painting, but ends up with the blank canvas again and Frog sends anonymous flowers and pictures with love hearts on to Duck. In the books, there are strong parallels between the images in which Elephant and Frog rush to the right, and by implication, onto the next page, though Frog, because his act is secret and under cover of darkness, is not yet fulfilled. As with 'The emperor and his new clothes', Elephant needs to be reassured by Crocodile that the all-white picture has more going on in it than in all the other paintings. The thinking process is shown framed, but in the next image, at the moment of revelation, Elephant rushes off, unframed, heading into the next page. Back in the framed, warm-toned room with his objects of comfort (tidy bookshelf, fresh flowers, cup of tea poured out, armchair and cat on lap) he is either looking at something outside of the frame, or somehow inwardly. It is Elephant who now seems blank: in which case he was right when he claimed that he did not need the painting in front of him except as a transitional object providing reassurance. *Crocodile's masterpiece* has a disappointing ending, in that is seeks too much closure. Having hung the art back on the wall, Elephant 'lives long and happy with his masterpiece' (the English translation actually reads 'he lived happily ever after'), and Crocodile has become a famous artist who has done many more white canvases. His smug image, paint-bespattered from his white paint pots, goes back to the artist's stereotype Velthuijs seemed to be satirizing. Where is the wit in this? ('*Wit*' is Dutch for 'white').

So the notion of 'something missing', the blank canvas, the apparent lack where there is in fact overloaded meaning, is a recurring theme for Velthuijs. For post-Freudians like Jacques Lacan, the motif, a characteristic detail which repeats itself, is the 'sinthom' mentioned earlier, a 'constellation of signifiers without implying a common meaning'. Do motifs therefore define the limits of interpretation, and are specific visual pleasures inscribed on the texts and readers of image and print?

Perhaps naked Pig is the key to this sinthom, since Velthuijs never once implies how we are to read Pig's naughty nakedness/nudity. In *Little bear's birthday*, we are introduced to a naked Pig sitting in his armchair with his coffee, regarding a second, empty, Vincent Van Gogh-like chair facing him. Motifs in the room seem expectant of company: the two chairs, the way Pig is gazing at exactly the space where a visitor would be, and the two pieces of fruit in the painting on the wall, a pear and an apple. Pig decides to bake a surprise cake for Bear, and the text reads as innocuously as a recipe book: 'Little Pig greased a cake pan with butter, dusted it with a little flour, and poured in the cake mixture. Then he put it in the oven.

However, the images of Little Pig tying his apron and popping his cake in the oven demonstrate that by wearing the apron, his nudity is accentuated, perhaps particularly since he is drawn in both cases featuring his bottom cheeks and tail. Nothing appears to be missing in Pig's life: invariably he is contentedly cooking or collecting strawberries and passing conservative comment in Velthuijs's stories. It should be remembered that it is Pig who says a Frog cannot love a Duck, and it is Pig who distrusts the newcomer, Rat, in *Frog and the stranger*. Perhaps Pig's life is less problematic because he does what he knows and no more, unlike Frog, Elephant or Crocodile. If Pig's nakedness is marked, given all the other animals bar the birds are clothed, is Velthuijs implying that, like the blank canvas and the loving heart, some motifs reveal certain motives? Is Pig the reverse of the emperor, happy in his own skin? Is that the bare truth?

When a class of nursery-school three-year-olds was asked about the recurring motif of Pig's nakedness, at first the children went for logical explanations: 'real pigs don't wear clothes'; 'pigs get dirty and like to roll around in the mud and that would spoil clothes'; 'maybe he knows he's going to be hot'. But when asked about the apron, things get more Freudian: 'he has to wear an apron or he'll have the cake all over his body and he'll have to eat it all off and it won't be fair because his friends and little Bear won't have any'.[16] This is a skilled and knowing reading of Pig's apron as a portent, given that the story is about how Pig, Rabbit and Duck eat almost all the cake in the act of testing whether it's good enough for Bear's birthday. Here the apron is an example of motive-bearing motif.

Motifs and motives, having the same roots in language, and interconnected in the companionable counterpoint between text and image in the picturebook, are linked as the 'trigger' which drive the reader/viewer towards a certain goal, or allow us a sneak preview into that which moves a person to act or respond in certain ways. This is how motifs reveal a great deal about motives.

Frog in love ends with Frog and Duck in that time-honoured romantic arrangement, rowing together on a lake. 'A frog and duck … Green and White. Love knows no boundaries.' Tell that to Romeo and Juliet. It is a fact that too much children's literature ends with glib 'and they lived happily ever after' consolation, rather than with the questioning nature of the leap, or the blank canvas. Zizek's 'spatial image of a jumping place at the end of the world' (with which Hitchcock was fond of ending his films) 'leaving the world itself, as when, in medieval times, navigators approached the edge of the map'[17] should rightly form part of an uncensored children's literature, free from political correctness. We are not asking for incomplete and bitter ends, just some small recognition of the space of the unknown; some room for things other than happy ever after. We live in a strange world that requires some questioning. When the Mona Lisa was stolen from the Louvre, why did the visitors still queue to see the empty space?

So the sense in which it seems appropriate to inscribe this complex and unique space of the 'edge of the world' is as that impossible representation of absolute non-space, the 'other' of space, which is required for concrete space in order to constitute itself as meaningful language.[18] Metaphor makes this possible: because it speaks of something other than itself; it *stands for* space. Can Max Velthuijs's picture books resolve structuralist and post-structuralist controversies by bringing together in metaphor an extension of meaning, a growth in being, a *living* thing?

16 Discussion with three-year-olds at Columbia Primary School, London E2.   17 Zizek, *Everything*, p. 56.   18 Ibid., p. 57.

Artists' books for a cross-audience

SANDRA L. BECKETT

The innovative picture book examined in this paper challenge the boundaries not only of the picture book, but of the book itself. The artists Bruno Munari, Warja Lavater, and Katsumi Komagata are interested in the book as a three-dimensional object. Their intriguing and innovative experiments with format and design have resulted in picture books that are also art objects and are often termed 'artists' books' for children,[1] although they appeal to a cross-audience of all ages.

BRUNO MUNARI

The multi-talented Italian artist, Bruno Munari, whom Picasso called 'the new Leonardo', was a painter, sculptor, designer, maker of toys, and architect, as well as an illustrator and author for both children and adults. He began his career as a Futurist artist, experimenting with a wide variety of techniques and materials. Early on, the book assumed an essential place in his work. As a young painter, he was involved in the Futurist experiments with bookmaking, illustrating Tommaso Marinetti's metal book *L'anguria lirica* (*The lyric watermelon*, 1934). For Munari, the material and the feel of a book are as important as the content and the visual element. The daring innovation that marks all his books is particularly evident in those he targeted at children. A special place is devoted to Munari by Corraini, which describes itself as a 'contemporary art gallery as well as a publishing house' that brings out 'both "artist"s' books and children's books'.[2]

Having worked as a book designer, Munari was interested in every aspect of the book and paid close attention to typography, page layout, and paper texture. His first books for children fell into the category of what he calls the *libro-gioco* (game-book), such as *Toc toc, chi è? Apri la porta* (*Who's there?*).[3] His renowned *libri illeggibili* (illegible books) are wordless books that tell visual stories by means of lines, colours, paper cutting techniques, transparencies, cotton threads and other inserts.

---

1 Annie Pissard Mirabel, '"À quoi sert un livre?" La réponse de Bruno Munari', *Livres d'enfance* (Saint-Yrieix-la-Perche: Pays-Paysage/ Centre National du Livre d'artiste, 1998), pp 35-42.   2 See http://www.corraini.com/chisiamoi.htm. Although some of his books have been published or reissued in the United States (he had a book co-published by the Museum of Modern Art in New York about the same time as Lavater), the work of this Andersen prize-winner has not received the critical attention that it deserves in the English-speaking world.   3 Bruno Munari, *Toc, toc, chi è? Apri la porta* (Mondadori, 1945).

The first edition of the famous *Libro illeggibile bianco e rosso* (Illegible book in white and red) was published in 1953.[4] A cotton thread carries the thread of the narrative in several of these remarkable books. *Nella notte buia* (*In the darkness of the night*, 1956) has taken on cult status and become a landmark in children's publishing. The story is told as much by the different types of paper and the cutting and piercing techniques as by the text, as the reader is led through the 'darkness of the night'. One of his best-known *libri-oggetto* (object-books) is *Nella nebbia di Milano*,[5] which actively involves the reader—'adult or child' (Corraini catalogue) — in a story that leads through the milky opacity of Milan's fog, evoked by the use of translucent pages, to the colourful world of the circus, created on bright-coloured heavy paper that is cut and perforated in an ingenious manner.

Munari experiments with a variety of materials in his famous *I prelibri*,[6] a series of twelve small books in a case, which were published in four languages. Intended to be a child's very first books, they invite children to experience books not just with their eyes, but with their other senses as well. A red thread runs through *Book 1*; in *Book 9* thin sheets of plywood replace paper so that the act of page-turning creates a noise; and *Book 12* contains a fur tail between pages of black and white paper. Munari takes the concept of the book the furthest perhaps in his *libroletto*, which has the double meaning of a 'read book' and a 'bed book'. This very large format book actually converts into a bed, giving the term 'bedtime story' new meaning.

WARJA LAVATER

The Swiss artist, Warja Lavater, is best known for the series of *imageries* based on Perrault's fairy tales that she began publishing in the 1960s, mobile and versatile works, which she herself referred to as 'radical' books.[7] In actual fact, Lavater does not consider them books at all, but rather 'book-objects' or even sculptures. She has experimented with a variety of innovative formats, including what she calls the modulated-book, the standing-book,[8] and the mural book. The colourful pages of her *imageries* unfold from left to right like the bellows of an accordion. Lavater got the idea from the prefabricated folded books used by calligraphers in New York's Chinatown, which, in addition to the 'double pages' of standard books, provide

4 Bruno Munari, *Libro illeggibile N.Y. 1*. (New York: The Museum of Modern Art, 1967).   5 Bruno Munari, *Nella nebbia di Milano*, 1968. Published in English as *Circus in the mist* (New York: The World Publishing Company, 1969).   6 Bruno Munari, *I prelibri* (Milano: Edizioni per Bambini-Danese, 1980).   7 *Le Petit Chaperon Rouge: une imagerie d'après un conte de Perrault* (Paris: Maeght, 1965); *Cendrillon: une imagerie d'après un conte de Perrault* (Paris: Maeght, 1976); *Le Petit Poucet: une imagerie d'après un conte de Perrault* (Paris: Maeght, 1979); *La Belle au bois dormant: une imagerie d'après un conte de Perrault* (Paris: Maeght, 1982); *Blanche Neige: une imagerie d'après un conte de Perrault* (Paris: Maeght, 1974); *La Fable du Hasard: une imagerie d'après un conte de Perrault* (Paris: Maeght, 1968); *Passion et raison* (Paris: Maeght, 1985); *William Tell* (Bale: Editions Heuwinkel, 1991): all by Warja Lavater.   8 Warja Lavater, *Passion et raison*, a book based on Descartes, was published by Adrien Maeght in 1985 as 'un livre ... debout'.

'non-interrupted flowing tales, from left to right or from top downwards'.[9] The artist stresses the mobility and versatility of the unique format of her *imageries*. The signs can be followed by viewing the pages in a conventional manner, but the artist points out that it is also possible to go backwards 'with much more continuity than in the classic book.'[10] The new and exciting possibilities of these innovative books explain their appeal to children, who quickly appropriated the expensive luxury books meant to be sold in museums to art lovers.

In Lavater's *imageries*, the stories are retold by means of 'pictorial language' or what the artist also calls 'pictograms'.[11] A former student of the École des Arts et Métiers in Zurich, Lavater, like Munari, was influenced by the Bauhaus movement. At a very early stage, she felt that the combination of codes and signs linked to forms and colours could create a kind of new language that would no longer be verbal, but visual. *Le Petit Chaperon rouge: une imagerie d'après un conte de Charles Perrault* (Little Red Riding Hood: an imagery adapted from a tale by Charles Perrault) was published in Paris in 1965, and the final tale in the series, *La Belle au bois dormant* (Sleeping Beauty), in 1982. All of the *imageries* are printed by Arte from original lithographs by Lavater and the entire set of six can be purchased, for several hundred euros, in a colourful cardboard case illustrated by the artist. Art lovers can now also buy Lavater's *imageries* pre-mounted on wood as murals.

The only text in Lavater's *imageries* is found in the legend on the flyleaf at the beginning, and it explains the elementary code based on colours and forms. Guided by the symbolic icons, readers construct their own version of the story. The code remains the simplest and most effective in the first story she rendered using this technique. In *Le Petit Chaperon Rouge*, there are only eight icons and they are limited to dots (Little Red Riding Hood is symbolized by a red dot and the wolf by a black dot), with the exception of one rectangle and a squared U shape for the bed. In later books, there is a proliferation of icons and they tend to become increasingly more complex and less easily decoded by readers. In *Blanche-Neige* (1974), Snow White is a black, white, and red dot that represents her three distinguishing physical features, the 'bad queen' is a yellow dot with a black centre symbolizing her black heart. The elaborate nature of the visual language of *Cendrillon* is illustrated by the scene that portrays Cinderella's arrival at the ball: in a colourful, fancy swirl of orange gown, the heroine enters the ballroom where the prince is surrounded by his guests and flanked by the two stepsisters in their gold ornaments, the king's servants and soldiers stand at attention, the king and queen occupy a podium, and the proletariat gathers outside the palace walls.

With basic geometric forms, Lavater skilfully interprets the archetypal motifs

---

9 Letter from Warja Lavater to Clive Phillpot, former Chief Librarian at the Museum of Modern Art in New York, August 6, 1986.   10 Warja Lavater, 'Tête à tête: entretien avec Warja Lavater', interview by Bernadette Gromer, *La Revue des livres pour enfants* (Winter 1991), pp 137-48, p. 42.   11 Warja Lavater, 'Perception: when signs start to communicate', in *The faces of physiognomy: interdisciplinary approaches to Johann Caspar Lavater*, Ellis Shookman (ed.) (Columbia, SC: Camden House, 1993), p. 186.

of the traditional tales. In her rendition of the story of Snow White, the motif of the magic mirror, represented by a simple yellow rectangle, is particularly effective. The folded format allows a striking juxtaposition of the two double-spreads in which the queen consults her mirror. In a later juxtaposition that covers four folds, the queen witnesses in the mirror the scene taking place in the forest, as the prince's kiss literally projects the poisoned apple from Snow White's throat. The treatment of the motif of the glass slipper in *Cendrillon* is both effective and humorous. Amusing scenes represent each of the stepsisters trying on the slipper while Cinderella sits on the sidelines in the hearth with the matching slipper that is virtually invisible because it is represented on a much smaller scale and covered in ash. The following scene is situated entirely within the hearth, where a resplendent Cinderella (almost the only figure not covered in ash) takes centre stage to try on the slipper in front of the prince, whose proportions are humorously reduced so that he is no larger than the slipper.

In *La fable du hasard*, based on Perrault's 'Les souhaits ridicules' (The foolish wishes) revised and corrected by the Brothers Grimm in 'The poor man and the rich man', the symbols are not only more complicated, but the amount of text is greatly increased in the legend, where detailed explanations are given along with the interpretation of the symbol. Beside the poor man and his wife, portrayed as two complementary green swirls that seem to hold hands, the reader is informed that their generous hospitality led Fortune to reveal its identity and to grant three wishes to the couple, who had only two modest wishes. Beside the rich man and his wife, represented by two unequal and detached jagged lines, the author explains that they were jealous of their neighbours' happiness and so the rich man mounted on his horse to overtake Fortune (whom they had turned away) to ask for three wishes as well, a request that was granted. The author obviously feels that the visual code is not adequate to tell what is Perrault's least known tale. Further, it is the only book in the series that contains any text beyond the legend: Lavater includes Perrault's moral on the final two-page fold.

While expanding the boundaries of the book, Lavater's unique *imageries* transcend geographic and cultural boundaries. *William Tell* was published with either an English or a German legend and the Perrault tales appeared first with a French and then an English, German, and Japanese legend. Lavater's unconventional books also transcend the arbitrary boundaries that attempt to divide readers into specific age categories. Lavater now claims that the 'pictorial language' of her *imageries* appeals to all ages,[12] but she was initially astonished when, after the co-publication of the luxury edition of *Le Petit Chaperon Rouge* in Paris and New York, people began telling her that their children not only liked it, but also understood it.[13] As many critics now point out, children are often more receptive to untraditional visual and verbal narratives than adults.

12 Lavater, 'Tête à tête', pp 42, 44. *Le Petit Chaperon Rouge* was followed by *Blanche Neige*, *Le Petit Poucet*, *La Belle au bois dormant*, *Cendrillon*, and *La fable du hasard*.

Lavater manages to infuse her illustrations with suspense, drama, and energy. The impression of movement is particularly striking in *La fable du hasard*, where the very first image draws viewers into a spiral as they follow a wandering Fortune, disguised as a poor beggar, first to the house of the discordant rich couple who turn him away and then to the house of the harmonious poor couple who immediately bid him enter. A series of very dynamic double-spreads depicts the rich man jumping on his horse and riding after Fortune in ever-larger loops that evocatively imitate the galloping horse, and then his three foolish wishes. The colourful, dramatic illustration of the bloody scene in which the huntsman arrives to rescue Little Red Riding Hood and her grandmother reminds us of a smouldering volcano about to erupt, whereas a similar scene in *Le Petit Poucet* evokes an actual eruption. In both cases, the contents of the villain's stomach are released unharmed in a spectacular graphic display of dazzling colour and dynamic movement.

It has been suggested that Lavater's object-books represent 'a twenty-year advance in computer icons and menus'.[14] The birds that eat the trail of bread left by Le Petit Poucet look strikingly like Packman in the popular video game developed later. The wild beasts that surround Snow White menacingly in the forest where the hunter abandons her have the same familiar form. Lavater's *imageries* have recently inspired a number of very interesting multimedia projects by IRCAM-Centre Pompidou. The first was an award-winning series of six digital image movies with music by the composer Pierre Charvet, who, using sound synthesis software, composed specific sounds that correspond to the geometrical 'codes' of Lavater's work. Currently, the *imageries* are the object of an interactive CD-ROM project.[15]

KATSUMI KOMAGATA

Katsumi Komagata is a Japanese artist who started his own company, One Stroke, in Tokyo to publish his innovative books. He began creating books for children when his first child was born in the hope that they would expand children's imagination.[16] They are nonetheless cross-audience works since the artist 'expect[s] both adults and children to be flexible when they read [his] picture books'.[17]

The three books in Komagata's Paper Picture Book Series (1994) are luxuriously made 'especially for lovers of paper'[18] and resulted from what the artist calls a 'fortunate encounter with a paper company.'[19] Each page is made from a different paper so that the texture and colour changes constantly. The books have been marketed as being suitable 'for interior design' as well as for children, although they

13 Lavater, 'Tête à tête', p. 44.   14 http://www.ircam.fr/produits/technologies/multimedia/imageries-e.html   15 Ibid.   16 Katsumi Komagata, *Blue to blue* (Tokyo: One Stroke, 1994), blurb.   17 Katsumi Komagata, 'Messages within picture books,' *Bessatsu taiyo 'nihon no kokoro'* no. 108 (Winter 1999) special issue: *Ehon to asobou: me to te de tanoshimu ehon-shu* [Let's play with the picture books: let's enjoy them with eyes and hands] (Tokyo: Heibonsha, 2001), p. 134.   18 www.one-stroke.co.jp/komagata.html. Accessed 20 October 2003.

are not in the holding of the International Institute for Children's Literature, Osaka, because of the potential risk of paper cuts. As the title *Yellow to red*[20] suggests, the story of the little chick who wakes up alone one morning and goes in search of its mother, is told on pages that range in colour from yellow to red. The pages are graduated in size so that the range of colours is visible when the book is opened. On its journey, the chick encounters other birds in a variety of colours that are inset at varying heights throughout the book. The changing colours evocatively express the passage of time, as the sun travels from east to west. Like Munari, Komagata delights in surprising readers: the blue page hidden behind what seemed to be the final red page of *Yellow to red* is quite unexpected. When it is turned, the reader finds two cut-outs of a rooster and a hen that can be viewed crowing against the blue night or the final sunny yellow page that was also hidden. This brings us full circle and starts the cycle of another day, as the chick awakes to the crowing of its parents. *Green to green*[21] is the story of a black cat that appears as a cut-out at the beginning of the book where he peers up at a window. Through this the viewer catches a glimpse of the graduated green and salmon pages of the landscape against the blue sky of the final full page.

The final book in the series, *Blue to blue*, tells the story of the life of salmon. The single hole in the cover provides a glimpse of the blue and white pages cut in wave shapes behind the first translucent full page, as if the viewer was looking through a porthole at the sea shrouded with mist. A large grey salmon swims between the pages, the numerous cuts in its tail creating the impression of movement as it lays eggs in the river. The baby salmon are small holes in the blue paper, their eyes formed by tiny red dots in the water on the page underneath. The baby salmon do not know their own parents, explains the narrator, and when they meet a mother swan and ducklings on their way down the river to the sea, they wonder where their moms and dads are. Some illustrations are formed by an elaborate superposition of multiple intricately cut pages. When the smaller brown and green pages arc turned, more salmon are revealed cut into the blue page. As they head northward, they are guided by a whale, highlighted against a shiny, textured white paper that evokes the icy, frozen sea. *Blue to blue* offers another of the cyclical stories of which Komagata is so fond: the salmon, now large fish, have returned to the river where they were born and it is their turn to be parents. 'Now they know what parents are,' writes the author humorously.

Holes are used very cleverly throughout several of Komagata's books. *Story of a tear*[22] evokes a child's inexplicable sadness, and the tear that is the protagonist of the charming story infiltrates the pages of the entire book. From the child's eye, the tear falls toward her dog and lands on the ground near an ant. It is absorbed into the ground where it nourishes the roots of a tree; it falls from dark clouds as a

19 Katsumi Komagata, *Blue* (Tokyo: One Stroke, 1994), blurb.   20 Katsumi Komagata, *Yellow to red* (Tokyo: One Stroke, 1994).   21 Katsumi Komagata, *Green to green* (Tokyo: One Stroke, 1994).   22 Katsumi Komagata, *Histoire d'une larme* [Story of a tear] (Tokyo: One Stroke 2000).

raindrop in a storm; it falls as a raindrop or a tear from the eye of the same dog and lands at the feet of the same child; it sits on the stem by an ant and then falls from the ant's eye in the next double spread; eventually it makes its way to the sea and then into a tap. The artist suggests that tears are part of life, nourishing plants and animals, and becoming part of the cycle of water, from the sky to the sea. But one also has the sense that the child's sorrow has somehow been eased because it has been shared with nature. Komagata's very simple *Story of a tear* succeeds in evoking strong emotions in readers of all ages.

Found it!,[23] published in 2002, is entirely composed of translucent pages that allow the images clearly painted on one side to be viewed in reverse and less distinctly from the other side, as though 'through a mirror dimly.' *Boku, umarere-yo!* (I am going to be born, 1995),[24] inspired by Komagata's four-year-old daughter's account of her memories of the time she had spent in the womb, evokes birth from the point of view of the baby, on transparent paper in warm, orange shades. Like many of Komagata's books, this one also had a device that posed a technical problem: the artist wanted the umbilical cord to be cut into the book in such a way that it would lengthen. *Snake*[25] is a wordless book constructed from a single sheet of paper that has been cut and folded to form the shape of a snake that is yellow on one side and white on the other. A hole has been cut out for the eye and holes of varying sizes occur the entire length of his body along with spots that are painted on in various colours. *Tsuchi no naka niwa*[26] (Adventures underground) is formed by a spiral cut into one big square sheet of paper. In order to follow the bug underground, the viewer has to turn the book around and around. Komagata has produced other spiral books, and explains that he created 'the spiral format book' hoping to change 'the one-way movement' that the artist is forced to pay heed to when 'the texts are typeset vertically' and readers use their 'right hand to turn the pages and follow the story that goes from right to left'.[27]

Artists' books, such as those by Munari, Lavater, and Komagata, offer young readers innovative, challenging books of exceptional aesthetic quality, but the artists who create them often have to overcome major obstacles. Komagata raises the problem of the perception of 'three dimensional action books' by the public, which tends to be suspicious of books that seem to rely on format to appeal to children, often classifying them in the 'temporary goods category'.[28] When Komagata exhibited at the second Artists' Book Fair in New York, he felt that the attention his books drew was due to the public's curiosity as to whether or not an artist can maintain the quality of his art in works that address children. Some problems are of a

23 Katsumi Komagata, *Found it* (Tokyo: One Stroke, 2002).   24 Katsumi Komagata, *Boku, Umarere-yo!* (Tokyo: One Stroke 1995).   25 Katsumi Komagata, *Snake* (Tokyo: One Stroke, 1995).   26 Katsumi Komagata, *Tsuchi no naka ni wa* (Tokyo: Kaiseisha, 1993).   27 Katsumi Komagata, 'Messages within picture books', *Bessatsu Taiyo 'Nihon no Kokoro'* no. 108 (Winter 1999): special issue: *Ehon to Asobou: me to te de tanoshimu ehon-sh* [Let's play with the picture books: let's enjoy them with eyes and hands] (Tokyo: Heibonsha, 2001), p. 134.   28 Katsumi

very concrete nature. When he sent his books, including the featured *Little Eye (or I)*[29] series, by airmail to the '1,2,3 Komagata' exhibition held in Lyon in 1994, the customs officer labelled his card-style books as toys, which have a much higher tax rate than books. Such innovative books often do not fit into conventional book marketing systems. To illustrate that his books do not conform to the Japanese distribution system, Komagata points to his books like *Snake* that do not have a spine on which to put the title. Lavater's fluid books had to be contained in transparent, plastic cases. Production costs are quite high and mass-producing such books is extremely difficult. Mobile books obviously damage much more easily than ordinary books because of their elaborate devices and complicated shapes, and libraries are more reluctant to lend them. In spite of all the problems, Komagata insists that three-dimensional action books are essential because they express the pleasurable and unique experience of the high-tech age.[30] The Japanese artist does question their categorization as '*hikake-ehon* [picture books with gadgets or devices], mobile books' because, as he puts it: 'books are books, that's all'.[31]

After limiting the corpus of this paper to Munari, Lavater, and Komagata, I was intrigued to learn that there were links between these artists from such diverse backgrounds and cultures. Komagata describes his discovery of an 'old-fashioned bookstore' in Paris, where 'some wonderful books' that had been produced by an artist using lithographs were treated as 'art objects' by the bookshop owner.[32] He can only be referring to Lavater's books in the Librairie Maeght on rue du Bac. In New York, Komagata had discovered and been strongly marked by the books of Munari, whom he calls 'the pioneer' in the field of 'three-dimensional action books'. He could not initially believe that Munari's *prelibri* had been produced for children, but successive readings changed his mind and he began to dream of the day when he could 'play together with [his] own children using [Munari's] books'. Komagata's dream was eventually realized and he says that Munari's books are now 'old and worn out, but still [a] treasure' that he intends to give his daughter as a wedding gift.[33] In France this summer, I discovered that the affinities I had sensed between these three artists have not gone entirely unnoticed. A French company, Les Trois Ourses, has recently marketed the 'Boîte verte' designed by Bruno Munari, containing twelve artists' books, in which Munari, Lavater, and Komagata all have a prominent place.[34] At €600, only an elite adult audience buys this box of books. However, the innovative picture books of these artists have a universal language that appeals to all ages and cultures.

Komagata, 'Messages within picture books', *Bessatsu Taiyo 'Nihon no Kokoro'* no. 108 (Winter 1999). **29** Komagata, Katsumi, *Little Eye [or I]* series (Tokyo: Kaiseisha, 1990). **30** Katsumi Komagata, 'Messages within picture books', *Bessatsu Taiyo 'Nihon no Kokoro'*, no. 108 (Winter 1999), pp 135-6. **31** Ibid. p. 137. **32** Ibid. p. 135. **33** Ibid. p. 136. **34** Munari had previously designed a box for Les Trois Ourses, 'Valise Munari', in which Alix Romero organized the space so that fifteen books and a game each have their own spot. They have also produced 'Livres en valise de Katsumi Komagata'.

Notes on contributors

ANN ALSTON is a PhD student at Cardiff University. Her dissertation is concerned with aspects of family in children's literature, 1818–2000, among them the family meal, and it is here that her paper concerning obesity and the colonialization of food in children's fiction originates.

SANDRA BECKETT is professor of French at Brock University (Canada) and the out-going president of the International Research Society for Children's Literature (IRSCL). She is author of several books on contemporary French literature and the editor of *Reflections of change: children's literature since 1945* (1997) and *Transcending boundaries: writing for a dual audience of children and adults* (1999). Her most recent book is *Recycling Red Riding Hood* (2002). She is currently writing a book on crossover literature.

MARGARET BURKE has completed an MA in children's literature at St Patrick's College, Drumcondra, Dublin. Her dissertation focused on the writings of Patricia Lynch. At present she works as a resource teacher for travellers in Blanchardstown and is cataloguing the Patricia Lynch collection at the National Library of Ireland.

SEBASTIEN CHAPLEAU researches children's literature and critical theory at Cardiff University. His research focuses on the way the child-reader is considered in children's literature criticism. He is part of the Groupe de Recherche de l'Institut Littératures d'Enfance (GRILE) at the Institut International Charles Perrault in Eaubonne, France.

VICTORIA DE RIJKE, originally a primary school teacher, is principal lecturer in English, Education & the Performing Arts and also coordinator of the REALL Centre (Research in Education, Arts, Language & Learning) at Middlesex University. She is a member of the editorial board of *Children's Literature in Education*. Her PhD was on metaphors of childhood.

ROBERT DUNBAR is Head of English at the Church of Ireland College of Education, Rathmines, Dublin, and also teaches children's literature at Trinity College Dublin and St Patrick's College, Drumcondra. A founder member and twice president of the Children's Literature Association of Ireland, he edited fifteen issues of *Children's Books in Ireland*, and the anthologies *First times*, *Enchanted journeys*, *Secret lands*, *Skimming* and, with Gabriel Fitzmaurice, the poetry anthology *Rusty nails and astronauts*. He co-edited with Celia Catlett Anderson the Irish children's literature edition of *The Lion and the Unicorn* (1997). He has published numerous articles and is a regular children's books reviewer for the *Irish Times* and RTÉ radio.

CAROLE DUNBAR is a tutor in the English Department at St Patrick's College, Drumcondra. Her doctoral thesis explored the depiction of the working classes in nineteenth-century British children's literature.

MARY FLYNN has completed an MA in children's literature at St Patrick's College, Drumcondra. Her dissertation is concerned with Talbot Press publications for children.

HOWARD HOLLANDS, originally a secondary arts teacher, is principal lecturer in Art and Design Education, and co-coordinator of the REALL Centre in the School of Lifelong Learning & Education at Middlesex University, London. His PhD study is on the depiction of the visual arts in children's literature.

CELIA KEENAN is a lecturer in English and director of the MA in children's literature at St Patrick's College, Drumcondra. She co-edited *The big guide to Irish Children's books* (1996) and *The big guide 2: Irish children's books* (2000) with Valerie Coghlan. She reviews for *Inis* and has contributed articles on the work of Michael Mullen, Don Conroy, Maeve Friel and Eoin Colfer. She is a founder member and current president of ISSCL.

DECLAN KIBERD is professor of Anglo-Irish Literature at University College Dublin, and former Parnell Fellow at Peterhouse College Cambridge. He is currently a senior research fellow of the Irish Research Council for Humanities and Social Sciences. He is author of *Irish classics* (2000), *Inventing Ireland* (1996), *Idir dhá chultúr* (1993), *Men and feminism in modern literature* (1985), and *Synge and the Irish language* (1979). Among his numerous literary awards are *The Irish Times* Award (1997) for non-fiction, the Rhodes Award of the American Committee of Irish Studies (2002) and the Capote Award (2002). He is a frequent contributor on Irish culture to Irish, British, and American periodicals.

CIARA NÍ BHROIN was awarded an MA in children's literature by St Patrick's College Drumcondra, and an MS Ed. by New York State University, where she specialised in the teaching of reading and writing. Her background is in primary school teaching and she is currently lecturing at Coláiste Mhuire, Marino. She is particularly interested in the illuminative perspective afforded the study of Irish children's literature by postcolonial theory.

ÁINE NIC GABHANN has completed an MA in children's literature at St Patrick's College, Drumcondra. She is a lecturer at Coláiste Mhuire, Marino. Her MA thesis is on the adult/child dynamic in the work of Frances Hodgson Burnett.

JANE O'HANLON is education officer with Poetry Ireland. She has worked with early school leavers, in adult education and in the prison education service. She completed her MA in women's studies in 1997 and her MA in children's literature in 2003.

A.J. PIESSE is a Fellow of Trinity College Dublin where she has lectured in Renaissance literature and children's literature since 1994. She has published on Kyd, sixteenth-century identity, Tyndale and allegory; she regularly reviews for *Inis* and has published articles on Mark O'Sullivan and Siobhán Parkinson, and is currently preparing a piece on Eilís Dillon. One of her current projects is Shakespeare and children, and the notion of children and childhood in the Renaissance.

KIMBERLEY REYNOLDS is Director of the National Centre for Research in Children's Literature and current president of IRSCL. Her research interests are in the history of children's literature and childhood, the history of the children's book industry, representations of gender, Victorian arts and letters, and boundary breaking narratives directed at a juvenile audience. Recent books include *Frightening fiction* (ed.) (2001); *Representations of childhood death* (ed. with Gillian Avery) (2000) and *Children's book publishing in Britain since 1945* (ed. with Nicholas Tucker) (1998). She is currently editing a book for Palgrave-Macmillan called *Contemporary children's literature: an introduction*, which will be published next year.

DAVID RUDD is a senior lecturer in the Department of Cultural and Creative Studies at Bolton Institute, Lancashire, where he teaches courses on education and literature, including children's literature. Aside from some sixty articles on the topic, he has written books on Roald Dahl and, more recently, Enid Blyton (*Enid Blyton and the mystery of children's literature*). He is an editor of *Children's Literature in Education*, and member of the editorial boards of *The Lion and the Unicorn* and *New Review of Children's Literature and Librarianship*.

DEBORAH THACKER holds the Field Chair for English Studies at the University of Gloucestershire. Her research in children's literature is concerned primarily with theory and poetics. She is co-author with Jean Webb of *Introducing children's literature from romanticism to postmodernism* (2002).

MARY SHINE THOMPSON is college co-ordinator of research and lecturer in English at St Patrick's College, Drumcondra. Her research interests include twentieth-century Irish literatures. She is former editor of *Arista: Journal of the Association of Teachers of Philosophy with Children*, and has published several articles on the textualization of Irish childhood. She is a founder member and current secretary of ISSCL, and a regular reviewer for *Inis*.

PÁDRAIC WHYTE studied English and Drama at Trinity College Dublin and at the University of Glasgow. He is currently undertaking doctoral research in the area of Children's Literature and Film in Ireland with Trinity College. He is vice-president of ISSCL.

Index